Yoga for Trauma

Yoga for Trauma Recovery outlines best practices for the growing body of professionals trained in both yoga and psychotherapy and addresses the theoretical foundations that tie the two fields. Chapters show how understanding the safe and effective integration of trauma-informed yoga and somatic psychotherapy is essential to providing informed, effective treatment. Uniting recent developments in our understanding of trauma recovery with ancient tenets of yoga philosophy and practice, this foundational text is a must read for those interested in the healing capacities of each modality. Readers will come away from the book with a strong sense of how to apply theory, philosophy, and research to the real-life complexities of clients and students.

Lisa Danylchuk, LMFT, E-RYT, is the founder of The Center for Yoga and Trauma Recovery in Oakland, California. A graduate of UCLA and Harvard University, she offers training on yoga and trauma treatment internationally. She serves on both the Board and the UN Task Force for the International Society for the Study of Trauma and Dissociation. Learn more about Lisa and her work at www.howwecanheal.com.

Yoga for Trauma Recovery
Theory, Philosophy, and Practice

Lisa Danylchuk

Routledge
Taylor & Francis Group

NEW YORK AND LONDON

First published 2019
by Routledge
52 Vanderbilt Avenue, New York, NY 10017

and by Routledge
2 Park Square, Milton Park, Abingdon, Oxon, OX14 4RN

Routledge is an imprint of the Taylor & Francis Group, an informa business

Library of Congress Cataloging-in-Publication Data
Names: Danylchuk, Lisa, author.
Title: Yoga for trauma recovery : theory, philosophy and practice / Lisa
    Danylchuk.
Description: New York, NY : Routledge, 2019. | Includes bibliographical
    references and index.
Identifiers: LCCN 2018051626 (print) | LCCN 2018053160 (ebook) |
    ISBN 9781315166773 (E-book) | ISBN 9781138707191 (hbk) | ISBN
    9781138707207 (pbk) | ISBN 9781315166773 (ebk)
Subjects: | MESH: Psychological Trauma—therapy | Yoga | Resilience,
    Psychological
Classification: LCC RC552.T7 (ebook) | LCC RC552.T7 (print) | NLM
    WM 172.5 | DDC 616.85/21062—dc23
LC record available at https://lccn.loc.gov/2018051626

ISBN: 9781138707191 (hbk)
ISBN: 9781138707207 (pbk)
ISBN: 9781315166773 (ebk)

Typeset in Sabon
by Swales & Willis Ltd, Exeter, Devon, UK

To the possibility of healing, which exists within the heart of us all.

Contents

PART III
Growth: Keeping Joy Alive in the Face of Trauma   149

Foreword

I often marvel at the ways yoga practices have evolved and become increasingly popular during my lifetime. You can now practice yoga with goats, while wine tasting – even on a slack line stretched high above the Grand Canyon. These aspects of yoga incorporate the outside world, while much of yoga requires the deep internal work of sensing subtlety: the search to perceive ourselves, our inner world, and our circumstances with clarity. Given the depth of suffering caused by trauma, offering yoga for trauma recovery is one of the most powerful innovations that I have seen arise in recent years. By applying the wisdom and knowledge passed from teacher to student for centuries to modern science and humanitarian needs, we create an opportunity to foster deep, lasting well-being in our students. Each small change in the direction of health has an impact, and these increments of healing help to cultivate awareness of how we treat ourselves and others, and how we move through the world. Most modern yogis fall in love with the *asana*, or postural aspects of the practice, just as I did initially. By deepening our understanding of the mental, emotional, and psychological components of yoga, along with their applications to trauma recovery, we can tailor the wide range of philosophical principles and yogic practices to people facing deep adversities. In choosing to practice and teach yoga for trauma recovery, we skillfully place attention and care on the aspects of practice and teaching that cultivate inner healing.

I cannot think of a better guide to walk you through the theory, philosophy, and practice of applying yoga to trauma recovery. Lisa practiced with me at the BKS Iyengar Yogamala while she was a graduate student at the Harvard Graduate School of Education in Cambridge, Massachusetts, and continued to attend my workshops and retreats after moving back to her home state of California. Early in her time practicing with me, I noticed her experiencing sadness, and often she left the room crying in the middle of class, to return a few moments later. She appeared to be struggling with some very difficult emotions. As she continued the practice of *tapas* – of showing up and dedicating energy to the practice,

I began to witness a shift in her energy. It was not until years later that I learned what she was working through: the tragic loss of her brother, who had overdosed on heroin when he was 25. As I shared with her after I learned of this loss, that could have been me in my twenties; instead, yoga found me.

When I met B. K. S. Iyengar I was still working through my own difficulties with life. There was a light in his eyes that drew me in; I wanted to connect with that light, with him, and with the zest for life and practice he carried. At the time, I was suffering from depression. In my first class with him, while we were in *Tadasan*, he made a statement that I'll never forget: "If you open your armpits, you'll never get depressed." Many people thought, "What is he talking about?" Of course, what he meant was that if you stand straight and your armpits are lifted, which helps you open your chest, it will impact your mental state. It was the idea that what you do with your body affects your mind. That was my first introduction to yoga being about more than just the body. That's what hooked me in.

In my years studying with Guruji, I learned increasingly more about the many healing pathways available through yoga. The postures, breath work, and teacher–student relationship are central aspects of this practice, and the philosophy outlined here and in other yogic texts helps guide the subtle workings of these elements. There are countless practices in yoga that can help guide our minds in the direction of presence, acceptance, and contentment. They can truly promote mental and emotional health.

My hope is that this book, and your practice of yoga, guide you to self-reflect, see your students' needs clearly, and respond skillfully as you support those who have endured traumatic experiences. As teachers of yoga, we are bound to come in contact with people who have suffered tragic circumstances, or who are struggling with mental and emotional challenges. Like me, and like Lisa, many people look to yoga to inspire feelings of joy and connection to life, and each other. As the yoga practice continues to evolve, I hope that we, as teachers, can keep the jewels of wisdom our teachers shared with us alive, and practice yoga in a way that keeps our hearts, and our armpits, open. With this, we access an inner capacity for resilience, which helps us endure challenges when necessary, let go of patterns that bind us to pain, and enjoy our lives to the fullest. This is my wish for each of my students, and for you.

I wish you well on your path through this rich text, and throughout your journey of yoga and life.

Peace and blessings.
Patricia Walden
Senior Advanced Iyengar Yoga Teacher
President, B. K. S. Iyengar Regional Association of New England

Foreword

I have had the pleasure of knowing Lisa for the past decade, and I have watched her teachings on yoga and trauma recovery evolve to reflect the principles covered in this book. With her unique skills as an excellent trauma therapist, yoga teacher, and teacher trainer, she communicates depth in each of these two fields and seamlessly bridges the connections they share.

Lisa and I have taught countless workshops on dissociation, mindfulness, yoga, and complex trauma together, and have broached the discussion not only of how these modalities are helpful, but how they can, even with positive intention, invoke more harm than good. Over the past decade, I have experienced frequent encounters with clinicians who either extoll the miraculous benefits of these modalities, or approach them with a great deal of caution. This caution is warranted when we factor in the many potential implications of complex trauma and dissociative symptoms. Unfortunately, dissociation is a process that is too often overlooked or misunderstood within the field of mental health, even within some trauma-specific communities. This book incorporates this crucial understanding of the dissociative response to trauma.

And yet, even trauma therapists skilled in dissociative processes can become perplexed when applying these skills. Colleagues often ask, "how can I offer yoga or meditation without further harming the client?" Others don't feel comfortable with these practices as a whole, or bemoan the difficulties with statements like, "this is too challenging for my clients," or, "that's great for other people, but my client's symptoms are too severe." At the same time, experts in the field of mental health and mindfulness assert that if you're not practicing mindfulness with clients, you're doing a disservice. If you don't fully understand *how* to apply yoga and mindfulness practices to trauma recovery, you're likely to fall into one of these two camps, all for or all against bringing yoga and mindfulness practices into trauma recovery.

In this book, Lisa has brilliantly set out the foundational theories, philosophies, and practices that fill these gaps in understanding so that everyone, from yoga enthusiasts to specialists in dissociative identity disorders, can apply the knowledge of these ancient practices to even the most sensitive populations. This book will assist teachers of trauma survivors in understanding the body's mechanisms for protection. It puts post-traumatic responses into biological context, which lead you to the solutions that yoga can provide for each individual, given the needs of their nervous system. While you will find an abundance of books that discuss yoga, and shelves of texts speaking to the needs of trauma survivors, you will find very few that connect these two topics, and none that provide the depth of philosophical and theoretical foundation that you will find in the pages to come.

We can all benefit, personally and professionally, from the knowledge, wisdom, and skill contained in this book. My hope for the future of these fields: trauma therapy, yoga, and trauma-informed mindfulness practices, is that the information contained in this book becomes mainstream – I suspect that you, dear reader, may play a role in that process. I invite you to read, enjoy, and share the pages to come, and wish you well on your personal and professional path.

Christine Forner MSW, RSW
President, International Society for the Study of
Trauma and Dissociation, 2019
Author of *Dissociation, Mindfulness, and Creative
Meditations: Trauma-Informed Practices to
Facilitate Growth*

Acknowledgments

A deep thank you to each person who has supported my personal and professional path to date, who has helped me keep an open heart in the face of tragedy, and to everyone who helped this book come to fruition.

Thank you to Anna, senior editor at Routledge, for the invitation to write this book and all those who assisted with the editing process. To the colleagues and friends that answered questions, offered guidance, and provided inspiration at just the right moment – Noona, Christine, Claudia, Jade, Elaine, Ashley, Sue, Ween, and many more.

I feel deep gratitude for my many teachers – academic, yogic, spiritual, and otherwise. Dr. Mike Nakkula, thank you for modeling compassion and for co-creating the Risk and Prevention Program at HGSE. Dr. Jo Kim, thank you for your warmth, trust, and ongoing support. To Patricia Walden, Gianfranco Amaduzzi, Lisa Walford, Vinnie Marino, Laura Miles, Seane, Hala, Suzanne, and all the other teachers who supported me through the practice of building awareness, healing, and growing as a student and teacher.The process is truly never-ending and I hold what I have learned from each of you in my heart and cells. To my ISSTD colleagues and friends, thank you for creating a professional home and family that both understands the implications of trauma, and holds the capacity for healing.

To each of the students I have had the privilege to teach over the years – in yoga studios, juvenile halls, prisons, recovery centers, schools, orphanages, and beyond: thank you for welcoming me, for being open to learning together, and for trusting me enough to try. To the clients who have shared their stories and hearts with me, thank you. The wisdom you have gleaned informs this text, and enriches my life along with yours. To every student in the Y4T Online Training Program, your questions and feedback within the training have shaped this offering. To those I have mentored and been honored to support and learn from, in particular the Founding Members of the Center for Yoga and Trauma Recovery: Tara Tonini, Meghan Delaney Zipin, and Molly Mahoney – wishing each of you strength of mission and vision, laughter, many spoons, and an abundant supply of your favorite comfort foods.

Thank you Mom, Dad, Mike, and always Matt, as well as friends who have become family, ancestors, and all those who have provided guidance along the way. I deeply appreciate your love and support throughout my life and unique career path. To Alex, Noah, and Iris: thank you for accommodating the life of a writer over the past few years and for making our home such a peaceful and comfortable place to be.

My deepest gratitude and love to each person who has touched my heart, and to every one of you doing the important work of healing in the world. Thank you for your efforts to support one another. May you be happy, may you be well, and may you feel free. *Namaste*.

Part I

Foundations

Understanding Trauma and Recovery

Introduction

The Evolution of a Field: Trauma-Informed Yoga

Begin Anywhere.
  – John Cage

I arrived at Massachusetts Correctional Institution (MCI) Framingham, ready to teach yoga to a group of female offenders after months of logistical emails. Dressed simply with my hair tied back, I followed the correctional officer through the gates and entered a large visitation room, where the program participants would soon arrive. I was used to working with adolescents; instead, I had a group of shy children eager to see their mothers, and mothers awaiting a moment of connection with their daughters. The girls filed in first, then the women, quietly. I had expected more commotion. The correctional officer immediately directed everyone's attention towards me. "This is Lisa and she is here to teach you yoga." All 26 pairs of eyes, with mixed emotional expressions, rested on me.

A colleague recruited me to teach this class on behalf of the Girl Scouts Beyond Bars program; this was a mother–daughter group with ages ranging from 6 to 60 – a unique population for a correctional facility. We stood in a circle as I led the group to move, breathe and explore different shapes. Perhaps because of the rare opportunity for these families to connect, everyone was on their best behavior. It was clear that the yoga practice was difficult for them, and I could see their faces cloud over with self-doubt when falling out of postures. I did my best to encourage them and to teach the yoga poses as experiences, rather than shapes to be perfected, and modeled this by stepping in and out of tree pose, myself. The clouds in a few eyes cleared.

The children's presence magnified the vulnerability of the group: love and desire to connect filled the room, as did a pervasive feeling of sadness and longing. This was their family time: supervised in a locked facility, barely allowed to touch. Two generations stood before me, and while I was not in a place to read any case files, I'd worked with the Department of Justice enough to know that these women and girls faced immense adversity, and could safely assume that most, if not all, were coping with the effects of neglect, abuse, and other forms of systemic, intergenerational, and personal trauma.

We didn't call it trauma-informed yoga then, but it was happening. Step by step, volunteers like me carried yoga practices into schools, prisons, mental health programs, and beyond. Soon classes became programs, programs became trainings, and research and books began to sprout about the topic. It's been a decade and a half since the class at MCI-Framingham and, as a field, we've learned so much. This book serves to collect the wisdom of theory, research, and practice into a digestible guide for your work in the field of yoga and trauma recovery. Whether you are a yoga teacher, studio owner, or mental health clinician, this book will help you understand the connections between the fields of yoga and trauma treatment, and will guide you as you support your students and clients on a path of healing.

***

Yoga's popularity has grown in recent years and, as classes like the one above become more commonplace, curiosity about how it plays a role in trauma recovery has increased in stride. In 2003, 15 million people were practicing yoga in the US, a number that blossomed to 36 million in 2016 (Yoga Alliance, 2016). Researchers estimate that for every one current teacher, there are two people interested in becoming one (Harris Interactive Service Bureau, 2003). As yoga's popularity has grown, trauma-informed care has become a mental health phenomenon, and the collective understanding of post-traumatic stress has broadened and deepened. Over these past 15 years, professionals in the field of mental health have grown an increased appreciation for the need for physical and somatic work; simultaneously, yoga teachers have sought training on trauma in order to respond to students' emotional experiences on the mat. These two fields have steadily come closer together as clinicians seek to bring yoga into treatment while yoga teachers, many with mental health backgrounds, teach classes like the one I offered at MCI-Framingham. This increasing overlap led to the rise of the integrative field of trauma-informed yoga (TIY). As the aphorism attributed to John Cage at this chapter's opening encourages, teachers began where they were, and in doing so, created a movement of yoga, service, and trauma-responsive care.

As yoga studios have blossomed throughout the world, the term "trauma-informed" has nudged its way into article titles, nonprofit mission statements, and agency task forces. I've listened to many people, including friends and colleagues, with a superficial understanding of yoga and trauma-informed care question how they can connect. Of course, if you think of yoga as flexibility training and trauma as something that only happens to a limited number of suffering souls, you would not see the connection at first glance. How could being able to do the splits help someone recover from early childhood abuse? As a simple action, it can't; however, when we are fully informed in the theory, philosophy, and subtle teachings in each field, we come to understand how even a single posture can play a role in one's healing.

Thankfully, researchers, teachers, and clinicians continue to develop an understanding of the mechanisms of healing that yoga provides. As researchers and practitioners in the fields of yoga and trauma recovery continue to understand yoga's healing components in more detail, we all can make increasingly well-informed choices. Important conversations about how to apply TIY are now happening in conference rooms, courts, and in makeshift yoga spaces in schools, jails, and disaster relief settings. As in any human relationship, in order to understand how these two disciplines connect, we must look to the depth of their organizing principles, belief systems, and goals, rather than rest on superficial observations. This book will walk you through some of the many decisions you can make to bring these two practices together in a thoughtful, educated, and purposeful manner.

Trauma Therapists Reach Toward Yoga Practice

While I was quite young, I had the opportunity to follow my mother, a psychologist with a gift for working with Dissociative Identity Disorder, to psychology conferences. I loved her colleagues; they were genuine, heartfelt, respectful, and good listeners. By the time I got to college, I began to join these professional organizations, and developed a network of friendships with fellow young professionals. My love for the process of trauma recovery and the people I worked with deepened and, yet, there remained a significant challenge: sitting all day in conference chairs was simply not an option for me. It's so uncomfortable! I became known as the person sitting on the floor in the back of the room in some form of a yoga posture. As we spoke of dissociation and disconnection, I wondered, "Are we dissociated from our bodies, or is my body stuck in a 6-year-old state?" My body screamed, "Movement! Dance! Anything!! Energy, vibrancy, please!" At psychology conferences, I yearned for more physical movement, more ability to respond to my own body and its need to not sit in a conference chair for five days straight. As you may have heard your yoga teacher say, sitting is quickly becoming the new smoking. Unless you're sitting to meditate. So, the message becomes "Stop sitting and move the body so you can sit and still your mind. Then you can move with more clarity and intention." Oh, how complicating it all becomes!

I recall a conversation with a prominent psychologist at a conference in 2005. I explained that I taught yoga to youth with trauma; she paused, then offered,

"You know, I have a client who found herself doing yoga postures during a hypnosis session. I recognized them because I took a class in college. I wondered what that could mean, but never quite knew what to make of it. Soon after, the client moved so I never had a chance to learn more. But I've always wondered what the connection was."

At this point, if we are to use the motivational interviewing model of change, the mainstream mental health field was in either pre-contemplation or, as in the case of the psychologist above, the contemplation stage of change (DiClemente & Velasquez, 2002). Yoga was not a popular approach to trauma recovery and, yet, many clinicians had personal, or professional, stories that they felt comfortable sharing with me. At this time, yoga was still viewed primarily as either flexibility training, stress management, something people do in an ashram, or something people do in a spa. Perhaps you see it continuing to fit into these categories. In a number of conversations similar to the one above, I heard a mixture of curiosity, dismissiveness, ignorance, and interest, as our collective understanding of the therapeutic role of yoga in trauma recovery slowly deepened.

Over the following five years a fascinating shift occurred – more yoga teachers began appearing at the psychology conferences I frequented. At a conference in Montreal, hosted by the International Society for the Study of Trauma and Dissociation (ISSTD) in 2011, I attended a session on creative visualizations for use with dissociative clients and found the instructor teaching in yoga language, using colors and images I had learned directly from my yoga teachers. I raised my hand and asked, in one part bold, one part timid fashion, "Are you using the chakras as a template for these visualizations?" "Yes." The instructor replied simply and directly, smiling. A simple affirmative response, but it felt like an opening, and the metacommunication I received was, "It's okay to use yoga with clients." I breathed a sigh of relief and connected with the presenter after class. We've since collaborated on conference presentations, webinars, and educational efforts to bring yoga and mindfulness practices to severely traumatized clients in a skilled and educated manner. The presenter was Christine Forner, who is now president of the ISSTD. She also happens to be a warm, hilarious, heartfelt human being. That presentation remains a turning point in my mind, a moment where the cultural shift moved beyond contemplation and preparation to the action stage: yoga was appearing on the scene.

I witnessed as the culture of mental health and trauma conferences continued to evolve to include morning yoga, more yoga practitioners on the floor or doing gentle dynamic movement in the back of the room with me, dance parties in the evenings and (sometimes) more comfortable chairs. During the same time frame, the culture evolved from accepting yoga, but rejecting my proposals to speak about it, first to accepting speakers like me who teach about yoga, and then to inviting keynotes and day long intensives about the topic. In fact, I've just returned from teaching an in-depth post-conference session on yoga, vicarious trauma, and self-care, where we explored how therapists can incorporate movement practices into their own healing and growth. The progression continues.

Yogis Reach Toward Trauma Theory

Although psychology conferences lacked movement, the opposite was true of yoga conferences. True to the pace and values of western culture, at yoga conferences I would hop from session to session to bend, twist, sweat and move my body until it called uncle. I had a policy of registering for at least one restorative, meditative, or discussion-based practice each conference day, but the offerings in general were very dynamic and *asana* (posture)-centric. At these conferences, I yearned for more stillness, investigation, research, and theory.

It was also not unusual to have, or to witness, what some would call a healing crisis on the yoga mat – tears, shakes, upsetting memories, psychological projections onto the teacher or a nearby student, or struggles in connecting with the body. Yoga, like meditation, gives space for internal monologues, dialogues, and diatribes to come to the surface and into consciousness. Some teachers spoke to this; others did not. Some were able to catch mini-crises building and offer appropriate tools, preventing students from becoming overwhelmed or flooded. Others, though thoroughly trained in teaching *asana*, missed these opportunities to facilitate healing, or even worse, exacerbated the crises with misguided responses.

I discovered that the teachers who were catching the subtle psychological experiences were also developing an interest in trauma recovery. Through their own personal journeys with psychology, and through reading and training, they were developing new ways of communicating these very common human experiences to their students. Pop psychology is popular in yoga culture. As my own training in psychology gained depth, I developed an increasingly refined ear for helpful guidance, as compared to gross overgeneralizations and pithy clichés, and witnessed as well-intentioned phrases landed as invalidating at best, and infuriating at worst.

Some sayings that were meant to be helpful could be sharp, shame-inducing tools – "crooked mind, crooked body" comes to mind. Others served to create an air of purported wisdom around the teacher. I recall a highly-anticipated class I took with a world-renowned teacher. His comment, "Sometimes fear keeps us alive – *dramatic pause* – but sometimes, it keeps us from living," fell flat on my ears. The words are true in some contexts, but the oversimplified and dramatic delivery insulted the intelligence of the group. At the time, I was working with youth who lived in oppressive conditions and experienced constant fear of all kinds, and his words were targeted to situations where the people have the luxury of feeling physically safe. Fear of growth and fear of violence are not one and the same, and should not be called by the same name. Luckily, other teachers were more skillful in responding to trauma resurfacing on the mat; I even recruited some of them to teach at my favorite psychology conferences and in a program for juvenile offenders where I worked as a counselor. Moments such as these bridged gaps in care and brought yoga into the world of trauma recovery.

Combining the Two All Along

While I noticed the strengths and limitations of each of these worlds, I felt blessed to have them both in my life, and to be able dive deeply into both fields. Each is a practice of connection and compassion, and both have heart and purpose. Throughout my training and career, I have always felt they balanced and complemented each other in a way that kept my work sustainable, skilled, and embodied. Committing to one practice to the exclusion of the other was not a viable option for me; I would be forced to abandon part of myself to do so. Combining a deep focus on the mind with movement, all in efforts to build consciousness, created a beautiful opportunity for me to experience mind–body healing.

Even from this simplified viewpoint of mind and body, yoga and trauma recovery contribute to one another quite well. They help to bring the mind to the body and the body to the mind, and, as we'll discuss in Chapter 4, both directions of practice are important. By straddling these two cultures, I found a way to keep attention on the body, mind, and heart, and to keep both a rational and intuitive perspective of my life and work. For me, having these two worlds together feels holistic, integrative, and healing.

Blossoming Sub Specialties

Numerous subfields have emerged under the umbrella of yoga and trauma recovery, each applying yoga to a group at risk of experiencing symptoms of post-traumatic stress. We now have yoga for veterans, incarcerated populations, victims of sexual assault and intimate partner violence, first responders, law enforcement, homeless individuals and families, students across all age ranges, and those in 12-step recovery. Nowadays, you can find restorative yoga in a military hospital in Washington DC, *hatha* yoga in the library of an inner-city school in Oakland, *jnana* yoga in a maximum-security prison in Louisiana, vinyasa yoga at a women's shelter in Harlem, and the list goes on. Related fields sprouting alongside trauma-informed yoga include: yoga service (also known as *karma* yoga), yoga and social activism, yoga for medical issues including HIV, cancer, chronic pain, and fibromyalgia, yoga for traumatic brain injury (TBI), as well as yoga for autism and developmental difficulties.

This list is not exhaustive and related fields will continue to emerge. The content of this book relates to people across contexts, as it focuses on the impacts of developmental experiences on the body, mind, psyche, and spirit. Many of the people in the populations I describe above have experienced traumas that occur more than once and many have experienced trauma or neglect earlier in life, in addition to experiencing challenges as adults. Trauma-informed principles apply across these subgroups, and I encourage you to refine the principles in this book to respond to the unique needs, contexts, and cultures of those you serve.

What's in This Book

This book is divided into three sections: Foundations, Applications, and Growth. In **Part I: Foundations**, I'll explain how we think about trauma and recovery to provide an understanding of the how to address health needs through a yoga practice. Chapter 1 outlines the foundations of mental *health*, and describes how the field is growing towards an emphasis on strength-based treatment. Chapter 2 details the manifestations of post-traumatic stress and describes what we know about Post-Traumatic Stress Disorder (PTSD) and complex trauma, with an emphasis on how this applies to development. Chapter 3 covers the nuts and bolts of the nervous system and stress response, while Chapter 4 explains how somatic interventions can safely and effectively integrate the body into treatment.

In **Part II: Applications**, I'll teach you how to use yoga to recover from trauma and extreme stress. Chapter 5 spells out how yoga philosophy sets the tone for trauma-informed practice. In Chapter 6 you will find answers to questions such as, "What's the best sequence to teach?" And "How do I help a student or client when they get triggered?" Chapter 7 discusses the importance of trust, outlining how to build healthy relationships and address attachment needs with students and clients (it's not just about being kind). **Part III: Growth** provides suggestions on how to resist being impacted by the negative aspects of trauma; cycles of abuse and pain, when left unchecked, can pass down through generations and even impact providers with no personal history of childhood trauma. Chapter 8 describes trauma-informed principles for group and individual work, and Chapter 9 provides frameworks for promoting resilience in yourself and those you serve. Chapter 10 offers recommendations for creating sustainable systems to support the growth of students, clients, and professionals alike. Chapter 11 explains why cultivating joy is the ultimate phase of trauma treatment and, in Chapter 12, we will close with hopes for the future of the field.

At the end of each chapter, you will find **Reflection Questions** and **Resources**. I encourage you to journal or converse with a colleague in response to the reflection questions, which I've designed to help you apply the material in each chapter to your work and life. Taking the steps to complete these in verbal or written form will enhance your understanding of the material and facilitate deeper clarity in your work as you apply this knowledge to your unique setting and population. **Resources** for each chapter are accessible online at www.howwecanheal.com/y4tr. I've designed each of these tools to help you integrate the material we cover in the book. These resources serve to engage aspects of learning beyond reading comprehension, which, obviously, is the primary learning pathway of a print or e-book. While I encourage you to engage with the practices and answer the reflection questions, if any of them do not feel right for you, you're welcome to move on, or revisit when the time is right.

As I explain more in Chapter 1, learning about trauma can bring up our own memories and response patterns, so notice how you feel as you read through this book, and be sure to nourish yourself with rest and appropriate self-care. Even the word trauma can trigger negative associations, so, particularly if you have a personal history of trauma, be sure you are well supported as you move through this material. Keep in mind that all names of clients and students, along with identifying details, have been changed to protect confidentiality, and that, though we cover the details of the PTSD diagnosis, nothing written in these pages is intended to diagnose or treat a specific individual or group. Instead, I've shaped the material in this book so you can make informed decisions and skillful choices as you respond to individual and group needs in the wake of trauma. Should you, or anyone you serve, need medical or psychiatric care, please contact your appropriate local emergency service provider.

***

In the process of reconnecting with old colleagues to prepare this book, I came to find out that a Massachusetts-based yoga and mindfulness training program has now trained 10 inmates at MCI-Framingham to teach yoga and mindfulness classes to the women detained there. Trauma-informed yoga is not just a young field, but part of an evolution in the way we approach healing. When students and clients learn these tools in a safe and supportive environment, they can practice them anytime, and can even share them with others, expanding the reach of the practices. Based on the exponential growth I have witnessed over the years, I am confident that this field will continue to develop and integrate information from complementary fields, and that the reach of these accessible practices will blossom to serve those who have experienced trauma, including those who may not yet be aware of how trauma has impacted them. It is an honor to witness the expansion of this young field and to share its foundations, spanning ancient wisdom and modern science, with you now.

Reflection Questions

1 What is your role and how do you see yourself fitting in to the development of this field?
2 What are your professional and personal needs?
3 How do the communities you're a part of contribute to your development?
4 Which subgroups of yoga and trauma work interest you?
5 Which population(s) do you feel most passionate about serving?

Additional resources available at: http://howwecanheal.com/y4tr

References

DiClemente, C. C., & Velasquez, M. M. (2002). Motivational interviewing and the stages of change. *Motivational Interviewing: Preparing People for Change*, 2, 201–216.

Harris Interactive Service Bureau (2003) *Yoga in America*. In International Association of Yoga Therapists (2004). *IAYT Yoga Statistics and Demographics*. Retrieved from: https://c.ymcdn.com/sites/iayt.site-ym.com/resource/resmgr/bibliographies-members/stats.pdf.

Yoga Alliance (2016). *The 2016 yoga in America study*, conducted by *Yoga Journal* and Yoga Alliance. Retrieved from: www.yogaalliance.org/Portals/0/2016%20Yoga%20in%20America%20Study%20RESULTS.pdf.

1 Foundations of Mental *Health*

The secret of change is to focus all of your energy, not on fighting the old, but on building the new.

– Dan Millman

I walked into the group home on Saturday at 7:00 AM, ready to meet the day and the children I was there to serve; I was greeted by an 8-year-old with a mouthful of expletives. It's a fond memory, actually, one that simultaneously makes me chuckle, smile, and shake my head with sadness. Hugo was one of many challenging clients in the group home – he had transferred housing placements multiple times, and had been in this house less than three weeks. I had the chance to review his file – it was thick, filled with diagnoses, medication changes, and reports about aggressive behavior towards staff. My mama bear instincts quickly fired: this stack of paper represented a boy who had been hurt and needed care. With one parent in jail and the other struggling with substance recovery, it made sense that he was angry, and having trouble regulating his emotions and behaviors. While I knew that he needed something even more than what I could offer as an employee, I made a silent vow to work with the other staff members to provide as much consistency and support as was possible, given the group home setting.

Back in 2003, there was little talk of developmental trauma in these settings. Hugo's case file didn't have a PTSD diagnosis, but he had been diagnosed with Attention Deficit Hyperactivity Disorder (ADHD), Reactive Attachment Disorder (RAD), Major Depressive Disorder (MDD), and Oppositional Defiant Disorder (ODD). His file, like most of the kids in the home, was a cocktail party of mental health diagnoses. While the notes in the file answered the question, "What's wrong with this kid?" they did little to capture the depth of what had happened to him. This, I gathered from conversations with him, and with the counselors, social workers, and other professionals who learned through the process of working with Hugo and his family. As we added this information to our case formulation – our understanding of him and his behaviors – it humanized Hugo and made our work with him more responsive to his deeper needs. While the case file did a wonderful job outlining what people perceived to be wrong with his mind, emotions, and behavior, a few of us on staff felt passionate about honoring the resilient spirit we saw before us, and championed the effort to repeatedly raise the question, "What's right with him?"

***

A Solution-Focused, Integrative Approach

In this chapter, we explore the key components of an approach rooted in mental *health*. With a foundational focus on resilience, prevention, and early intervention, we combine trauma-informed, attachment-focused principles with healthy power dynamics to set the stage for healing. We'll also begin to explore the truth that mental health has physiological, mental, emotional, social, and spiritual components, and we'll continue to explore how to respond to the needs of these layers skillfully in future chapters.

While mental health, from an insurance standpoint, centralizes its focus on mental illness and diagnosis of disease, practitioners on the leading edge across disciplines are finding it necessary to promote whole-person health, from as early an age as possible, in order to facilitate lasting health and healing. This does not mean, in the case of trauma, that we ignore or deny the truth of painful experiences; rather, that we seek to bolster students and clients to a place where they can process painful memories without becoming consumed or overwhelmed in a lasting way. Throughout the book, we will discuss how to facilitate this foundation of health, both in theory and in practice.

Just as Eastern medicine approaches like Ayurveda and Traditional Chinese Medicine (TCM) encourage us to develop an everyday practice of facilitating health to balance the energies of our system, we, as teachers and mental health practitioners, need to create and maintain a comprehensive picture of what mental *health* looks like and build in that direction. There is value in understanding dysfunction and challenges; in the case of trauma, it is important to understand what it is in order to respond in a way that promotes healing. However, it does a disservice to everyone when we, as providers, become consumed with the problem, rather than holding a broader, solution-focused perspective. The international field of mental health, like eastern medicine and modern integrative medical practices, increasingly incorporates strength-based perspectives into mental health treatment. This strength-based, solution-focused approach is both the way of the future and the way of healing. It is the "secret" the character Socrates shared in Dan Millman's book, *Way of the Peaceful Warrior* (1984); to focus our energy on building the new.

With this evolution, resilience-focused practices are gaining traction and being put to the test in clinics and research labs alike. This shift is akin to transitioning from seeing students and clients as carrying a glass half full of health, or one half empty. How would you prefer to see those you serve – as deficient or lacking in some capacity, or as accessing tools to cultivate strengths? Given that self-worth and esteem can be negatively impacted by trauma, and that our brains carry an inherent negativity bias (Rozin & Royzman, 2001), it is crucial that we maintain an orientation towards each person's potential for health and healing.

Rooted in Resilience

Resilience, as a word, speaks to elasticity and recovery. The term "bouncing back" comes up in many definitions of the word, though, when describing psychological resilience, there is more at hand than the simple recoil of a spring or rubber band. The American Psychological Association (APA) defines resilience as "the process of adapting well in the face of adversity, trauma, tragedy, threats or significant sources of stress." The most common misconception of resilience is the belief that you either have it, or you don't. This oversimplified, all-or-nothing perspective (yes, it's a cognitive distortion, Cognitive Behavioral Therapist friends) prevents us from seeing the many shades and flavors of resilience that support people in recovery from difficult life experiences. In fact, the APA goes on to explain, "Resilience is not a trait that people either have or do not have. It involves behaviors, thoughts and actions that can be learned and developed in anyone" (APA, 2018).

While mental health texts have succeeded in identifying mental, emotional, and behavioral problems, slotting them into categories of diagnosis, this shift in attention toward positive psychology and mind–body interventions continues to pave a path from diagnosis toward resilience. With this evolution, there is a shift in zeitgeist from the question, "What's wrong with this patient?" to "What happened to this person?" This is one key tenet of trauma-informed care: to understand the impact of trauma and to hold the client's presentation and behavior in this context. When we ask the question, "What happened?" we humanize the client and become aware of the impact of challenging experiences and life circumstances. We can go on to ask the client questions like, "How did this experience impact you? What sense did you make of it? What did you need to do in order to survive?" (Johnstone & Boyle, 2018). Once we have an understanding of the person's context – environment, upbringing, significant relationships, and experiences – we can learn about the tools they have used to cope, and begin to sort out which of these tools are helpful now, as well as which ones no longer serve, or create current experiences of suffering or harm. Perhaps most importantly in this process, we can ask the question my colleagues and I posed on behalf of Hugo: "What is right with this person?"

When we pay attention to what someone has done well, and to their capacity to survive, we begin to shine light on their resilience. Going further to explore the physical, emotional, and social resources they have access to, and supporting them in getting fed the positive psychological reinforcements everyone needs, helps us keep our focus on health and promote their well-being. We do not discard the value of understanding problems or of feeling difficult emotions; rather, we resist the pull of inertia to stay in the problem-focused mindset, and move to identifying strengths, resources, and supports that serve to soothe and stabilize. This shift from focusing on the problem to exploring and practicing solutions is invaluable; it helps us apply the knowledge and research we've gathered about mental illness to promote true mental *health*.

When we, as providers, understand our clients' and students' behaviors as a reaction to a toxic situation, we begin to support them in developing agency and an internal locus of control in the present moment. If we do not instruct them to identify with their feelings and behavior, they are free to make a change without risking a loss of self. When we understand someone's reaction to difficult experiences, we can help them do the difficult work of distinguishing "What is me?" from "What is a response to my experience?" This can manifest in the simple difference between a 10-year-old saying, "I am depressed" or "I feel depressed"; it is much easier to respond with solutions to the second statement. This process helps people clarify identity and reduce the negative impact of shame, which we'll discuss more in Chapter 7. When we support clients and students in connecting with a sense of self that lies beneath experiences and reactions, we can help them answer important questions like, "What do I like about myself?" and "Who do I want to be in the world?" This cultivates healthy self-esteem and self-worth. As providers, by keeping our minds oriented to resilience, we shine a spotlight on strengths and resources, and encourage those we serve to connect with these qualities within themselves.

Is It Truly *Mental* Health?

In addition to a habit of framing things from an illness perspective, the term mental health reinforces a false, but common, western belief – that it's all in your head. There are select moments when simple thought switching and self-talk can solve the problem of the moment – both yoga and psychology offer this as a tool. However, a new thought does not necessarily have the power to change the experiences of the past, the emotions you unconsciously associate with that thought, or the way other people behave. When you are feeling deep grief, one of the worst things someone can say is, "Cheer up! Think positive." Contrary to these limited understandings and applications of positive psychology, deeper feelings do well when given space to process and move through us. The aphorism "feel it to heal it" helps remind us that even emotions that we commonly label as negative – sadness, fear, anger, disgust – can teach us something, and often transform when given attention, care, and space.

If it's not all in your head, then where is it? In the case of most experiences of trauma, it's in the brain, body, mind, psyche, energy field, and relationships. I would elect to use the term biopsychosocial health over mental health and, even then, I see a need to incorporate the subtle body (as mapped in TCM, yoga, and Japanese shiatsu, among other traditions), and spiritual health. The reality is that trauma impacts us on all levels: physical, mental, emotional, social, psychic, and spiritual, and that each of these layers are inter-connected. Mental health is whole-person health, and by paying attention to the many layers, we can more readily identify and access the supports people need when recovering from trauma.

Prevention

Another shift occurring in the field of mental health is from a focus exclusively on treatment, which will always be an important piece of trauma recovery, to a broader understanding of how we can prevent mental health problems before they start. Prevention programs, when working well, keep participants healthy and developmentally on track. Prevention also builds our toolkit, so we have ways to manage stress in case of an emergency. Just as a first aid kit rests in a cabinet in the bathroom – it is both comforting to know it is there, and that we have a plan to respond when crises arise – the simple act of being prepared is preventative. Prevention efforts work to recognize components of mental health that are at risk in a given population and identify ways in which groups are disproportionately exposed to traumatic experiences. They then work to bolster coping skills prior to the risk or exposure, aiming to subvert challenges with preparation.

By providing psycho-education and training to maintain health, we bolster resilience skills before recipients face potential challenges. Preventative skills can include social and emotional teachings woven into curricula for young children, along with mindfulness and somatic resourcing practices, like yoga. It's important that we teach these skills to young children and continue to reinforce them, creatively, with teens and young adults as their brains develop and undergo neural pruning. When we teach young children how to appropriately recognize, respond to, and process their emotions, and then support them in this ongoing practice, we give them a solid foundation on which to recover from traumatic experiences and prepare them to lead a healthy adult life. Prevention often includes education for families and entire communities, as well as connecting those in need to programs and resources that can help promote whole-body health. Research indicates that effective prevention programs can have powerful impacts; they can prevent depression (Raes et al., 2014) and address the mechanisms underlying PTSD (Feldner, Monson & Friedman, 2007).

Early Intervention

Despite our best efforts to cultivate health and do preventative work, life experiences will continue to pose challenges. Even if we could control for every type of violence and abuse, circumstances and experiences will remain that facilitate a stress response, including loss, accidents, and natural disasters. Psycho-educational protocols promote prevention when we can offer them en masse, like vitamins, they ensure healthy development and bolster immunity. When we practice early intervention, we seek out signs that something negative is on the rise, or might occur if we do not intervene. With early intervention, in addition to providing services that promote healthy growth and development, we seek to identify problems in their early stages and call in supports to course-correct before the challenges become significant.

Early intervention can be in response to physiological challenges like speech difficulty, developmental issues like autism, or experiential challenges like exposure to trauma. To use the nutrition analogy, early intervention is akin to noticing one's hemoglobin count is low and deciding to supplement with iron to stave off anemia. A study we'll discuss in a moment has helped the medical world become more aware of relational and familial experiences that lead to physical and emotional difficulties later in life; programs that seek to respond to these familial challenges and relational needs in their early stages are also early intervention programs and can have a crucial positive impact on youth and families.

A wonderful example of programs focused on these two important aspects of mental health are Head Start and Early Head Start. Both are federally funded programs with a focus on prevention and early intervention. Through these programs, economically disadvantaged families with infants or toddlers, along with pregnant women, are eligible to receive services that offer training to parents and direct support to promote children's healthy social and emotional development. Through speech and language evaluations, psychological referrals, and counseling, the Head Start program helps identify, support, and solve early signs of problems, in order to encourage optimal development (Office of Head Start, 2018). These programs allow youth and families to get professional support in maintaining healthy development, and in identifying and responding to challenges quickly and effectively. They are excellent examples of effective prevention and early intervention efforts.

Adverse Childhood Experiences

What service can prevention and early intervention programs provide? The Adverse Childhood Experiences (ACE) study conducted in collaboration between the Centers for Disease Control and Prevention (CDC) and Kaiser Permanente identified abuse, neglect, and family/household

Abuse

- **Physical abuse:** A parent or adult living in your home pushed, grabbed, slapped, threw something at you, or hit you so hard that you had marks or were injured.

- **Emotional abuse:** A parent or adult living in your home swore at you, insulted you, put you down, or acted in a way that made you afraid that you might be physically harmed.

- **Sexual abuse:** An adult, relative, family friend, or stranger who was at least 5 years older than you touched or fondled your body in a sexual way, made you touch his/her body in a sexual way, attempted to have any type of sexual intercourse with you.

Household Challenges

- **Parent treated violently:** Your parent was pushed, grabbed, had something thrown at them, was kicked, bitten, hit with a fist, hit with something hard, repeatedly hit, or ever threatened or hurt by a knife or gun by another adult in the home.

- **Household substance abuse:** A household member was a problem drinker or alcoholic or a household member used street drugs.

- **Mental illness in household:** A household member was depressed or mentally ill or a household member attempted suicide.

- **Parental separation or divorce:** Your parents were ever separated or divorced.

- **Criminal household member:** A household member went to prison

Neglect

- **Emotional neglect:** There was no one in your household who helped you feel important special, loved. People in your family seldom looked out for each other or felt close to each other.

- **Physical neglect:** No caretakers protected or cared for you. You did not have support accessing food, medical care, or your parents were too drunk or too high to take care of you, or you had to wear dirty clothes.

Figure 1.1 Categories of Adverse Childhood Experiences (CDC, 2016a)

challenges as adverse experiences and found that, the more of these a child had in their early life, the more negative their physical health outcomes (Felitti et al., 1998). Figure 1.1 lists the experiences measured in the ACE study, and Figure 1.2 displays the findings related to these experiences. In short form: ACEs set the stage for challenges in neurodevelopment, which can impact social and emotional development, and can even correlate to a shorter lifespan. When prevention programs address or resolve problems described in the study, we can deduce that they improve the physical outcomes of the child.

In essence, the study found the higher the exposure to these childhood experiences, the higher the risk for heart disease, depression, suicidality, and more negative physical health outcomes. In turn, the data emphasize the importance of nurturing, love, and care for children, and highlight the powerful impact that relationships have on our development as human beings. We now know that the higher the exposure to these ACEs (and, likely, others not listed here), the more important early intervention and treatment interventions that provide positive relationships and consistent support become.

The data collected in the ACE study point to a public health problem whose scope goes beyond children's experiences, to impact adults and communities. Nadine Burke Harris, pediatrician and champion of ACE education, founded the Center for Youth Wellness in San Francisco's Bayview district in an effort to identify ACEs and cultivate health in the community. The organization advocates for ACE screening and early intervention, and describe this as a "critical step to prevent and undo the existing and future harm to children's brains and bodies caused by toxic

Mechanism by Which Adverse Childhood Experiences
Influence Health and Well-being Throughout the Lifespan

Figure 1.2 The ACE Pyramid (CDC, 2016b)

stress" (Center for Youth Wellness, 2018). If we detect ACEs early, we can recognize and respond to the needs of children at risk, and even prevent life-long health issues. This is the essence of early intervention. The impact of implementing ACE screening measures could significantly decrease health costs and even play a role in intercepting intergenerational cycles of trauma. While the ACE data may not feel initially uplifting, it makes solutions to mental – and physical – health challenges abundantly clear.

Figure 1.3 lists resilience factors that draw from the ACE study and cultivate the opposite, identifying what *does* facilitate healthy development in young children (ACEs Too High, 2018). This practice of cultivating the opposite is a yoga practice we will continue to discuss in Chapters 6 and 7. The items on this resilience questionnaire highlight just a few aspects of resilience. We can use questions like these as ways to assess resilience, to identify supports, and to provide options that guide young people in the direction of actively coping with the challenges life presents.

This is just one example of how we can shift the focus to resilience, assess for resilience factors, and direct energy toward reinforcing these supports in order to meet the needs of those we serve.

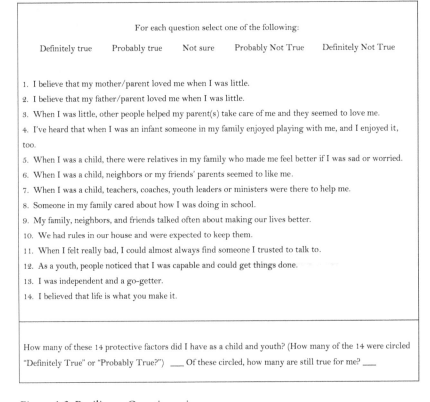

For each question select one of the following:

Definitely true   Probably true   Not sure   Probably Not True   Definitely Not True

1. I believe that my mother/parent loved me when I was little.
2. I believe that my father/parent loved me when I was little.
3. When I was little, other people helped my parent(s) take care of me and they seemed to love me.
4. I've heard that when I was an infant someone in my family enjoyed playing with me, and I enjoyed it, too.
5. When I was a child, there were relatives in my family who made me feel better if I was sad or worried.
6. When I was a child, neighbors or my friends' parents seemed to like me.
7. When I was a child, teachers, coaches, youth leaders or ministers were there to help me.
8. Someone in my family cared about how I was doing in school.
9. My family, neighbors, and friends talked often about making our lives better.
10. We had rules in our house and were expected to keep them.
11. When I felt really bad, I could almost always find someone I trusted to talk to.
12. As a youth, people noticed that I was capable and could get things done.
13. I was independent and a go-getter.
14. I believed that life is what you make it.

How many of these 14 protective factors did I have as a child and youth? (How many of the 14 were circled "Definitely True" or "Probably True?") ___ Of these circled, how many are still true for me? ___

Figure 1.3 Resilience Questionnaire

Trauma-Informed, Attachment-Focused

Given recent developments across disciplines – in medicine, neuroscience, biology, mindfulness, psychology, and beyond – our understanding of human beings' response to violence and trauma has become clearer and our responses more skilled. The movement towards trauma-informed care encourages us to simply become aware of, and respond to, trauma and its impacts. The Substance Abuse and Mental Health Services Administration (SAMHSA) identifies three components of trauma-informed care: realizing the prevalence of trauma; recognizing how trauma affects individuals, organizations, or systems, including its own workforce; and responding by putting this knowledge into practice (SAMHSA, 2012). When we understand the potential impacts of trauma and maintain awareness of the environment and experiences the people we serve have been steeped in, we are better able to respond to their needs. Mental health professionals with this training can assess for trauma history and differentiate between diagnoses to craft responsive treatment, and adjunct providers can facilitate a safe, supportive environment and better respond to the needs of those they serve.

Trauma-informed principles, which we discuss in detail in Chapter 8, help us respond the needs of those who have suffered through overwhelming experiences and create a safe space where healing can occur – but they do not occur in a vacuum; they take place within the context of human relationship. TIY principles provide a pathway to understand ourselves, the human body and the human experience, and to connect with others and share in our common humanity.

For many people, relationship plays a key role in the experience of trauma, at times giving rise to challenges in attachment patterns or expectations of trust. Trauma too often occurs at the hands of other human beings, which makes reaching out to another human being for support more challenging. By cultivating healthy relationships, we support clients and students in healing the wounds of ruptured attachment and promote equality in our communications. This type of attachment-focused care respects how trauma can impact the experience of bonding, and supports those we serve in creating relationship in their own time. Chapter 7 offers an in-depth discussion of these relational aspects of healing work.

Healthy Power Dynamics

When we are in the role of holding space for someone, we have power and influence. What we say and do matters, particularly when people are exploring wounds, feeling vulnerable, or sharing a tender aspect of themselves. This puts us in a position of power and, rather than deny or exploit that, we must respect it and practice using the authority we have in service of those we serve. Philosopher Eric Fromm writes about this in his description of *rational authority* (Fromm, 2013a). He writes, "Rational authority is based on competence, and it helps the person who leans on it to grow. Irrational authority is based on power and serves to exploit the person subjected to it." By recognizing that we do have power, committing to our own learning and competence, and helping those who look to us for support to grow in the ways that best serve them, we practice rational authority. Fromm goes on to distinguish authority based on having – skills or competence, to authority based on being – the totality of the person: "Being-authority is grounded not only in the person's competence to fulfill certain social functions, but equally so in the very essence of the personality that has achieved a high degree of growth and integration" (Fromm, 2013b). Our own development is at the core of our capacity to lead.

In addition to establishing dynamics of rational authority, it serves us to develop awareness of the roles of Victim, Perpetrator, and Rescuer, and how these dynamics can play out as modeled in Karpman's triangle (Karpman, 1968). It is important to recognize that this model outlines a negative cycle between the three roles it describes, and that the definitions to follow define each role within this negative cycle. Perhaps most importantly, we distinguish them from legal terminology of victim, which describes the person harmed by the criminal activity of another. In a similar way, someone rescuing another person is often a positive thing, yet this model points to an approach and cycle that impedes, rather than facilitates, the healing process.

In Karpman's model (1968), the Victim is placed in a powerless role, without the ability to make decisions, find insight, or solve problems. The Rescuer responds to the Victim's needs largely out of guilt, and can enable the disempowering feelings of the Victim. This keeps the Victim in a dependent role, and takes focus off of the Rescuer and any emotions they may be feeling; in fact, the Rescuer often plays this role largely to avoid feeling their own emotions. The Persecutor plays the role of blaming the Victim, often with criticism, anger, rigid thoughts, and a stance of irrational authority.

As we consider this triangle, it can be helpful to keep the axiom in mind that "hurt people hurt others." Many perpetrators have experienced significant trauma and are reenacting aspects of their own abuse; this is *not* to excuse their behavior, but to humanize the cycle of abuse and to include the roots of each problem in our awareness. In seeking holistic solutions to problems that involve a perpetrator, we must include their healing and behavior change in our awareness, as difficult as that can often be. In addition, people in the Rescuer role, as described in this model, can have difficulty valuing their own needs, trusting others, and expressing their emotions. For those in the Victim role, we must remember that trauma can induce feelings of powerlessness, and that an experience of powerlessness does not equate to a lifetime of it.

Identifying these roles helps us to recognize the needs of each member of the triangle; remaining connected to the emotional roots of each position gives us a map to move forward, when possible, in a healthy and holistic manner.

Watch for these roles and dynamics in your own work; in cultivating your own personal growth, you reduce the risk of being in an avoidant, enabling, Rescuer role. By reminding the client or student of their power to choose and to problem solve, you prevent this form of Victim identity (different from the reality of having been victimized) from developing or continuing. Also, it is common for those who have experienced abuse to internalize messages of abusers, so watch for not only the person or people who play the Perpetrator role, but the way their thoughts and behaviors can show up within those they target, as a remnant of the abuse.

An Important Truth About Trauma Work

When I started leading yoga and trauma recovery workshops, I was teaching to a largely clinical population (psychologists, social workers, psychiatrists, etc.) and would excitedly jump into a review of our concepts and definitions of trauma. With this population, it was a review of core concepts, and it was necessary to set the stage for the related yoga philosophies. However, as I took this workshop into yoga studios, to people who were not as familiar with the Diagnostic Statistical Manual of Mental Disorders (DSM-V) and the common markers of post-traumatic stress, it took me a moment to reorient to the group before me. For the most part, these students had not spent years studying the ins and outs of trauma recovery via a masters or doctoral degree. I quickly recalled a truth I'd learned long before: **studying trauma can bring up our own reactions to life's most intense experiences.** With that, I began to prepare people more, shifted the focus of the beginning of the workshop to resourcing, a foundational concept in healing trauma, and something we will continue to address throughout this book and in detail in Chapter 8. As in Fromm's concept of being-authority, we must attend to our own trauma recovery, needs, and growth if we are to be effective leaders.

Prepare Your Self-Care

The truth is, trauma responses are powerful and we all experience exposure to some degree of trauma in our lives, even if it's just through supporting others who are coping with its effects. As we will revisit throughout the book, your self-care, self-awareness, and ongoing personal development are essential in your role as service provider. To make your healing work sustainable, I recommend identifying supports on each level of being: physical, mental, emotional, social, creative, energetic, and spiritual. Proactively identifying your needs keeps you healthy and your feet planted firmly in a field of health; which is what we seek to facilitate in others. Even if you are familiar with the content we cover in this book, reading may bring up emotional reactions of your own, and facilitate a deeper process of integration. If you make your primary purpose to observe these responses, without judgment, and to make the conscious and preventative choice to care for yourself, you are more likely to prevent overwhelming triggers, to increase your experience of self-awareness and to have a positive experience moving through the material. In studying or practicing trauma recovery, going slow and taking care tends to improve the experience of integration.

Embodied Leadership

Combine being-authority with the truth that trauma work tends to bring emotional material to light, and it becomes clear why it is crucial that we practice self-care and continue to do our own work. Seek to identify your blind spots. Learn from clients and invest in your own growth and healing. Trauma is not something that happens to a set group of people; we are all at risk and we are all exposed. This is the truth of human vulnerability. If we place ourselves too high on a pedestal as teacher or leader, we risk increasing blindness to our own process. We teach from the light of our own self-discovery. We become aware of our deepest wounds and challenges when we seek to connect with other human beings, and bring our whole selves into relationship. In order to teach in an integrative way, we must also keep an open mind to new approaches and how they might serve, and be open to entirely new ways of thinking and seeing the world. The truth of trauma is painful; cultivating the strength to move through it is something we can ask for support with, and consciously choose. The choices you make can facilitate personal development and, if you are in a leadership role, they can influence others' trajectories, as well. Continue to observe, reflect, and integrate as you go. No one is *done* or has perfected this process of evolution.

***

You'll be happy to know that Hugo, the delightful child who greeted me with expletives at 7:00 AM that Saturday morning, stayed in the group home for the full year that I worked there, and he made significant progress. As staff began to praise his ability to self-express and share with us how he was feeling, he became more selective with his words and, with support, started naming the feelings, instead of just acting them out. As he slowly and consistently received more praise and positive reinforcement, his outbursts of anger became directed less at staff and more at inanimate objects. I worked with him on deep breathing a number of times, and witnessed him using it in a heated argument with his room-mate about a missing Pokémon card. Hugo made progress, and we made sure that he knew it and received recognition for his efforts. He practiced and earned resilience skills that I trust are still with him to this day. When I left, he maintained the diagnoses in his file, but we managed to add in notes about how well he responded to our interventions and charted the progress he had made. We made a point to list what was *right* with him, so whoever looked through the file next would see a perspective on Hugo that was more resilience-focused, and would help them to pick up where we left off. In these cases of what we now call complex, developmental trauma, it takes a village to support one healing path, and each experience of support can help create a healing shift.

Reflection Questions

1   Identify three aspects of mental *health* in yourself or in those you serve.
2   Brainstorm three aspects of resilience that are not included on the ACE Resilience Score.
3   How does it feel for you to be in a leadership role? Identify one to three ways you can encourage a healthy power dynamic between you and the people you serve.
4   What happens when you become triggered?
5   Which self-care practices are essential for you?

Additional resources available at: http://howwecanheal.com/y4tr

References

ACEs Too High (2018). *What's your resilience score?* Retrieved from: http://acestoohigh.com/got-your-ace-score/.

American Psychological Association (2018, February). *The road to resilience.* Retrieved from: www.apa.org/helpcenter/road-resilience.aspx.

Center for Disease Control (CDC) (2016a). *Adverse Childhood Experiences presentation graphics.* Retrieved from: www.cdc.gov/violenceprevention/acestudy/ACE_graphics.html.

Center for Disease Control (CDC) (2016b). *ACEs definitions.* Retrieved from: www.cdc.gov/violenceprevention/acestudy/about.html.

Center for Youth Wellness (2018). *What the science tells us.* Retrieved from: www.centerforyouthwellness.org.

Feldner, M. T., Monson, C. M., & Friedman, M. J. (2007). A critical analysis of approaches to targeted PTSD prevention: Current status and theoretically derived future directions. *Behavior Modification, 31*(1), 80–116.

Felitti, V. J., Anda, R. F., Nordenberg, D., Williamson, D. F., Spitz, A. M., Edwards, V., . . . & Marks, J. S. (1998). Relationship of childhood abuse and household dysfunction to many of the leading causes of death in adults:

The Adverse Childhood Experiences (ACE) study. *American Journal of Preventive Medicine, 14*(4), 245–258.

Fromm, E. (2013a). *Man for himself: An inquiry into the psychology of ethics.* London: Routledge.

Fromm, E. (2013b). *To have or to be?* London: A&C Black.

Johnstone, L. & Boyle, M. with Cromby, J., Dillon, J., Harper, D., Kinderman, P., Longden, E., Pilgrim, D., & Read, J. (2018). *The Power Threat Meaning Framework: Towards the identification of patterns in emotional distress, unusual experiences and troubled or troubling behaviour, as an alternative to functional psychiatric diagnosis.* Leicester: British Psychological Society.

Karpman, S. (1968). Fairy tales and script drama analysis. *Transactional Analysis Bulletin, 7*(26), 39–43.

Millman, D. (1984). *Way of the peaceful warrior: A book that changes lives.* Los Angeles: H J Kramer.

Office of Head Start (2018). *Head Start programs.* Retrieved from: www.acf.hhs.gov/ohs.

Raes, F., Griffith, J. W., Van der Gucht, K., & Williams, J. M. G. (2014). School-based prevention and reduction of depression in adolescents: A cluster-randomized controlled trial of a mindfulness group program. *Mindfulness, 5*(5), 477–486.

Rozin, P., & Royzman, E. B. (2001). Negativity bias, negativity dominance, and contagion. *Personality and Social Psychology Review, 5*(4), 296–320.

SAMHSA (2012). *Trauma and Justice Strategic Initiative: SAMHSA's working definition of trauma and guidance for trauma-informed approach.* Rockville, MD: Substance Abuse and Mental Health Services Administration.

2   Defining Trauma

Human beings are tender creatures. We are born with our hearts open.
And sometimes our open hearts encounter experiences that shatter us.
Sometimes we encounter experiences that so violate our sense of safety, order,
predictability and right that we feel utterly overwhelmed, unable to integrate
and simply unable to go on as before, unable to bear realty. We have come
to call these shattering experiences trauma. None of us is immune to them.
  – Stephen Cope, in the foreword to Overcoming Trauma
  Through Yoga *(Emerson & Hopper, 2011)*

Sandra sat with her shoulders to her ears, gripping with what appeared
to be every muscle in her body. She began to breathe the deep sighs that
precipitate a sob, then got quiet and still, tears streaming from her eyes.
We hadn't discussed details of the event before, but they came pouring
out now, in a wave of release. As she spoke, I took long, deep breaths.
I had a sense that she was ready for this and that this movement of emotion was essential to her healing process. She asked questions aloud as she
recounted the situation, dynamics, and mysteries of the experience. "Who
does that?" "Why did no one intervene?" and "There was no way I could
have known." These comments revealed the part of her reflecting, maintaining a present moment perspective while feeling the intense emotion
from the event, which flowed through her body in patterns of tension and
release. I continued to breathe, saying very little, just enough to remind her
that I was there, feeling compassion and empathy for her. There was no
magical resolution to the story I could provide, but I sought to remind her,
with simple cues, that she was in a safer space now. After moving through
a few rounds of sighs, deep breaths, and tears, she opened her eyes, looked
at me, and said, "I've never told anyone that before. It's been 16 years."

***

Experiences that shatter us don't happen every day and yet, each unique
life has its brush with neglect, violence, heartbreak, or overwhelming

experiences, and the resulting re-ordering of beliefs and expectations about ourselves and the world. The fact of the matter is that timing, circumstance, and relationship impact our response to trauma, and our stage of development when trauma occurs shapes its influence on our personal and professional trajectory. For a variety of reasons, some responses to trauma are frozen in time, left for us to deal with at a later date. As Stephen Cope describes in the foreword to *Overcoming Trauma Through Yoga* (Emerson & Hopper, 2011), "None of us is immune" to traumatic experiences.

In this chapter, we outline core components of post-traumatic stress, and build a foundational understanding of trauma that you can apply to the wide array of experiences your students and clients have experienced. We'll define different types of stress, comb through the details of the diagnostic criteria for PTSD, and explore the more complicated presentations of complex and developmental trauma. These foundations provide us with guidelines to organize how we think about the experience of trauma and recovery, so that we can build the road of resilience with skill and purpose.

This is a dense chapter, one that honors the depth of suffering that exists as a part of life. It is essential both that we stand rooted in mental *health*, and that we understand the ways our bodies, minds, and beings respond to overwhelming experiences. This material is not meant for you to get lost in, or to use as a diagnostic tool; rather, it helps us to clarify how trauma shows up so that we can respond intelligently to its manifestations, and access the appropriate coping strategies to facilitate healing. If you are skipping around in this book, note that, as we discussed in the previous chapter, studying this material can bring up our own memories. Set up your self-care before jumping in here.

Why Disorder?

Like Hugo, whom you met at the beginning of Chapter 1, many of the youth I served early in my career had thick case files and multiple diagnoses. In a time where they were exploring a sense of self in relationship to the world, I often heard them describe themselves in the context of their current mental health challenge. It is incredibly sad to hear a 9-year-old say, "Hi, my name is Dominic, I have ADHD," or a 13-year-old say "It's just who I am; I'll always be depressed."

Diagnostics have value and help us to understand, categorize, and research problems, but they do not encompass resilience factors, and are not intended to become identities. As we covered in the last chapter, when we lead treatment with diagnoses, and introduce these concepts in a heavy-handed way while youth are developing, we facilitate the experience of illness becoming internalized to identity. Even in adult treatment, there is value in rephrasing the words, "I am depressed," to,

"I have depression." The language of the latter increases agency and labels the diagnosis as an experience, rather than a core aspect of self. When we are able to look at a symptom with a bit of distance, we can create space to understand the multi-layered impact of an experience, and to remain rooted in a deeper sense of a healthy self.

Another common misunderstanding associated with the word "disorder" is that it makes those diagnosed different from other people who are in similar shoes. In most all cases, post-traumatic stress is a common reaction to an uncommon or extreme experience. Recall the question, "What happened to this person?" Traumatic experiences can, indeed, have a profound impact and lead to experiences of post-traumatic stress. However, it is important for those who are diagnosed with PTSD to know that they are not alone, that many of these reactions to stress are deeply rooted in biology, as we'll explore in Chapter 3, and that there *is* a pathway to healing. A diagnosis is not intended to function as an identity or a point of comparison, yet is often interpreted in this way.

What is Stress?

While I was in graduate school, I called into a radio station thinking I had the winning answer to their question, "In a survey of 1,000 people, what was the most stressful life experience people reported?" When the DJ picked up the phone and I guessed, "The loss of a loved one?" He paused, "Funny, no, that didn't even make the list." "What made number one, then?" I asked, curious to know what could possibly be worse than saying goodbye to those we hold nearest and dearest, "Moving," he responded. Clearly my understanding of stress was quite different from the radio listeners' – I had just moved across the country and it was one of the most thrilling and adventurous experiences I'd had to date! In addition, I was certain that, had they shared my understanding of the definition of stress, many of the listeners would have agreed that experiencing a loss was more stressful than a move.

Since PTSD is classified as a disorder of stress (American Psychiatric Association, 2013), we need to have a deep understanding of the word and the phenomenon. Stress is a common household word, and can refer to a myriad of experiences and reactions. Studying for a test? You must be stressed! Getting ready to give a speech? That's stressful, too. Breakups? Those are so stressful. Common definitions of stress speak to physical and emotional strain, emphasis, pressure, and tension. It's easy to lump all forms of psychological stress into one category, but it's important to understand that not all stressors are created equal, and not all stress is experienced in the same way. Some research points to the influence of our perception and understanding of stress on experience. While stress, as an internal experience, is on a spectrum and we can choose how to interact with it, there are important differences between everyday stress and traumatic stress.

All stress is meant to help us respond to, or cope with, the situation at hand, but when stress responses get stuck, healing can warrant significant effort. For the purposes of this book, we will differentiate among three types of stress: eustress, distress, and traumatic – or toxic – stress.

Eustress

Eustress is moderate psychological stress that brings some benefit to the person experiencing it. Simply put, it's positive stress. Even when change is welcome, it can be challenging and require us to adapt in ways we do not foresee. Adapting to our own development and to natural changes in life can be an experience of eustress, if we choose to meet the challenge of growth, and adapt. Adjusting to a new job or relationship, getting married, or having an eagerly-anticipated child can be stressful. In fact, not anticipating the stress that comes with positive change can lead to distress, or the perception that something is wrong. Accepting the reality that change poses the challenge of adaptation makes it easier to embrace the experience of eustress.

In addition to major life events, we all need to respond to daily demands – to wake up, make lunches, get kids to school, exercise, submit a report to the boss, or complete an assignment for class. Each of these activities requires us to organize, relate to time, and use our brain power to respond to the demands of our environment. We can also experience positive social stress in daily interactions when we connect in close relationship, seek to understand one another, and seek to forge a path forward with respect for all parties involved. Life involves growth, and eustress is a fact of life across the lifespan.

Distress

Distress describes the stress we feel in association with negative life events and often involves anxiety, sorrow, or pain. Distress could result from losing a job, or a relationship ending. It is an internal experience that could come about as a result of misplacing a wallet, having a fight with a coworker, or getting pulled over by law enforcement. Distress rarely carries with it a clear benefit, as eustress does, and we tend to perceive events that cause distress as primarily negative. Distress can involve mental or emotional suffering, including, but not limited to, loss or harm. Experiencing distress can bring up uncomfortable emotions, which we may choose to feel and process, or to avoid and suppress. In the case of mild and moderate distress, the choice to address, contain or avoid feelings associated with the stressor are often conscious and involve thoughts like, "I'll deal with this later," or, "I've had a hard day, I deserve a drink." There is a spectrum of intensity of distress, and a range of healthy to unhealthy ways of coping with the emotions and situations it presents.

Traumatic Stress

Traumatic stress describes the reaction to significant and marked experiences of intense distress. Examples include a car accident, loss, experiences of violence or harm, or of natural disaster. Contrary to everyday distress, traumatic stress results from heightened and, for most people less common, negative experiences. Traumatic experiences have a marked impact on our physiology; recovering well from them requires significant external support in addition to internal coping skills. While an experience of distress may impact us for a day or two, the impact of traumatic stress often lasts longer and takes time and resources to resolve.

Research indicates that exposure to interpersonal violence increases the risk of developing PTSD (Kilpatrick et al., 2003); as a long-time provider for the California Victims of Crime program, I see the negative impacts of exposure to violence in clients on a regular basis. While nurturing promotes healthy development, violence and neglect negatively impact neurological development in a lasting manner (Perry, 2002). Occasionally, clients express a desire to return to the scene of harm and not be negatively impacted by it, saying things like "It shouldn't have impacted me this much," but this goes against our human biology. Having seen the fallout from emotional, physical, and sexual abuse firsthand for decades, it is clear to me that violence is toxic and not something we should normalize or dismiss. We should not be expected, or expect ourselves, to tolerate abuse. It is harmful to our bodies, minds, and emotional well-being, and is not a stress that we should normalize or talk ourselves into enduring. As we'll discuss in the diagnostic criteria for PTSD, violence is one of the central causes of PTSD.

Cumulative Stress

Allostatic load is the term we use to describe the cumulative effect of stress on an individual. When someone is exposed to repeated or chronic stress, there are physiological consequences, including changes in neuroendocrine responses. Since we cannot easily see brain areas impacted by stress – the hippocampus or the hypothalamic pituitary adrenal (HPA) axis for example – it serves us to draw analogies to things that are more visible. If you had a broken arm, would you go to the gym to do bicep curls? Even if they were a regular part of your routine before the injury, you'd need to adapt to meet the needs of the healing bone. Similarly, when your system is in a state of extreme distress or trauma, it is helpful to modify daily demands, reduce additional stressors, be gentle with yourself, and avoid exposure to distressing circumstances, whenever possible.

For someone experiencing PTSD, the load of daily demands – making lunch, getting to work on time, submitting the report by the deadline – may feel overwhelming. As a result of the collective load that the violent experience or traumatic event has left in its wake, mundane tasks that felt approachable in the past may no longer feel so, and what felt like eustress or distress before the trauma may feel much more challenging after the fact. This is normal. An important part of trauma recovery is to respect the overall needs of your system so it can heal. Often, as is true of a broken bone, the healing process can feel painstakingly slow and, yet, the more we respect it, the more thorough the healing experience, and the less we disturb the slow steady progress being accomplished on a daily basis.

A student recently shared *spoon theory* with me – a simple way to conceptualize the impact that traumatic stress and chronic illnesses can have on the system (Miserandino, 2003). Spoon theory gives us a tangible way to understand how the long-term impacts of trauma can impact energy. Imagine, if you will, that everyone has 100 spoons to spend each day, energy to invest in whatever we so desire. For the healthy person, a workday morning may look like this:

- Spoon #1: Wake up & get ready;
- Spoon #2: Drive to work;
- Spoon #3: Respond to email; and
- Spoon #4: Work on current project.

That same morning for someone experiencing complex PTSD or chronic illness may externally appear the same, while this internal experience is quite different, resembling something closer to:

- Spoon #1: Open eyes;
- Spoon #2: Roll to one side;
- Spoon #3: Stand up;
- Spoon #4: Take a shower, and so on throughout the day.

By noon, the person coping with post-traumatic stress or chronic illness may have spent all their spoons, while others may have spoons to spare after work. Spoon theory offers a simple, tangible representation of the internal experience of energy and how it can change for those recovering from trauma and dealing with chronic illness.

How We Think About Stress

Studies focusing on the importance of how we perceive stress – as negative or positive, debilitating or motivating – report that when we believe stress is harmful, we are more likely to die from stress-related health conditions (Keller et al., 2012). This information could come across as empowering for some clients and invalidating for others. When you look to the examples of eustress and distress above, it's easier to see how our perception of the event might change, and the experience of stress could bring growth. Many people lose their jobs and find better ones, or learn about themselves in the process of ending a relationship. This research highlights the need to distinguish between the stress of high demands and the stress of witnessing or experiencing violence, the former being something we can perceive as motivating, while the latter goes against the relational needs of human beings. In the next chapter, we will explore Polyvagal Theory, which describes the differing physiological experiences that accompany relational connection and experiences of threat.

Violence and the experience of traumatic stress are not good for the body. At the same time, it is helpful when we understand that our bodies respond to toxic stress by *trying* to keep us safe, which is sometimes impossible. Our bodies don't always do what we would have liked them to, but accepting that the body's response is deeply wired helps us to know that the responses do not mean anything negative about us; it is simply the way we are wired to respond to a toxic situation. By befriending ourselves and acknowledging physiological responses without judgment we create room for healing experiences that honor the body's attempt to keep us alive in the face of overwhelming threat, danger or shock.

Criteria for PTSD: DSM-5

While any diagnostic manual has its constraints, a considerable amount of effort has been dedicated to developing these manuals, along with the conceptualizations they contain. They are never perfect, always viewed through the lens of the authors, and they can help us to identify core themes that other professionals have observed, discussed, and deduced, over a significant period of time. The American Psychiatric Association published the first Diagnostic and Statistical Manual of Mental Disorders (DSM) in 1952, and included the PTSD diagnosis in 1980. The concepts we cover here represent 61 years of observation and evolution in the field of mental health, and 33 years of refining this concept of post-traumatic stress.

According to the fifth version of the DSM, PTSD requires exposure to either death, threatened death, or violence. This exposure can be direct or indirect, or occur during the course of vocational duties. After an experience of death, threatened death or violence, four common patterns emerge: re-experiencing, avoidance, changes in thought and mood, and changes in arousal or reactivity. While the manual does not discuss social or emotional threat, I have observed reactions to social violence, like teasing and bullying, follow strikingly similar response patterns to threats of physical violence – you may observe this in yourself, your students, or clients as you read through these criteria. Notice what comes to mind as you read. If the thoughts that arise in reaction to this content feel in any way overwhelming, I encourage you to pause, get support, and come back at a later time.

Re-Experiencing

The first response to stress included in the DSM-5 diagnosis of PTSD is re-experiencing, which can occur in the form of nightmares, flashbacks, or an intrusion of a mental, emotional, or somatic nature. An intrusion is a remnant of past experience that comes to awareness without conscious volition, bringing with it images or sensations related to the experience. While Hollywood's favorite way to dramatize PTSD is through dramatic nightmares, intrusions can appear during fully awake daylight hours, and can manifest as memory, thought, emotion, somatic impression, or even as a physiological experience.

Intrusions may take many forms and indicate that there is some emotional material related to the event that has yet to process. To imagine a less disturbing example, let's pretend you once threw up cotton candy at a carnival – and, for the sake of this example, let's call that traumatic. You thought you were going to die and, despite years of therapy, it still upsets you to think about cotton candy to this day. Intrusions could manifest in a myriad of ways:

- You may drift off in the middle of a conversation, overcome by a cloud in the sky, and see it as pink, fluffy, sugary, vomit-inducing cotton candy.
- You might wake up at night to a dream of the cotton candy machine whirling and the memory of the server handing you the cone with its sticky crystals reaching out to you.
- You may also find the emotion of terror gripping you as you lean over a drinking fountain, not even aware that it was a drinking fountain you threw up in all those years ago, when you thought the cotton candy had brought you not only to your knees, but to your last day on earth.
- You may feel a lurch in your stomach any time you see an advertisement announcing that the carnival is in town.
- You may break out in a cold sweat at the taste of artificial cherry flavor.
- You may feel the urge to flee when you see someone eating cotton candy.

There are as many examples of intrusions as there are factors of unique human beings and personal experiences. As the examples above demonstrate, intrusions can have physical, mental, and emotional presentations, and some spiritual approaches consider trauma to have an impact on the soul itself. The examples above also serve to illustrate that an experience one person finds to be happy, safe, and comforting (i.e., going to the carnival and eating cotton candy as a kid), could trigger intrusions and a full post-traumatic reaction in another person with a different experience.

This truth makes it difficult to predict triggers, and virtually impossible to avoid upsetting a group of people with diverse trauma histories.

Avoidance

It's overwhelming to take on any large task, particularly one that includes difficult emotions, so often there is a part of us that would rather wait, or pretend that the task is not there. Avoidance symptoms related to trauma manifest when we do not want to face the full range of emotion related to an experience, so we may choose to not to drive down a specific street, or visit a pocket of the world where something upsetting occurred. It could also involve avoiding people – an ex-girlfriend, the neighbor who witnessed your cotton candy vomit-spree, or even an entire race, gender, or vocational group that relates to the experience of trauma.

Avoiding people, places, things, words, and even areas of the body, is common in the wake of exposure to trauma and/or extreme stress. After a female client of mine experienced an assault at the hands of law enforcement, there were times when she described wanting to jump into the shadows – a place she used to assume to be dangerous – to avoid walking past a police car. She would not let herself get close enough to attempt to distinguish if there was anyone in the car, because any semblance of trust that she would be treated with respect had been obliterated. The experience of being assaulted by someone in police uniform changed her expectation of all those who wore it.

This desire to distance or disconnect from pain may lead us to avoid a certain street, person, or group of people. But what if the trauma occurs to the body? This is often the case with physical and sexual violence, though the phenomenon is not constrained to these types of trauma. I had a client who was pregnant but lost her child in the early stages of the third trimester. Her primary memory of being happily pregnant was peering over her belly, unable to catch a glimpse of her feet. Since she'd lost the baby, she could not look down, or "feel into her feet" as we so often instruct in efforts to help those we serve ground, without overwhelming feelings of sadness arising. For her, the things she wanted to avoid were the very same body parts that carried her around from day to day. Any attention placed on her feet brought an overwhelming experience of grief straight to the surface.

In prolonged or extreme cases, people may cease to live in an area of the body that relates to the experience of trauma. In the clinical setting, this could be a manifestation of *somatoform dissociation*, which often presents as loss of feeling, numbness, or pain in an area of the body exposed to trauma (Nijenhuis et al., 1996). Knowing this, and knowing that any part of the body could potentially hold a trauma-laden memory, consider the risk of yoga practices, which ask us to connect in increasingly refined detail with the various areas and actions of which our bodies are capable. While it is important to become familiar with the ways trauma might manifest physically for your students and clients, it is impossible to instruct physical forms and avoid all potential somatic triggers at the same time.

Changes in Thought and Mood

Negative changes in cognition and mood are also common reactions to traumatic experience. Changes in thought can manifest in thoughts about the self, others, or the world at large. Examples include thoughts such as "I am bad," "other people are bad," or "the world is unsafe." Such beliefs can persist to contribute to a negative sense of self, negative assumptions about others' behaviors, and a negative world view. These beliefs can go on to impact self-esteem, self-worth, relationships with individuals and groups, and life outcomes related to those relationships.

Changes in mood speak to differences in emotional experience after a traumatic event. Mood changes may include heightened affect, like anxiety, anger, and sadness, and may also include flattened affect, a feeling of restricted range of, or access to, emotion. These feelings can be specific, and change rapidly, or can exist as a general experience, like a cloud hanging over one's head or a buzz of anxiety constantly in the background. These emotional experiences and expressions are in contrast to what was common or typical for the person prior to the traumatic experience, and are typically apparent to those who know the person well. You may also hear students or clients say things like "I just don't feel like myself lately," when their mood shifts significantly. Listen for comments like these.

Changes in Nervous System Arousal

The last area of change noted in cases of PTSD is changes in arousal of the nervous system, often leading to changes in reactivity and the ability to self-regulate. The nervous system's response to trauma aims to keep us safe from physical harm; as a result, people often experience symptoms of hypervigilance, fatigue, and the more complicated freeze response. We cover this in detail in the next chapter, accompanied by a few different models of the nervous system's response to trauma. Often, these symptoms are apparent in the body and can change posture, physical tension, and facial expressions in a significant way. Photographers have captured images of soldiers' faces before, during, and after their service in combat zones (Snow, 2012). These images speak to some of the ways traumatic experiences can impact the nervous system and facial expression.

These are the four primary components of PTSD. When intrusions, avoidance, changes in thought and mood, or changes in reactivity occur after the fact and last longer than a month, it may be time to seek professional help. We often call a single event that leads to these post-traumatic experience a "simple trauma;" examples include a car accident, assault, or witnessing a one-time act of violence. When a client has a single-event experience, and little to no prior exposure to trauma, healing tends to be more straightforward. When multiple traumas occur, treatment can become more complex.

Complex Trauma

The term *complex trauma*, introduced by Judith Herman (Herman, 1992) evolved as a way to describe what happens when one endures multiple traumatic events. It speaks to the complexity of coping with the impact of more than one experience, and to the potential for more wide-ranging and intertwined symptoms. Complex trauma often refers to trauma that is relational in nature and, thus, impacts the attachment system in addition to the symptoms outlined above. Complex trauma can result from the ACE experiences outlined in Chapter 1, including but not limited to childhood physical, emotional or sexual trauma, challenges within the family, or neglect. Thus, complex trauma tends to have a more long-term impact than single event trauma and, as a result of its interpersonal nature, can involve difficulties relating to providers seeking to help in the healing process.

Attachment trauma speaks to symptoms related to the loss or absence of a parent, while the term *betrayal trauma* describes the impact of having lost trust in those closest to protect us, or to act in our best interest. Betrayal can occur in many ways; one unfortunately common manifestation occurs when parents are perpetrators and deny abuse, manipulating the child and leaving them to question their own memory and experience. Both betrayal and attachment trauma are deeply interpersonal, so the task of healing in therapy or in relationship to others in a supportive role involves cultivating a healthy relationship and overcoming challenges related to the initial relational wound.

Developmental Trauma

The term *developmental trauma* emerged to speak not only to the cumulative relational aspects of trauma, but to the context of development during which they occur. Development speaks to the biological, social, emotional, and behavioral changes that occur between birth and full brain development, which occurs around 26 years of age. Figure 2.1 shows the basic stages of brain development; keep in mind that these are norms and that individual experiences can vary. We can also apply the context of development to people across the lifespan, though the bulk of developmental milestones occur in earlier years.

If something happens at a crucial stage of development, it can impact the mastery of that stage, either delaying it as the system responds and

Age Range	Cognitive (Piaget)	Social (Erikson)	Implications
0–2 years	Experiencing world through senses and actions	Trust vs. mistrust	Attachment and bonding
2–6 years	Object permanence; Language development; Pretend play	Autonomy vs. shame and doubt; Initiative vs. guilt	Self-soothing; Academic success
7–11 years	Logical thinking	Industry vs. inferiority	Social competence
12–21 years	Abstract reasoning; Moral reasoning	Identity vs. role confusion	Loyalty, friendship
21 plus years		Intimacy vs. isolation	Maintaining relationships; Connection to community

Figure 2.1 Developmental Tasks of Cognitive and Social Development (Erikson, 1950; Piaget, 1964; Cozolino, 2014)

heals from the trauma, or shifting the course of the social, emotional, and psychological tasks associated with the developmental stage. Consider some of the developmental tasks that children move through as their brains and bodies develop (Figure 2.1).

In addition to the theories outlined in Figure 2.1, there are specific physical accomplishments children complete, including walking, talking, and learning to communicate. Since relationships facilitate learning and, in the case of attachment and betrayal trauma, relationships play a negative role, we can see how experiences of early trauma can have multiple impacts on the course of development. As the developing brain organizes around these negative experiences, it creates pathways that prune throughout adolescence and, when left unchallenged by positive experiences, result in a world view founded in the traumatic experiences of early childhood.

Bessel van der Kolk, founder of The Trauma Center in Brookline, MA, proposed a diagnosis of Developmental Trauma Disorder (DTD) to be included in the DSM-5 (van der Kolk, 2005). The proposed diagnosis was ultimately rejected, with feedback rumored to have been that it covered too much psychological territory and would be too confusing to differentiate from other disorders. Since DTD has a direct impact on brain development, with impacts on attention, mood, relationship, sense of self, expectations and experiences in the world, and physical health, it is indeed challenging to narrow down the effects. The proposed criteria for DTD are included in Figure 2.2; as you can see, the scope is much wider than what we discussed in the diagnosis of PTSD, yet there are common themes.

As the proposed diagnosis outlines, DTD's scope of impact is wide and far-reaching. As we learned in the ACE study, negative experiences

A. Exposure

    1. Multiple or chronic exposure to one or more forms of developmentally adverse interpersonal trauma (abandonment, betrayal, physical assaults, sexual assaults, threats to bodily integrity, coercive practices, emotional abuse, witnessing violence and death).

    2. Subjective Experience (rage, betrayal, fear, resignation, defeat, shame).

B. Triggered pattern of repeated dysregulation in response to trauma cues. Dysregulation (high or low) in presence of cues. Changes persist and do not return to baseline; not reduced in intensity by conscious awareness.

- Affective
- Somatic (physiological, motoric, medical)
- Behavioral (e.g. re-enactment, cutting)
- Cognitive (thinking that it is happening again, confusion, dissociation, or depersonalization)
- Relational (clinging, oppositional, distrustful, compliant)
- Self-attribution (self-hate and blame)

C. Persistently Altered Attributions and Expectancies

- Negative self-attribution
- Distrust of protective caretaker
- Loss of expectancy of protection by others
- Loss of trust in social agencies to protect
- Lack of recourse to social justice/retribution
- Inevitability of future victimization

D. Functional Impairment

- Educational
- Familial
- Peer
- Legal
- Vocational

Figure 2.2 Developmental Trauma Criteria (van der Kolk, 2005)

in early childhood can cause immediate harm, as well long-term developmental challenges related to physiology, psychology, and social outcomes. Even if a parent tells a child that they are hitting them out of love, or that leaving them alone cultivates independence, the stress of abuse and neglect is unhealthy for children. Physical, emotional, and sexual abuse cause harm. Once abuse has occurred, the best thing to do is to address the harm done, attempt to repair any relational strain, meet the child's needs, and bolster the child's access to resilience factors.

Intergenerational Trauma

Another important layer of trauma is the intergenerational transmission of it. At times, people refer to *intergenerational trauma* as *historical* or *transgenerational*, all pointing to the truth we've revealed that traumatic stress can impact offspring through history and across generations. Intergenerational trauma conversations center around experiences like war and genocide, and include experiences of violence, slavery, and imprisonment. Slavery in the United States, the Holocaust in Europe, and apartheid in South Africa are all systems of oppression that included physical abuse, emotional abuse, and neglect. Studies measuring genetic alterations in Holocaust survivors and their children have identified epigenetic alterations in both survivors and their offspring (Kellermann, 2013; Yehuda et al, 2016). The field of *epigenetics* studies both environmental and hereditary factors and provides us with the context of how biology and experience intersect. As we further understand the impact of traumatic stress, we can explore factors for both risk and prevention.

If we are apt to explore the impact of intergenerational trauma on humans, cells, and genes, it is important to include a conversation about *intergenerational resilience*. In Chapter 9, we'll discuss post-traumatic growth, the field that explores the growth people report experiencing in the wake of trauma, including but not limited to feeling grateful for life and loved ones, or feeling a renewed sense of purpose. There is markedly little research on intergenerational resilience, and very little on how coping skills are passed down through generations in the absence of traumatic stress. As the field of psychology places increasing value on positive emotions, and research measuring their impact on health, we will hopefully find more ways to measure and encourage intergenerational resilience. Just because we are not looking at, or measuring it yet, does not mean it is not happening already.

The conversation of intergenerational trauma sheds light on the reality that entire groups of people have been subjected to traumatic experiences, with little systemic support in recovering from the negative effects. Unfortunately, the rational authority we explored in Chapter 1 is not always what is practiced in leadership structures, and entire communities can be harmed by a group or single leader who practices exploitive, irrational authority. As we engage in healing work, it is important to recognize the systems of oppression that impact people on the basis of race, ethnicity, sex, gender, sexual orientation, ability, disability, body size or appearance, and other factors. Honoring the pain, recognizing its impact, and exploring the realm of intergenerational resilience can help. Knowing that group experiences do not always reflect the individual experience is also helpful, and approaching with curiosity and compassion can help you to learn about the unique experience of the individuals or groups you serve.

It is also tempting to think that only groups who have experienced extreme events – war, trauma, or political violence – will experience post-traumatic stress, or that resolving trauma is not a collective priority because it only applies to marginalized groups. On the contrary, and as Nadine Burke Harris shares in her discussion of ACEs, "we marginalize the issue because it *does* apply to us" (Harris, 2014). There are inequalities and systemic challenges that put some groups at higher risk of poverty, violence, and neglect and, at the same time, facing difficult emotions, dynamics, and life experiences is a challenge for everyone; trauma occurs across boundaries of race, religion, culture, age, gender, socioeconomic status (SES), and sexual orientation. In order to move forward, we must acknowledge that there was, and is, pain, and each of us must do our own healing work. The empathy that stems from facing our own struggles helps to build bridges across perceived differences.

***

In Sandra's session following the disclosure, she appeared softer and more at ease. She spoke indirectly of her experience now, sharing reflections from the week since we'd last met. "I called my mom. I didn't tell her, but I cried. I feel like she must know. How could you not? Everything changed for me that year." She filled this session with many deep breaths, pauses, and sighs. Something had shifted within her. "It's like I've been carrying Pandora's box on my shoulders. Last week I put it down, and opened it. It's not gone, but somehow it holds less power. I don't know if or how people recover from these things, but I think this is progress."

In our time together, she never revisited the narrative of this trauma. She did, however continue to process layers of emotion, and to build a sense of peace, resilience, and self-worth into her everyday life. She took steps towards goals she hoped to achieve, which had been a challenge for some time. Her posture shifted in subtle ways that left her looking taller, more expansive, and less fearful. After three years of working together, she moved out of state. "I've had this big antique chest in my closet for years," she told me. "I've always loved it but, for some reason, I decided I don't want to take it with me. Almost like it represents the weight of holding things in. I donated it to a shelter around the corner from my house. It can help someone else hold things now." For Sandra, this was an important act that symbolized her release of the emotions related to her traumatic experience.

Reflection Questions

1   What is the most common manifestation of traumatic stress that you see in the people you serve?
2   Based on what you know about their exposure to trauma, what aspects of development may have been impacted?

3   How can you recognize, access, and foster intergenerational resilience within yourself and those you serve?

Additional resources available at http://howwecanheal.com/y4tr

References

American Psychiatric Association. (2013). *Diagnostic and statistical manual of mental disorders* (DSM-5). American Psychiatric Publications.

Cozolino, L. (2014). The neuroscience of human relationships: Attachment and the developing social brain. New York: Norton.

Emerson, D., & Hopper, E. (2011). *Overcoming trauma through yoga: Reclaiming your body*. New York: North Atlantic Books.

Erikson, E. H. (1950). *Childhood and society*. New York: Norton.

Harris, N. B. (2014). How childhood trauma affects health across a lifetime. Retrieved from: www.ted.com/talks/nadine_burke_harris_how_childhood_trauma_affects_health_across_a_lifetime/discussion?quote=1941https://www.ted.com/talks/nadine_burke_harris_how_childhood_trauma_affects_health_across_a_lifetime/discussion?quote=1941.

Herman, J. L. (1992). Complex PTSD: A syndrome in survivors of prolonged and repeated trauma. *Journal of Traumatic Stress*, 5(3), 377–391.

Keller, A., Litzelman, K., Wisk, L. E., Maddox, T., Cheng, E. R., Creswell, P. D., & Witt, W. P. (2012). Does the perception that stress affects health matter? The association with health and mortality. *Health Psychology*, 31(5), 677.

Kellermann, N. P. (2013). Epigenetic transmission of holocaust trauma: Can nightmares be inherited? *The Israel Journal of Psychiatry and Related Sciences*, 50(1), 33.

Kilpatrick, D. G., Ruggiero, K. J., Acierno, R., Saunders, B. E., Resnick, H. S., & Best, C. L. (2003). Violence and risk of PTSD, major depression, substance abuse/dependence, and comorbidity: Results from the National Survey of Adolescents. *Journal of Consulting and Clinical Psychology*, 71(4), 692–700.

Miserandino, C. (2003). The spoon theory. *But You Don't Look Sick*. https://butyoudontlooksick.com

Nijenhuis, E. R., Spinhoven, P., Van, R. D., der Hart Van, O., & Vanderlinden, J. (1996). The development and psychometric characteristics of the Somatoform Dissociation Questionnaire (SDQ-20). *The Journal of Nervous and Mental Disease*, 184(11), 688–694.

Perry, B. D. (2002). Childhood experience and the expression of genetic potential: What childhood neglect tells us about nature and nurture. *Brain and Mind*, 3(1), 79–100.

Piaget, J. (1964). Part I: Cognitive development in children: Piaget development and learning. *Journal of Research in Science Teaching*, 2(3), 176–186.

Snow, L. (2012). *We Are Not the Dead*. Retrieved from: https://lalagesnow.photoshelter.com/gallery/We-Are-The-Not-Dead/G0000_eT5QooYacY.

Van der Kolk, B. A. (2005). Developmental Trauma Disorder: Toward a rational diagnosis for children with complex trauma histories. *Psychiatric Annals*, 35(5), 401–408.

Yehuda, R., Daskalakis, N. P., Bierer, L. M., Bader, H. N., Klengel, T., Holsboer, F., & Binder, E. B. (2016). Holocaust exposure induced intergenerational effects on FKBP5 methylation. *Biological Psychiatry*, 80(5), 372–380.

3 Stress and the Nervous System

Until we understand that traumatic symptoms are physiological as well as psychological, we will be woefully inadequate in our attempts to heal them. The heart of the matter lies in being able to recognize that trauma represents animal instincts gone awry. When harnessed, these instincts can be used by the conscious mind to transform traumatic symptoms into a state of well-being.

– Peter Levine

Her body bristled at the sound. Just a 4-month-old puppy, this was the first time my partner and I let Iris off-leash on the trails – it wasn't my idea. I saw her body stiffen, called to attention by the sound of something big moving through the bushes. As leaves fluttered in the canopy, she froze and her eyes darted to follow the sounds. Her tail rose up like an antenna, then lowered between her hind legs, then rose again. What had been a sweet domesticated pup moments before with shining eyes became a wild animal again, aware of the dangers of the natural world. Before I could lure her back to us with a treat, she darted off, obscured immediately by the brush.

"Iris!!!" We both called. All we had was the sound of her collar, the jingle that tells you she is awake, nearby – or scratching to try to get it off. This time, it meant we had not lost her, but within a minute, the air fell silent. "Oh, shit," I thought, "We've lost our new puppy – my stepson's birthday gift, at that!" Now she was either still running, or hidden behind one of the many trees engulfing us, and had forgotten about the healthy meals we feed her, and the couch snuggling we caved to after swearing to a strict "no dogs on the couch" rule. In an instant, she'd forgotten that we exist. She had snuggled her way into our hearts and home; and with a stirring of the bushes, she was gone.

The Nervous System: An Overview

If you've been in the yoga or trauma recovery community for long, chances are you have heard mention of the nervous system. Even beyond these communities, we often describe shifts that occur in the nervous system in common language. Someone tapping a pencil on the desk is *nerve wracking*, people *get on our nerves* when they frustrate us, and we collapse after a deeply physical effort or emotional experience into *nervous exhaustion*. Western models of fitness often focus on the muscles, heart, and lungs, but fail to address the importance of a healthy and balanced nervous system. Holistic wellness efforts, like those we find in most yoga communities, recognize that we are more than muscles and bones, even physiologically speaking, and incorporate awareness of the nervous system into teaching choices and wellness efforts.

Our nervous system has a number of subcomponents with different structures and functions. Unless you have deep anatomical or medical training, it can easily get confusing, so we'll explore the different names, categories and functions here. This section serves as a resource to review or reference when sorting through the different functions of this complex, essential system. Understanding what happens when these "animal instincts," as Dr. Peter Levine refers to them in his book, *Waking the Tiger* (1997), become activated, is key to understanding trauma and recovery.

Structurally, when we refer to the **Central Nervous System (CNS)** we are talking about the brain and spinal cord, while the **Peripheral Nervous System (PNS)**, refers to the nerves that extend out into the limbs and more distal parts of the body. *Afferent neurons* relay messages from the body to the CNS, giving the brain information about the body's experience, while *efferent neurons* transmit messages from the CNS to all parts of the body, instigating action.

The **Somatic Nervous System (SoNS)** is part of the PNS and manages voluntary body movements and involuntary reflexes like a blink, knee jerk, gag or startle response. The **Autonomic Nervous System (ANS)**, regulated largely by the hypothalamus, is also part of the PNS and regulates involuntary, unconscious functions such as digestion, respiration, heart rate, and sexual arousal. The ANS is comprised of the sympathetic nervous system, the parasympathetic nervous system and enteric nervous system.

The **Sympathetic Nervous System (SNS)** activates the fight or flight response when exposed to significant mental and emotional stress, or when a situation arises that threatens physical safety. Both the fight and flight response come with an increase in heart rate and blood flow to the muscles, decreasing energy delegated to activities that are not dependent on immediate survival, like digestion. Its job is to give us the energy to fight or to flee to safety. When we are able to escape threat, the parasympathetic system, often referred to as the "rest and digest" system, kicks in to restore equilibrium. When we are unable to escape, or when the stressor repeats or becomes chronic, as it often is in the case of complex trauma, adrenaline, norepinephrine and cortisol flood the body, and the fight or flight response remains activated, without the opportunity for the parasympathetic nervous system to bring the necessary balance.

We've come to understand the **Parasympathetic Nervous System (PSNS)** as being in charge of the "rest and digest" response and, yet, this is only part of its function. Dr. Stephen Porges' Polyvagal Theory (Porges, 2011), which we will explore in more detail later in this chapter, outlines two branches of the vagus nerve responsible for two different parasympathetic responses. *Myelin*, a fatty sheath coating the axon that protects and helps send signals efficiently, plays a key role in differentiating the two branches of the nerve. The more recently evolved branch, the myelinated vagus, is involved in the rest and digest response, and connects to our ability to socially engage. In this state, digestion activities increase while heart rate lowers, and sympathetic responses decrease. The unmyelinated vagus, the "older software" so to speak, governs the parasympathetic freeze state, which relates to many of the numbing and distancing symptoms of post-traumatic stress.

The lesser known **Enteric Nervous System (ENS)** is located around the digestive tract. This system allows for local control without input from the sympathetic or the parasympathetic branches, though it can still receive and respond to signals from the rest of the body. There are more than 30 neurotransmitters in the enteric system, which is often referred to as the "gut brain" and is responsible for various functions related to the gastrointestinal system. Research suggests that the enteric nervous system interacts with the central nervous system and can impact experiences of anxiety, memory, and neuro-endocrine responses to stress. The same research identifies the possibility that some probiotic strains could have a positive impact on neurologic disorders (Carabotti, Scirocco, Maselli, & Severi, 2015).

This basic understanding of the key aspects and functions of the nervous system is essential in understanding our students' and clients' whole-body response to trauma and in building whole person solutions. If biology is not your interest or forte, I recommend putting some flash cards together, drawing some pictures, or trying to explain the above paragraphs to a colleague or loved one, in order to have this foundation in your toolbox. As this chapter progresses, we'll explore a few more complexities of the nervous system and its response to traumatic stress.

The Triune Brain

This three-part model of the brain is a wonderful way to simplify and categorize major functions, and evolutionary layers of the brain. Based on Paul MacLean's observations of sequential brain development in animals and humans (MacLean & Kral, 1973), this model organizes the brain into three key areas of engagement: the reptilian complex, the paleomammalian complex, and the neomammalian complex, also referred to as the brain stem, limbic system, and neocortex. The more neuroscientists learn about the complexity of the brain's structure and function, the less over-simplified models like these apply; so keep in mind that, while this remains an effective tool for teaching trauma responses to students new to brain function, it is a simplified model, and not a complete explanation of the true complexity that exists. Advancements in neuroscience continue to evolve and explain these functions in increasingly refined detail.

In this model, the brain stem – also referred to as the *reptilian brain* – describes the brain structures close to the spinal cord governing breath, heart rate, and reptilian behaviors like territoriality. In Figure 3.1, this is the section of the brain labeled at the left-hand side. The limbic brain, pictured towards the center of the diagram, refers to a group of structures in the midbrain associated with emotion, motivation, and long-term memory, as well as nurturing and social behaviors. The section on the right of the diagram, represents the "neocortex," the cluster of brain structures towards the front of brain that house advanced cognitions like planning, reflection, and analysis.

When teaching this simple model as a tool for self-regulation, we describe the generalized functions that apply to each of these three parts, and liken them to the experience of our client or student. The accompanying hand model uses the base of the palm, thumb, and fingers wrapped into a fist to create a model of the brain in our own hand. If you have

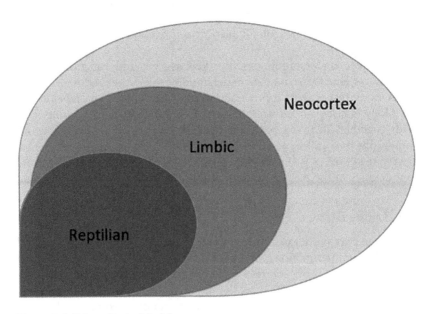

Figure 3.1 Triune Brain Model

yet to see this triune hand brain model, follow the resource link at the end of this chapter to follow along via video. We can use this three-part model, via a picture or a hand model, to describe a simplified version of what occurs when our nervous system responds to trauma. I have found this particularly helpful with youth, as they can take their hand model with them and model it to communicate their experience and needs in treatment sessions.

The trauma response involves deep-seated responses hard-wired into our nervous systems over thousands of years of evolution to help keep us safe. When we experience threat, the limbic and reptilian brain interpret and respond before we can reflect, analyze, and make a well-thought out plan of action. Evolution has created these responses over millions of years. When we fight, flee, or freeze, the lower brain structures are making the call, and when we are able to achieve safety, rest, and reflect, we engage the neocortex and have access to prefrontal functions like reflection and analysis. Accessing this prefrontal function, or getting it "back online" is a key way to engage self-regulation. As we'll discuss in the next chapter, there are both top down (brain to body) and bottom up (body to brain) avenues that those in helping professions can explore to facilitate this process. For an adult in trauma response, and particularly for a young person whose neocortex is in development, engaging awareness of the capacity to access the prefrontal functions of the neocortex, and to reflect and choose behavior, is a central treatment goal.

The Window of Tolerance Model

Now a foundational understanding in trauma treatment, Dan Siegel's Window of Tolerance model (Siegel, 1999) provides an excellent visual concept for understanding the SNS and PSNS. It provides a clear picture of how hyperarousal and hypoarousal of the nervous system relate

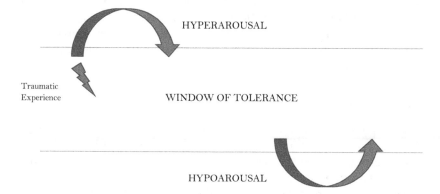

Figure 3.2 Window of Tolerance

to trauma and symptoms of post-traumatic stress. This model relates to yoga philosophy that will be explained in future chapters, and sets up a model of understanding that helps teachers and clinicians choose what type of yoga practices and postures will offer the most benefit.

Let's explore what this model can teach us about the SNS and hyper-arousal, the PSNS and hypoarousal, and the window of tolerance in the middle.

Hyperarousal

When a trauma occurs, most often the sympathetic system activates first, engaging fight or flight to respond to the circumstance at hand. We refer to hyperarousal, in this model, as being "above the line," and describe this as the nervous system's activation switch flipping to the *on* position. When a situation pulls the body from the Window of Tolerance and into hyperarousal, we see symptoms that present across many layers of experience. Physiologically, the heart rate and respiration increase, pupils dilate, and energy goes to the extremities. In the three-part brain model explored above, these responses are rooted in the brainstem and limbic brain. When the nervous system activates into fight or flight, we often experience an overwhelming rush of energy, and many people describe completing physical acts they would not normally attempt with success – jumping a fence, lifting an object, or pushing a person out of harm's way.

Common emotional experiences in hyperarousal include anxiety, fear, anger, rage, and at times, empowerment. Cognition, or thoughts, tend to be nonexistent, or quick, and related to survival. Some clients recounting traumatic experiences remember words or short phrases such as, "door" when eyes are locked on an exit point, or "must get out!" when fleeing. In my experience with clients, words are less common when engaged with a fight response as the body remains engaged, making split-second deci-sions in efforts to protect, though I had a client in physical struggle who repeated the word "No!" aloud, and another in an assault who stated "Stop, you're hurting me!" in efforts to communicate to the authority that they were not resisting. In each of these examples, the theme of returning to safety is clear, which underscores the nervous system's efforts in these cases: it activates in an attempt to bring our bodies to safety.

Hypoarousal

While traumatic encounters most often necessitate an active response, the system can transition to hypoarousal for a variety of reasons, com-monly related to either the perceived ineffectiveness of fighting or feeling, or the exhaustion of activation efforts over time. The first circumstance describes a freeze response, in which the body decides to shut down, or feign death, in efforts to preserve itself. The second describes collapse at the exhaustion of having the system activated for a prolonged period of time. Both manifest in physical symptoms of stillness, or lack of capacity for movement. This is the opposite of the fight flight response, where energy is in excess, and is as if the nervous system switch was flipped to the *off* position. In the freeze response, it can feel very challenging to access motion, as the body is now receiving the message that it needs to be still to preserve its life. In the collapsed state, the body has surrendered to stillness, after action proved to either not be safe, or not be effective in meeting the need for safety.

People experiencing a freeze response often appear depressed, despondent, or dissociated, and it can feel hard for them to connect with other people because of this. Polyvagal theory attributes this type of excess parasympathetic activation to the unmyelinated vagus. We can liken hyperarousal to the gas pedal of a car, hypoarousal to the brake, and a freeze response to having one foot on each pedal simultaneously. The freeze response, for this reason, is more complicated to treat, and when using yoga postures and breath work we must be careful not to exacerbate the trauma response in either the hyper- or hypo- range of the system.

Within the Window of Tolerance

When the nervous system is balanced, we refer to it in this model as being "within the Window of Tolerance," the space between the hyper- and hypo- lines. Here, we feel regulated, with access to coping skills, supports, and resources that help us respond to needs or challenges that arise. When we are "in the Window of Tolerance" we are able to appropriately respond to the needs of the moment, and connect with others. There is some fluctuation in activation, but these changes are generally smooth, as the nervous system coordinates gentle engagement of the gas and the brake, so to speak, when necessary. When trauma brings us out of the window, people in supportive roles can help identify ways to bring the nervous system back into the window. In Figure 3.2, this transition is represented by the arrows coming back into the Window of Tolerance. Over time, clients can develop habits of self-regulation that help them return to the window without external assistance. A primary goal of trauma treatment is to increase coping skills and access resilience, which we can define as accessing tools to re-enter the window, or liken to widening the window of tolerance itself, as in Figure 3.3.

Many clients experience both an initial narrowing of tolerance to external stimuli, followed by, as healing progresses, a widening of the window. Some clients describe this as little things not mattering so much anymore, as if their experience of trauma offered perspective over what is truly an emergency. Not everyone experiences this, and it is not something we should expect from those we serve, though diagrams like this help us to understand and reflect the phenomenon when it appears.

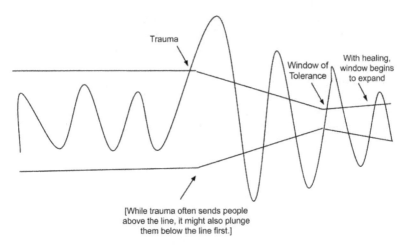

Trauma

Window of Tolerance

With healing, window begins to expand

[While trauma often sends people above the line, it might also plunge them below the line first.]

Figure 3.3 Window of Tolerance, Narrowing and Expanding

Dissociation and the Window of Tolerance

Let's take a moment to describe how a more complicated presentation of dissociation, like Dissociative Identity Disorder (DID) fits into the Window of Tolerance model. DID occurs when the intensity of a traumatic experience overwhelms a developing person's coping skills leading to different self-states, with part or total amnesia between the states. Of course, we all have various ego-state aspects of ourselves; you may be a wife, mother, teacher, and student, and adjust your sense of self and presentation to others based on these roles. The difference with dissociative states of identity is that there is often an entirely different sense of self, with a degree of an amnesia towards others, within the same body. We often describe trauma-induced dissociation as the "need to not know" (Forner, 2017) and, in fact, parts can hold information with the purpose of protecting other parts from the pain that comes with the truth of the traumatic experience. In the structural theory of dissociation, the emotional parts of the identity, or emotional personalities (EPs) hold memory and affect related to the trauma while the primary identity (labeled ANP, apparently normal part, or personality) can remain completely unaware (Steele, van der Hart, & Nijenhuis, 2009). Figure 3.4 charts how EPs can hold affect related to nervous system states induced by traumatic experiences.

As the ANP's Window of Tolerance widens, and coping skills help to regulate the EP's trauma responses, these parts can develop more communication and respect for each other's functions, in many cases facilitating some degree of integration across the self-states.

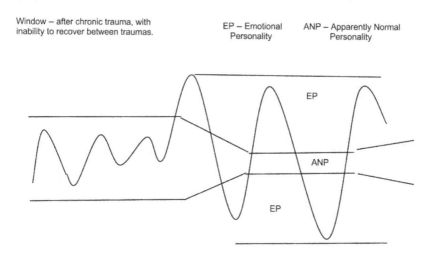

Window – after chronic trauma, with inability to recover between traumas.

EP – Emotional Personality

ANP – Apparently Normal Personality

EP

ANP

EP

Window of Tolerance is smaller. Person reacts in keeping with unresolved trauma, hyperarousal reactivity, or hypoarousal response. In dissociative disorders, EPs and the ANP may be separated by amnesic barriers, or may interact, experiencing different parts of the self as "me" and "not me".

Figure 3.4 Window of Tolerance with EPs and ANP

HPA Axis

In connection with the fight, flight, and freeze responses, the hypothalamic–pituitary–adrenal (HPA) axis plays a central role in the brain's response to stress. When exposed to high levels of stress, the hypothalamus triggers a release of hormones (corticotropin-releasing hormone, or CRH), which activates the pituitary gland, which then releases a rush of hormones (adrenocorticotropic hormone, or ACTH) to the adrenal glands. The adrenal glands then release the more familiar stress hormones cortisol, adrenaline, and noradrenaline. These hormones are helpful in the short term, but can weaken the immune system when continuously flooding the body over time (Tsigos & Chrousos, 2002).

Research indicates that early childhood trauma may alter HPA axis functioning (Tarullo & Gunnar, 2006; De Bellis & Zisk, 2014), which can in turn impact cognition, behavior, and immune function in response to stress (Lupien, McEwen, Gunnar, & Heim 2009). During critical times in HPA axis development, exposure to stressful or traumatic experiences may lead to long-term change in the function of the HPA axis, including increasing sensitivity to future stressors (Levine, 2005). In the Window of Tolerance model, we can describe this as a narrowing of the window, a phenomenon that is common for those experiencing both complex and developmental trauma. Further research indicates that early childhood trauma can lead to biological sensitivity to stressful experiences, which may in part explain how children exposed to ACEs become vulnerable to illness (Boyce & Ellis, 2005). At the same time, research suggests that mind–body practices may lead to a reduced risk of inflammation-related diseases (Buric, Farias, Jong, Mee, & Brazil, 2017), and that yoga can positively impact cortisol levels, and may contribute to healthy HPA axis function (Raghavendra et al., 2009).

Cascade Model of Defense

The Cascade Model of Defense adds more detail to the phases of response, and helps us to recognize stages of defensive systems, and their function in response to threat (Ratner, 1967; Bovine et al., 2014, Kozlowska et al., 2015). *Arousal* is the first step, occurring when the nervous system perceives a threat. *Fight or flight* follows, activating to respond to perceived threat; next the system will *freeze*, if the fight or flight does not solve the problem or threat increases; finally, *tonic immobility* or *collapsed immobility* serve as the last resort to inescapable threat, when all active defense responses have failed. *Quiescent immobility*, on the contrary, is a state of quiescence that promotes rest and healing. Each of these phases of response to threat has a unique neural pattern; understanding the patterns of these responses helps us respond to the need of the system and choose appropriate interventions. Facilitating shifts in the neural patterning is a key step in unlocking the trauma response and helping people heal.

Tracking these responses within yourself in non-traumatic circumstances can help you become more familiar with your own system and its activation. When connecting with your own system feels like too much, consider observing others, or animals, as in the example of Iris at the beginning of this chapter. Clinicians can also use art therapy to trace the client's experience of these stages, tracking emotional shifts and somatic cues through the process of illustrating, as a way to process in a measured, externalized manner.

Polyvagal Theory

The last and perhaps most integrative theory we'll cover in this chapter is Dr. Stephen Porges' Polyvagal Theory (Porges, 1995, 2011, 2017). Elements of other theories we have covered are present here, and while some of this will sound familiar, Polyvagal Theory provides a context that deepens our understanding of how the nervous system evolved to respond to threat, and how we can temper the defensive responses by accessing the more recent, mammalian brain circuits.

Polyvagal Theory looks to the evolution of humans and our vertebrate predecessors in search of explanations of nervous system function and behavior. It asserts that the ANS functions in a hierarchical way and consists of three defensive or protective systems, each with its own biological circuit. We are wired to use the more recently evolved circuits as a primary response, and to recruit older circuits when we need to defend or protect ourselves, or those we love. The oldest defense systems, seen in reptiles, is the immobilization, or feigned death circuit. This oldest circuit shuts down the body, immobilizing to appear inanimate and reduce risk of being seen or attacked. The mobilization, or fight flight, response, evolved next, followed by the mammalian social engagement system.

A central component of Polyvagal Theory is that the vagus nerve, the 10th cranial nerve, actually has more than one pathway with two important distinctions. Myelin, the sheath of fat that surrounds nerves and makes it easier for them to conduct messages, differentiates the two. The ancient unmyelinated vagus is responsible for the immobilization response, stemming from the dorsal vagal complex, while the mammalian myelinated vagus nerve, rooted in the ventral vagal complex, facilitates social interaction, with links to facial expression and prosodic speech. Dr. Porges asserts that, "The effectiveness of meditation, listening, chanting, posture and breath on fostering mental states and health is due to a common phylogenetic change in the neural regulation of the ANS" (Porges, 2016).

Neuroception

Dr. Porges coined the term *neuroception* (Porges, 2004) to describe the body's ability to detect risk in its environment, outside the realm of conscious awareness. Through neuroception, the brain picks up cues of safety, danger, or potential life threats, and recruits older circuits into defensive states when it deems necessary. These responses happen at a deep unconscious level, so they do not arise as conscious thoughts, but as implicit feelings in the body. Dr. Porges asserts that it is important to become aware of the body's responses and honor its interpretation of safety. We can then, if we perceive the threat to be unwarranted or related to an old cue, choose actions that are social in nature and help to downregulate the earlier, defensive systems. Creating a felt sense of safety and connection, or support, is one of the primary ways to begin to turn off defensive systems and encourage the autonomic NS to support health, restoration, and life, rather than using energy for defense.

Cultivating a Ventral Vagal State

Luckily for us, our nervous system responds to cues of safety, and we can use safety cues to help engage the mammalian system of the myelinated vagus. You can use these cues in a yoga class, a therapy session, on your own, or even with a scared child. According to Polyvagal Theory, voice, supportive social interaction, and breath are key ways to promote the ventral vagal, or myelinated vagal, response. In order to bring the "new neurological software" online, we can:

- Engage in dyadic (two person) face-to-face communication;
- Listen attentively;
- Speak in a prosodic way;
- Sing or chant;
- Exhale air slowly; or
- Play a wind instrument.

Did your yoga teacher training teach you not to use a sing-a-song voice when teaching? Now, you have reason to speak prosodically (in an authentic way, of course). This also gives you permission to interact, though keep in mind that forced interaction turns defensive systems on, so interaction that is helpful needs to be elective. Invited, bidirectional social engagement, caregiving and reciprocity stimulate the ventral vagal response and make us feel good. Mammals require the presence of other mammals; just knowing that a person is there, and you can reach out to them if you choose, offers benefit.

Regulators of physiology are embedded in relationships – think of the non-verbal gestures that extend kindness and connection, like reaching toward one another, or leaning on someone's shoulder. Cuddling even has a fun neurological name in this model – immobilization without fear. At a lecture I attended with Dr. Porges, he demonstrated this with a picture of a baby hippo and a turtle, who appeared to had developed quite a close friendship, in close proximity and both immobilized without indications of fear (Porges, 2013). The immobilized without fear response can only occur when the system detects safety via the social engagement system. When another being can appreciate our vulnerability and provide love and safety, our defense systems take a rest. Since physiology is a lens through which we perceive ourselves and the world, this rest is a necessary part of any biopsychosocial healing process. As we continue to explore how to facilitate safety while incorporating yoga into trauma recovery, keep these recent understandings of Polyvagal Theory in mind. When we seek to create an environment of safety, we seek to engage the ventral vagal response.

Applying Models of the Nervous System

Each of these models provide a way for clinicians and teachers to understand and communicate the body's response to trauma. A model is always a simplification and generalization, so it's important to understand the unique experiences of those you serve, and to use these models as a foundation for understanding. The fields of biology, neuroscience, and psychology are all involved in efforts to increase our comprehension of human behavior, and we can continue to look to them to deepen our understanding of ourselves and those we serve. Having covered many interrelated theories of the nervous system in this chapter, you may be craving some simple, real-time case examples. Consider observing your pet dog, or cat, or noticing the reactions of young children around you. I often appreciate the relevance of this work when observing non-trauma related human and animal behavior. Like Iris, who disappeared into the brush, we can observe instincts in other mammals and relate them to our own experience with life.

***

Luckily for me, and my partner, after six minutes of calling out her name, and increasing concern, Iris returned to us. Having not sensed any more large animals, and with nothing left to activate her most basic neurological instincts, she appeared as calm and connected to us as she had at the beginning of our walk. All of a sudden, she was responding to her name, to offers for treats, and to the walking pace of her human family. She was back online! While quite a different species, observing the nervous systems of animals gives us important information and context relative to our own brain development.

Reflection Questions

1   What brings your nervous system into your Window of Tolerance?
2   When your nervous system leaves the Window of Tolerance, where does it tend to go? Which symptoms arise first? Do they change over time?
3   What helps you downregulate your defense systems and connect to the mammalian social circuits governed by the myelinated vagus nerve?
4   How do you communicate safety to those you serve? Consider the principles of neuroception in your response.

Additional resources available at http://howwecanheal.com/y4tr

References

Bovine, M., Ratchford, E., & Mark, B. (2014). Peritraumatic dissociation and tonic immobility: Clinical findings. In U. Lanius, S. Paulsen, & F. Corrigan (Eds.), *Neurobiology and treatment of traumatic dissociation* (pp. 51–67). New York: Springer Publishing Company.

Boyce, W. T., & Ellis, B. J. (2005). Biological sensitivity to context: I. An evolutionary–developmental theory of the origins and functions of stress reactivity. *Development and Psychopathology, 17*(2), 271–301.

Buric, I., Farias, M., Jong, J., Mee, C., & Brazil, I. A. (2017). What is the molecular signature of mind–body interventions? A systematic review of gene expression changes induced by meditation and related practices. *Frontiers in Immunology, 8,* 670.

Carabotti, M., Scirocco, A., Maselli, M. A., & Severi, C. (2015). The gut–brain axis: Interactions between enteric microbiota, central and enteric nervous systems. *Annals of Gastroenterology: Quarterly Publication of the Hellenic Society of Gastroenterology, 28*(2), 203.

Danylchuk, L. S., & Connors, K. J. (2016). *Treating complex trauma and dissociation: A practical guide to navigating therapeutic challenges.* New York: Taylor & Francis.

De Bellis, M. D., & Zisk, A. (2014). The biological effects of childhood trauma. *Child and Adolescent Psychiatric Clinics, 23*(2), 185–222.

Forner, C. C. (2017). *Dissociation, mindfulness, and creative meditations: Trauma-informed practices to facilitate growth.* New York: Taylor & Francis.

Kozlowska, K., Walker, P., McLean, L., & Carrive, P. (2015). Fear and the defense cascade: Clinical implications and management. *Harvard Review of Psychiatry, 23*(4), 263.

Levine, P. A. (1997). *Waking the tiger: Healing trauma: The innate capacity to transform overwhelming experiences.* Berkeley, CA: North Atlantic Books.

Levine, S. (2005). Developmental determinants of sensitivity and resistance to stress. *Psychoneuroendocrinology, 30*(10), 939–946.

Lupien, S. J., McEwen, B. S., Gunnar, M. R., & Heim, C. (2009). Effects of stress throughout the lifespan on the brain, behaviour and cognition. *Nature Reviews Neuroscience, 10*(6), 434.

MacLean, P. D., & Kral, V. A. (1973). *A triune concept of the brain and behavior.* Toronto: published for the Ontario Mental Health Foundation by University of Toronto Press.

Porges, S. W. (1995). Orienting in a defensive world: Mammalian modifications of our evolutionary heritage. A polyvagal theory. *Psychophysiology, 32*(4), 301–318.

Porges, S. W. (2004). Neuroception: A subconscious system for detecting threats and safety. *Zero to Three (J), 24*(5), 19–24.

Porges, S. W. (2011). *The Polyvagal Theory: Neurophysiological foundations of emotions, attachment, communication, and self-regulation (Norton Series on Interpersonal Neurobiology).* New York: Norton.

Porges, S. W. (2013). *The Polyvagal Theory; implications for understanding and treating trauma and dissociation.* ISSTD 30th Annual Conference, *Navigating Development of the Therapist: Integration of Knowledge, Experience and Research in Complex Trauma and Dissociation.* Baltimore, MD, November 16, 2013.

Porges S. W. (2016). *The origins of compassion: A phylogenetic perspective.* The Science of Compassion: Origins, Measures, and Interventions. Telluride, CO, July 19–22, 2016.

Porges, S. W. (2017). *The pocket guide to the Polyvagal Theory: The transformative power of feeling safe (Norton Series on Interpersonal Neurobiology).* New York: Norton.

Raghavendra, R. M., Vadiraja, H. S., Nagarathna, R., Nagendra, H. R., Rekha, M., Vanitha, N., . . . & Ajaikumar, B. S. (2009). Effects of a yoga program on cortisol rhythm and mood states in early breast cancer patients undergoing adjuvant radiotherapy: A randomized controlled trial. *Integrative Cancer Therapies, 8*(1), 37–46.

Ratner, S. C. (1967). Comparative aspects of hypnosis. In J. E. Gordon (Ed.), *Handbook of clinical and experimental hypnosis.* New York: Macmillan.

Siegel, D. J. (1999). *The developing mind* (Vol. 296). New York: Guilford Press.

Steele, K., van der Hart, O., & Nijenhuis, E. R. (2009). The theory of trauma-related structural dissociation of the personality. In P. Dell & J. O'Neil (Eds.), *Dissociation and the dissociative disorders: DSM-V and beyond.* Chicago: International Society for the Study of Dissociation.

Tarullo, A. R., & Gunnar, M. R. (2006). Child maltreatment and the developing HPA axis. *Hormones and Behavior, 50*(4), 632–639.

Tsigos, C., & Chrousos, G. P. (2002). Hypothalamic–pituitary–adrenal axis, neuroendocrine factors and stress. *Journal of Psychosomatic Research, 53*(4), 865–871.

4 Somatic Psychotherapy
The Body's Influence on the Mind

The body always leads us home . . . if we can simply learn to trust sensation and stay with it long enough for it to reveal appropriate action, movement, insight, or feeling.

– Pat Ogden

The children appear shy and curious at first, then come out from behind corners, furniture, and each other to greet us. "Bonjou," they greet me in Haitian Creole, mixed in with other words I can't understand. Thankfully, Stella is with me to translate; she grew up here in Port-au-Prince and is a native speaker of Haitian Creole. I'm about to teach a yoga class to a group of orphans, and while I know yoga can be profoundly healing, seeing the buildings still in rubble six months after the earthquake, the sadness in the children's eyes, and the poverty that pervaded the area well before the earthquake, I fall silent. How is this going to help?

We begin, as most yoga classes do, with some breathing and movement. The children are engaged, looking back and forth between me and Stella. I'm overwhelmed by gratitude as she stands next to me, effortlessly repeating words that fall melodic on my ears, but fail to offer my linguistically-limited brain any information. We move through salutations, warriors, and twists until, as we make our way to the floor for backbends, I recognize an opportunity. "These poses are good for your heart" I say. "The heart contains love, but it also contains grief. When we lose things and people we love, it is normal to feel sad. These poses help us feel and slowly heal. Most importantly, they remind us of the love that is in our hearts. If you ever feel sad or depressed, try a pose like this one!" As we move out of camel pose and Stella translates my words, a few of the young eyes sparkle and I see that I have managed to make a connection between these seemingly random shapes and the reality of their emotional lives. Success! While it feels far from enough, it is something valuable: a spark of hope.

As we load into the car and begin our drive down the street, we pass a couple of the neighbors and a goat at the side of the road. Looking back,

I see a group of children following the car, shouting goodbyes. They wave, laugh, smile, and wave again. Then, spontaneously, one of them drops his knees to earth, falling gracefully into camel pose. The others follow suit, and soon there is a trail of children with chests lifted, smiles on their faces and laughter in their eyes. Our small volunteer group's presence could not touch the enormity of the suffering in Port-au-Prince post-earthquake. And yet, through yoga, Stella and I passed on a tool that could remain beyond our tenure. The children learned something to help them through a difficult moment, one that could meet them in their sadness. They had learned a way to use the body to support their emotional lives.

***

Now that we understand what trauma is and how it manifests in the nervous system, it is time to explore how physical shapes, postures, and felt experiences in the body play a role in healing. Physical postures are a big part of yoga – and the most visible aspect of yoga in the US. This chapter outlines somatic psychotherapy principles and examines how body movements and postures can influence trauma recovery and well-being.

Have you ever had butterflies in your stomach? A lump in your throat? These are some of the common ways we communicate somatic sensations that come with emotion. Gross and subtle, universal and unique, the experience of emotion in the body, and the nonverbal language of our physical bodies, brings us into the realm of somatic psychotherapy. The word *somatic* stems from the Greek word *soma*, which means *body*. While somatic theories and techniques vary, all approaches are centered in the power of bringing body awareness into psychotherapy, and may include exploration of movement, breath work, sensation, feeling, expression, touch, gesture, posture, and identity. Each of these layers of practice interact; with movement the breath changes, with feeling comes expression and postural shifts. Somatic work can involve analyzing and exploring these elements in a dyad, or in groups. With a focus on nonverbal facial and body communications, somatic psychotherapy guides us to become aware of the messages the body is sending us, and to notice how experiences and relationship impact us at a body level. As Pat Ogden suggests in the opening quote to this chapter (as cited in Knaster, 1996), even unpleasant sensations have a way of leading us home.

The Body Is Our Home

The body carries us through all of life's experiences. Even when attention or awareness leaves, the body remains, and experiences the things we may not be able to mentally or emotionally endure. Often in the wake of trauma, the body does not feel like a safe place to be and memories, as well as our response patterns to the trauma, remain trapped in the nervous system and tissues just outside of awareness. Like an iceberg, we often see the symptoms of trauma on the surface, while the roots in the body and subconscious mind reside below the surface. It can be difficult to only see part of the puzzle, and living in a body without access to the full extent of its knowledge takes its toll on a person's sense of internal ease. At the same time, knowing and feeling everything at once can lead to feeling overwhelmed and flooded with information. While it's common for people in search of healing to feel compelled to face everything immediately in efforts to move on, our minds repress memory and our bodies hold memories *because* of their difficult nature. For this reason, taking a consistent and gentle approach to understanding the body and psyche tends to be most beneficial for long-term healing. With body-based work, remember to respect the importance of building up psychological resources, and the guiding phrase, "The slower you go, the faster you get there" (Kluft, 1993).

The Body's Basic Needs

When we are not "in touch" with our bodies, physical challenges may result. Often clients may forget to eat, drink, or care for their bodies as a result of the distance between self-awareness and body sensation. Hunger, thirst, and other healthy impulses can become dampened in these cases; for this reason, maintaining awareness of the most basic needs of the body is helpful. This awareness helps us keep watch for physiological illness and refer to physicians, and helps clients develop awareness of the physical things they need to respond to in order to maintain health. I cannot count the number of times a client has come to a session in full distress and, upon my asking, has become aware that they have not eaten any food all day. This is one way trauma can perpetuate the body remaining in crisis mode, when psychological challenges contribute to physical ones, worsening the client's psychological experience. Recall Maslow's Hierarchy of Needs (Maslow & Lewis, 1987) and the foundational nature of basic physical needs, as pictured in Figure 4.1. Breath, food, water, and sleep are essential to access the higher needs of safety, social connection, esteem, and actualization.

When the nervous system is in crisis response, it is designed to prioritize safety over the mundane, daily functions of physiology. By keeping the base of Maslow's hierarchy in mind, we support our clients and students in creating a base for healing to occur.

Postures of Fear

In addition to the platform of physiological health, the shapes our bodies take from day to day and moment to moment can significantly impact our experience of the world. Our bodies take many forms throughout

Figure 4.1 Maslow's Hierarchy of Needs

the day – standing, sitting, lying down, and a number of movements in between. We carry our postural habits through these larger movements and both can have an impact on our emotional experience. Just as the nervous system activates differently in fear than in safety, our muscles, posture, and movements can change significantly based on our sense of safety, danger, or life threat.

As we discussed in Chapter 3, when our nervous systems go into fight or flight mode, the body activates and readies itself for these two activities. In both situations, blood goes to the extremities and the heart rate quickens, delivering energy to move the body to safety. It is common in both flight and fighting to flex at the hip in order to either lift the legs to kick or run, or in efforts to protect the vital organs, reducing their exposure to harm. Respiration also changes and the breath quickens. Dr. Tina Stromstead, psychotherapist and co-founder of the Authentic Movement Institute, speaks to the breath response to trauma:

> If we have suffered emotional wounding and lived in fear, we are likely to constrict our breath, keeping it high in our chest, with our diaphragm held tight. This not only perpetuates a state of fear; it also contributes to the process of separating us from our bodies and prevents our emotions from reaching awareness.
>
> (Sieff, 2014, pp. 51–52)

Thus, slow deep breath that expands the abdomen and brings flexibility to the diaphragm can be a significant challenge for someone with a history of childhood trauma; at the same time, it can be an opportunity to create safety and facilitate a healing response in the body.

It is common in hypervigilant states, due to the impulse for hip flexion, for the hips to tilt forward into an anterior tilt, and research indicates when bodywork targets a release in hip flexor tension, the parasympathetic nervous system function increases (Cottingham et al., 1988). While the freeze response induces low muscle tone and the body goes limp, it is also common here for the body to be in a posture that makes it appear small and uninteresting to the predator. In these protective postures, the chest caves and the shoulders roll forward to protect the heart and central organs; often the head moves forward as well. Dr. Stromstead explains, "When we repeatedly have to take on a posture in order to protect our self, that posture becomes part of who we are, shaping how we move in the world and ultimately how we experience it" (Sieff, 2014, p. 50). Yoga postures can work directly with the body to slowly open the areas that have contracted and bring balance to the body's postural patterns, changing the way we experience the world.

A recent study on the impact of posture found that participants in upright postures reported feeling more excited, enthusiastic, and strong, with higher reports of self-esteem, fewer reports of negative emotion, and decreased social fear, as compared to slumped participants (Nair et al., 2015). In this study, participants with slumped postures described feeling more fearful, hostile, nervous, quiet, still, passive, dull, sleepy, and sluggish. In linguistic analysis, the slumped participants used more negative emotion words and fewer positive emotion words than the upright participants. Those with upright posture also had stronger pulse responses than their slumped friends. The slump of shoulders can result from a fear response, but can also result from common modern habits like driving and computer use. This is another reason to practice patience while driving, or waiting for your computer to load: adding activation in the nervous system to the physical position of sitting – with hips already in flexion and the shoulders tending to roll forward – can exacerbate the posture and sensation of fear deep in the brain and body.

If you have any experience with a yoga asana practice, you are likely aware of the many postures that emphasize the upper spine moving in towards the chest, and the shoulders moving back and down. Many lineages speak to this action as an antidepressant. Geeta Iyengar, daughter of B. K. S. Iyengar – one of the most influential teachers of our time – in response to a student asking what to practice and teach when fear comes up during the practice, responded with, "When fear arises, you must lift your chest. You must lift your heart" (Sell, 2012).

When looking for postures of fear it is important not to become too rigid in our thinking of how fear will manifest for a person. Some people puff up, others shrink away when scared. Even the simple startle response, the way our bodies respond to a loud sound or sudden change, involves both extension of the spine and activation of the body, followed immediately by pulling inward in a protective manner. In slow motion, this activation and protection sequence gives us information about the body's immediate reaction to threat; if we were to freeze frame each small movement during this response, we would observe a posture of fear that is different from the frame before. As we have covered, impulses that are not completed and remain in the nervous system represent the body's efforts to bring us to safety. As we look to our client's, and student's bodies, observing what their posture communicates and how the body may be bracing for protection helps us to determine how the traumatic experience continues to live in the body.

Postures of Safety

When a body feels safe it tends to relax, expand, stretch out, and take up physical space, and when it does curl up – with a good book or a cup of hot cocoa – it does so without tension or bracing. Breath tends to move fully, into both the chest and the abdomen. Muscles relax and the parasympathetic "rest and digest" function is able to assume its role in growth, restoration, and healing. Since the system does not need to activate for defense, this is an opportunity for blood to return to the central organs. Postures of safety tend to leave the front of the body – the heart and central organs – open and at ease. *Savasana*, a common resting posture to practice at the end of a yoga asana sequence, positions practitioners in a supine position, with all the major organs exposed. In his book *Light on Pranayama*, B. K. S. Iyengar uses 22 pages to describe this posture, and often described *savasana* as one of the most challenging poses because it requires both full presence and full relaxation (Iyengar & Menuhin, 2003). Frequently, students feel challenged by this pose – the body feels fidgety or the mind has difficulty letting go of thought patterns. Bodies new to the practice, or those recovering from trauma, may not feel safe in their environments just yet. It is common for those experiencing hyperarousal to have a hard time with this final resting posture for these reasons.

These are common manifestations of bodily responses to fear and safety, and unique cases and exceptions do exist. As we learn these general responses, it is important to keep an open mind about how and why people respond the way they do to traumatic encounters. Many people will report feeling safe in a posture of fear because of the protective nature of the posture; however, this experience of safety is markedly different from one that does not require effort towards protection. As we covered in Chapter 3, Stephen Porges describes the myelinated vagal activation of the parasympathetic nervous system as immobilization without fear.

In this response, we are motionless and vulnerable, in the arms of another "appropriate mammal" (Porges, 2013). This speaks to the increasing popularity of animal therapies and yoga classes that include dogs, cats, bunnies, and even goats – each an opportunity for this type of contact.

As many master trainers in the field of somatic psychotherapy advocate, trauma therapy requires, above all, flexibility and the capacity to see and respond to the unique needs of each client (Rothschild & Oakes, 2002). Consider the posture of your students and clients and seek to become aware of how they need to move in daily life to respond to demands of work, family, or other activities. Consider their experiences and how their posture met, or continues to meet, a need for protection, defense, or perceived safety. Be aware that shifting posture can be empowering and may also bring difficult emotional material to light. Consider gentle ways you might offer your students and clients the opportunity to connect with their unique needs and develop a posture, and felt sense, of safety in the body.

Many symptoms result from the system's attempt to bring us to safety. All too common is the experience of shame at the body's response, which occurs at the deep brain level beyond rational thought, leaving little conscious choice. Many clients feel they should have, or could have, done something differently. It can be an important part of the healing process to recognize the deep brain's attempt to protect. Therapeutic movements can help connect us to un-acted impulses, and imaginative resourcing can help us visualize these actions and connect with their somatic sensations. Processing theses impulses and honoring the body can also involve acceptance of its function, and can contribute to reducing experiences of shame.

Modeling and Mirroring

In addition to developing awareness of our students' and clients' postural habits, ours, as providers, are also important. Naturally, our habits impact our experience of life, safety, or threat, and corresponding emotions, but they also can directly impact those with whom we share space. Beatrice de Gelder, a neuroscientist studying the impact of posture on behavior, observes, "Just like in the animal world, we also communicate through our bodies without our conscious minds being much aware of it" (Loygren, 2004). We often unconsciously mirror the posture of those we connect with, in therapy or otherwise, creating a sense of connection and shared experience. When we become conscious of the body, we can use this tool to guide ourselves and our clients into a posture of safety. One of Dr. de Gelder's studies demonstrates that "viewing fearful body expressions may automatically prepare the observer to respond to fear" (de Gelder, Snyder, Greve, Gerard, & Hadjikhani, 2004 as referenced in Loygren, 2004). Consider your own habits, not only in light of how they make you feel, but with the awareness that how you exist in your own body can directly impact those you seek to serve.

Bi-Directional Processing

As we discussed in Chapter 3, the nervous system has both afferent and efferent nerves, ones that send messages to the brain and ones that carry actions out to the muscles. In order to integrate awareness of both mind and body, it is important that we include practices that move in each direction: from body to brain, and from brain to body. Somatic practices represent the former, the pathway from body to brain. Both yoga classes and therapeutic interventions can focus on the mind telling the body what to do: place your foot there, take deep breaths to calm down, recognize negative thought patterns and interrupt them. We refer to this type of processing as *top-down*, when the brain directs the body and emotions. Practices that gather information and emotional experiences from the body and transmit it to the brain are an important part of the healing process. We call this type of processing, *bottom-up processing*. Through both top-down and bottom-up practices, yoga may be effective at down-regulating the system towards parasympathetic, ventral vagal dominance (Streeter et al., 2012; Gard et al., 2014; Schmalzl et al., 2015).

Top-Down Processing

Top-down processing initiates with our mind, or conscious thought, and flows from there to other senses, or into the body. Yoga offers a structured, guided way to experience the body, and many yoga practices are taught in a top-down orientation, guiding us from an idea of a form into the actual shape in our bodies. Instructors famously ask us to feel things we cannot yet access in yoga class, as in the classic (only mildly exaggerated) example I like to give of the instruction, "Root down through your inner outer left pinky toe." Thanks to many years of Iyengar practice, many of you reading could actually follow that instruction! One of my instructors used to call this "intelligizing the body"; bringing the intelligence of the mind into the tissues.

Top-down processing can happen with other senses, too. If you're walking down a back street in Paris and your friend says, "Do you smell that? Fresh croissants!" You are likely to use your mind to focus your attention on your sense of smell in search of a heavenly, fresh-baked inhale. Similarly, we can direct our vision, taste, or hearing to attempt to pick up subtleties or to focus on the desired object of attention. A wine novice will search for the flavor that might be tannins and scour the aftertaste for hints of a fruit flavor – other than grape. While we can use top-down processing with all five senses, most often, in yoga practice, we challenge our mind to travel into the felt sense of a body part.

Through asana practice and the ongoing practice of top-down instruction, we tend to improve our *proprioception*, improving the awareness of the position of our body and the felt sense of change as it moves through space. *Interoception* describes the ability to feel what is happening internally, listening to the body and becoming better able to connect with, and describe, its experiences. Since many people experience difficulty identifying and expressing emotions and sensations in the wake of trauma, building the capacity to identify internal experiences is an integral part of recovery.

Bottom-Up Processing

Bottom-up approaches in somatic psychotherapy begin with the body and allow it to inform the mind, strengthening interoception. Many cognitive therapies focus on the importance of narrative skills, the story or memory of the trauma, and fail to address the body's needs. A hyperfocus on the narrative and on cognitive coping skills dismisses the potential for powerful healing through movement and body awareness. Central works in the field of trauma recovery bear titles such as *The Body Bears the Burden* (Scaer, 2001), and *The Body Keeps the Score* (van der Kolk, 2014), highlighting the necessity to involve the body in the process of trauma treatment. This type of work can be particularly powerful in cases of somatoform dissociation, when sensation in a part of the body becomes disconnected from everyday awareness, holding some aspect, or memory, related to the traumatic experience. The challenge of bottom-up approaches is the potential they have to bring up too much emotion at once, making them potent, and heightening the importance of skill in this area. Possibly due to the stress responses in the brain, many trauma survivors experience *alexithymia*: not having words for feelings, or being unable to express them in a social context. Using body-based interventions bypasses the need for language and narrative, allowing another pathway to access healing. Relationship and attunement remain important in regard to pacing, containment, and co-regulation. Providers can cultivate a sense of safety by regulating their own bodies and tracking nonverbal cues.

Attention to experiences and changes in the body can help develop awareness and allow for the body's needs to become clear. When we approach the body with respect, acceptance, and non-judgement, we create space for healing. As a healing practitioner, paying attention to posture, gait, and muscle tone in the faces and bodies of those you serve can provide valuable information. Asking what the body would say if it had words, or how it wants to be positioned, or move, can inform the process of healing, as can tracking nonverbal shifts, and inviting changes or movement. Peter Levine, founder of Somatic Experiencing, speaks to the importance of discharging impulses held in the nervous system, stemming from a session in which he had a vision of a tiger and instructed his client to run to escape the tiger. Following his instruction, her feet tremored, her body shook, and her body cycled through waves of movement during which she reported that she could feel herself running. Dr. Levine came to understand that these impulses discharged the energy in her nervous system. As she took deep breaths following the experience, she came to recognize it to be related to an early experience of surgery (Levine, 1997). Body memory can remain stuck, but with skilled guidance can process to release. Often, these impulses exist just outside of conscious awareness, and methods like these create safety in relationship and support the client in accessing a pathway of release.

In what is now well-known research out of Harvard Business School, researchers looked into the impact of posture on hormones, comparing expansive postures (high power poses) and contracted positions (low power poses) (Carney, Cuddy, & Yap, 2010). In this study, participants who practiced high power poses demonstrated elevations in testosterone, decreases in cortisol, increased feelings of power, and increased tolerance for risk; while low-power posers exhibited the opposite pattern. While there has been some conflict in the field surrounding these results, they indicated that taking on a posture associated with a display of power led to adaptive psychological, physiological, and behavioral changes. The authors of the study note, "These findings suggest that embodiment extends beyond mere thinking and feeling, to physiology and subsequent behavioral choices" (Carney, Cuddy, & Yap, 2010). Call to mind an image of Wonder Woman: grounded, strong, and empowered, fearlessly gazing out over a battlefield. Then consider a victim in a horror film, covering the face and central organs, perhaps eyes closed in fear, ready to scream for help. The difference we feel when seeing, or even imagining, these contrasting postures is palpable, and scientists are continuing to gather data to understand these differing postures and physiologies.

There are a number of ways to encourage bottom-up processing; whichever we choose, the biggest challenges from this perspective are structure and containment. Practices like yoga, exercise, dance, and tai chi provide a structured way to make contact with the body and begin to explore what it holds. As we begin to connect with the body through the top-down structure offered by these practices, we can then learn to listen, and eventually track and follow impulses to release energy that has been trapped. It can be helpful to build a toolkit of body-based practices so that we can turn toward structured, predictable practices when we need containment and guidance, and choose open forms of movement when we feel ready to explore messages held in the body as unconscious material.

Bottom-Up Processing in Yoga

Even within a structured yoga class, we can learn to develop bottom-up cues. When I train yoga teachers and mental health professionals, this is one of the most common areas of confusion and questioning. Many yoga teachers express that this conflicts with their training. Many yoga teacher trainings, including the method I was trained in, place value on giving students clear directives: "Place your feet hips distance apart," and "Inhale as you lift your arms up" are common cues. While these involve the body, they remain top-down cues. Teachers often struggle to conceptualize bottom-up cues, so I've included a list of examples in Figure 4.2. A helpful structure to employ in a yoga studio class is to offer a directive, followed by a bottom-up cue, followed by an option or two for varying the posture to meet the body's needs. This is not only trauma-informed, it also helps people learn about their own anatomy and physiological needs.

In the only video class I've found that he has recorded, one of my early instructors says, "There is a point in every pose where you want to stop adjusting. Just be. Assume you are doing it correctly and be there and breathe and feel it" (Marino, 2013). This instructs students to stop sending messages from the brain to align the body and, rather, listen to the messages traveling from body to brain. Listening for cues like these can help you not only to develop bottom-up awareness, but to cultivate the skills to guide others in doing so.

	Top-Down Cues	Cues for Bottom-Up Awareness
Posture	Place your feet together	Notice how it feels to have your feet together, and hip's distance, and choose the distance that feels most supportive for your body today
	Lift your chest	How might it feel to lift and open your chest?
	Turn your back foot in	Notice what happens to your hips when you turn your back foot in
Breath	Breathe	Notice the rhythm (or rise and fall) of your breath
	Inhale, lift your arms	On your next inhale, lift your arms as far as you feel comfortable
	Breathe in and out through your nose	Breathe in a way that feels comfortable for your body
Experience	Rest your eyes on a point	Find a comfortable gazing point, or Notice where your gaze lands
	Pay attention to...	Listen
	Press, lengthen, lift, etc.	Feel, experience, tune in, get curious…

Figure 4.2 Bottom-Up Examples for Yoga Cues

Emotional Process and Release

Christine Forner, president of the ISSTD and specialist in treating trauma and dissociation, uses a bladder analogy to describe how many western cultures socialize us to respond to stressful situations (Forner, 2017). Many cultures teach us to behave in ways that make socializing smooth and that make other people more comfortable. This is functional in many ways, but falls short when we have physical, somatic, or emotional responses to stressful events that do not fit within an acceptable behavioral norm. We are taught to hold back emotions and impulses, but rarely given instruction on when and where it's okay to give our bodies permission to release. In essence, we learn to hold our emotional bladder half full most all the time.

What would happen to you, to your body, to your overall daily sense of peace, if you were trained to hold your bladder full rather than empty? It would be uncomfortable, but would also come to feel normal. Just as bladder function takes training, processing and releasing emotions takes practice. Psychotherapy offers a place to identify, express, and release emotional build-up, as most yoga classes do. The release offers relief, after which we can go about our day in a more relaxed and present mood, without being overwhelmed by sensation or disconnecting from our emotions and basic needs. Once we've discovered how and where that release is appropriate, we can begin the training of releasing at the earliest sign of stress, rather that walking around in a constant state of holding.

Following Healing Impulses

Upon learning this material, one of my students shared her husband Robert's experience with me. He had been riding his bike to work when a motorist sped by him and left him to topple over onto the street. This experience has the potential to create post-traumatic stress; in fact, I've worked with clients for whom similar experiences have led to symptoms of PTSD. Robert did not develop any symptoms, perhaps because of his ability to respond and express his body's genuine reaction. He got up, identified that he had not sustained any life-threatening injuries, and, as he describes it, "hulked out."

A roar and a deep squat arose from his body. He let out the impulse and expressed what his body, voice, and muscles needed to in order to respond to the life-threatening event he had just experienced. He let the impulses to respond to this traumatic experience and its impacts wash over him. Interestingly, he shared that, had others been around, he would have suppressed this urge, in efforts to not frighten them. This happens all too often and, while I do not suggest we forgo all socialization and dismiss the needs or concerns of those around us, it will serve us all to normalize the body's response to trauma and find a way to set these impulses free – be they vocal, emotional, somatic or physical (usually some combination). These reactions to trauma are deeply wired into our biology: shaking, breathing, and movement of this energy, while not the social norm, facilitate healing.

We need to model and teach how to cope with and process emotion in a way that moves the energy without harming others. Rather than holding back words, anger, tears, or shakes, we can hold space for, and encourage those we serve, to do these things safely. Facilitating this type of understanding at an early age sets the stage for healthy trauma recovery later in life.

The Energetic Impacts of Fear

Beyond gut feelings and bad vibes, eastern medicine measures the energetic imprints of fear in a very different way. As we discuss more in the next chapter, yogic traditions describe *nadis*, or energy pathways, that run through the body, as well as *chakras*, or energy centers, *vayus*, energetic winds, and *koshas*, energetic layers. While there are many diverse yoga practices and posture sequences, many have an underlying goal to bring balance to the energetic systems. Efforts to cultivate balance, explore areas of the body that feel blocked, and increase body–mind communication, are all practiced to reduce imbalances that come with disease, and increase health. In Chapter 6, we will explore sequences that can help foster this balance in a way that responds to the nervous system's needs following traumatic experiences.

Similar to yogic traditions, in TCM trauma impacts a number of the systems of the body, including the internal organs. Lungs connect to both grief and anxiety, while the large intestine is associated with letting go. The liver holds anger, while the kidneys absorb shock and fear. TCM uses acupressure, acupuncture, and herbs to help balance the organ systems and energies of the body. Randomized control trials testing the efficacy of acupuncture as treatment for PTSD provide promising results (Hollifield Sinclair-Lian, Warner, & Hammerschlag, 2007; Kim, Heo, Shin, Crawford, Kang, & Lim, 2013; Engel et al., 2014). TCM offers a non-exposure "bottom-up" treatment option for those struggling with symptoms of PTSD, and, for those experiencing depressive systems, or in a freeze response, it is one of few healing practices that require minimal to no physical effort or energy. If you find these practices being dismissed, recall the importance of cultural competence and inclusion. Our goal is to find what works best for each group or individual we serve; it may serve you and your clients or students to refer, consult, or incorporate complementary services that address the impact of trauma on these energetic systems.

Beyond Bi-Directional

When I offer training in TIY, one of the most common points of confusion is top-down and bottom-up processing. If the concepts don't feel

100 percent clear yet, allow the concept to settle into your practice and come back to re-read them later. In general, western cultures are more adept at the top-down approach, so bringing in more body to mind awareness is one of the huge opportunities that come with practices like yoga. To those of you well-versed in these two concepts, consider what other directions may exist in your practice and teaching. What about coming from the center? Seasoned psychologist Lynette Danylchuk (yes, also the woman who brought me into the world) shares,

> The center is located around the heart. Coming from the center, both the top and the bottom are accessible, and neither dominate. It's as if the center is there to take in both and respond in a way that is grounded, honest, and warm. Like our inability to fully understand the universe, we are also not able to fully understand ourselves. We look at pieces – the brain, the body, the DNA, epigenetics, etc., and fail to take in the whole person, including that intangible thing that happens when the heart speaks. It's intuition, a gut-response, a sense of something that's important – heart-felt.
>
> (Danylchuk, 2018)

When we are grounded, centered, and able to make the vulnerable gesture of opening our hearts, we receive information and foster connection. Consider, in addition to the connections between brain and body, where you feel your energetic center, and what you feel in your heart. Notice your experience there, including emotions and messages sent and received from this space.

***

We describe the tragedies of the world as heart-breaking, yet many psychological interventions are mental in nature. We cannot overlook that most healing techniques include the wisdom of the heart and the body. As we develop awareness, we can process and discharge intense emotion, releasing experiences that leave a hurtful impact. When mental strategies feel insufficient or inaccessible, and talking to others feels difficult or overwhelming, moving the body in a skilled and trauma-informed manner can support us in accessing awareness and processing emotions, or nervous system impulses, that have become lodged in the body with nowhere to go. For the youth in Haiti, a simple expansive posture gave them a moment of joy and a tool to use their bodies in the process of healing. It also gave them a way to communicate connection and gratitude – to salute us as we rode away from the orphanage. Recently, I was happy to come across research supporting our efforts in a study that found yoga can improve trauma-related stress for orphans in Haiti (Culver et al., 2015). How can your connection with your body support your own healing? How can your students and clients benefit from this information? In the next section, Applications: Using Yoga to Recover from Traumatic Stress, we'll address the many ways yoga responds to the impacts of trauma we've identified thus far.

Reflection Questions

1   Which positions, yoga or otherwise, make you feel powerful, expansive, or confident?
2   How can you invite the body into your work with individuals/groups in a respectful, body positive manner?
3   List three bottom-up cues you could offer in an individual or group session.
4   Free write about the last time you felt a heart connection, in session, in class, or otherwise.

Additional resources available at http://howwecanheal.com/y4tr

References

Carney, D. R., Cuddy, A. J., & Yap, A. J. (2010). Power posing: Brief non-verbal displays affect neuroendocrine levels and risk tolerance. *Psychological Science*, 21(10), 1363–1368.

Cottingham, J. T., Porges, S. W., & Richmond, K. (1988). Shifts in pelvic inclination angle and parasympathetic tone produced by Rolfing soft tissue manipulation. *Physical Therapy*, 68(9), 1364–1370.

Culver, K. A., Whetten, K., Boyd, D. L., & O'Donnell, K. (2015). Yoga to reduce trauma-related distress and emotional and behavioral difficulties among children living in orphanages in Haiti: A pilot study. *The Journal of Alternative and Complementary Medicine*, 21(9), 539–545.

Danylchuk, L. S. (2018). *From the center out*. Retrieved from www.howwecanheal.com/blog.

De Gelder, B., Snyder, J., Greve, D., Gerard, G., & Hadjikhani, N. (2004). Fear fosters flight: A mechanism for fear contagion when perceiving emotion expressed by a whole body. *Proceedings of the National Academy of Sciences of the United States of America*, 101(47), 16701–16706.

Engel, C. C., Cordova, E. H., Benedek, D. M., Liu, X., Gore, K. L., Goertz, C., . . . & Ursano, R. J. (2014). Randomized effectiveness trial of a brief course of acupuncture for posttraumatic stress disorder. *Medical Care*, 52, S57–S64.

Forner, C. C. (2017). *Creative meditations for complex trauma and dissociation: Fostering mindfulness to facilitate growth*. New York: Routledge.

Gard, T., Noggle, J. J., Park, C. L., Vago, D. R., & Wilson, A. (2014). Potential self-regulatory mechanisms of yoga for psychological health. *Frontiers in Human Neuroscience*, 8, 770.

Hollifield, M., Sinclair-Lian, N., Warner, T. D., & Hammerschlag, R. (2007). Acupuncture for posttraumatic stress disorder: A randomized controlled pilot trial. *The Journal of Nervous and Mental Disease*, 195(6), 504–513.

Iyengar, B. K. S., & Menuhin, Y. (2003). *Light on Prāṇāyāma: The yogic art of breathing.* New York: Crossroad Publishing Company.

Kim, Y. D., Heo, I., Shin, B. C., Crawford, C., Kang, H. W., & Lim, J. H. (2013). Acupuncture for posttraumatic stress disorder: A systematic review of randomized controlled trials and prospective clinical trials. *Evidence-Based Complementary and Alternative Medicine,* 2013.

Kluft, R. P. (1993). Basic principles in conducting the psychotherapy of multiple personality disorder. *Clinical Perspectives On Multiple Personality Disorder,* 19–50.

Levine, P. A. (1997). *Waking the tiger: Healing trauma: The innate capacity to transform overwhelming experiences.* Berkeley, CA: North Atlantic Books.

Loygren, S. (2004). Fear is spread by body language, study says. *National Geographic News.*

Marino, V. (2013). *Vinnie Flow #1.* Retrieved from www.myyogaworks.com/video/vinnie-flow-1/.

Maslow, A., & Lewis, K. J. (1987). Maslow's hierarchy of needs. *Salenger Incorporated, 14,* 987.

Nair, S., Sagar, M., Sollers, J. III, Consedine, N., & Broadbent, E. (2015). Do slumped and upright postures affect stress responses? A randomized trial. *Health Psychology, 34*(6), 632–641.

Ogden, P., as cited in Knaster, M. (1996). *Discovering the body's wisdom: [a comprehensive guide to more than fifty mind-body practices that can relieve pain, reduce stress, and foster health, spiritual growth, and inner peace]* (p.369). New York: Bantam Books.

Porges, S. W. (2013). *The Polyvagal Theory; Implications for understanding and treating trauma and dissociation.* ISSTD 30th Annual Conference, *Navigating development of the therapist: Integration of knowledge, experience and research in complex trauma and dissociation.* Baltimore, MD, November 16, 2013.

Rothschild, B., & Oakes, L. (2002). The body remembers: An interview with Babette Rothschild. *Psychotherapy in Australia, 8*(2), 26.

Scaer, R. C. (2001). *Trauma, dissociation, and disease: The body bears the burden.* New York: Haworth Press.

Sell, C. (2012) *A posture of courage.* In *Yoga International.* Retrieved from: https://elenabrower.com/a-posture-of-courage/.

Sieff, D. F. (2014). *Understanding and healing emotional trauma: Conversations with pioneering clinicians and researchers.* New York: Routledge.

Streeter, C. C., Gerberg, P. L., Saper, R. B., Ciraulo, D. A., & Brown, R. P. (2012). Effects of yoga on the autonomic nervous system, gamma-aminobutyric-acid, and allostasis in epilepsy, depression, and post-traumatic stress disorder. *Medical Hypotheses, 78*(5), 571–579.

Van der Kolk, B. A. (2014). *The body keeps the score: Brain, mind, and body in the healing of trauma.* London: Penguin Books.

Part II

Applications

Using Yoga to Recover from Traumatic Stress

5   Yoga Philosophy

Yoga is a journey of the self, through the self, to the self.
– Bhagavad Gita

"Am I doing this right?" Lana asks. "Are you breathing?" I respond. "I'm trying!" she replies. "Then you're definitely doing something right." She smiles.

Watching a teen girl slowly open up over the course of six months in juvenile hall is an incredible experience. She comes in to her first class avoiding eye contact, *way* too cool for you and, as you develop trust, starts to let her guard down. She slowly starts to practice, move, and breathe, and you get the gift of seeing a little more peace on her face after class, as the weeks go on. Her face slowly regains a childlike quality of innocence. Her language, on the other hand, doesn't tend to change so quickly.

> "No offense, but I kinda thought you were a bitch when I met you. Not really a bitch I guess, but I thought you were like those other yoga girls."
> I smile, "Oh yeah? Which girls?"
> "You know, the ones that think they are better than everybody else."
> "Oh, those girls."
> "Yeah. But you're not. And that's not even what yoga is about anyway."
> Now I'm curious. "What is it about?"
> "Just letting go of all the crap in our mind, I think. Being okay with who you are. I don't know. I actually kind of like it! But don't tell the other girls."

I wish I could tell Lana how many of the other girls have asked me to keep that very same word. Instead, I go along, "Of course not," smiling still. "And if yoga is making you okay with who you are, then you're definitely doing it right."

***

In this chapter, we define yoga and apply its theory and practice to the goals in we have established as central to trauma treatment. Yogis have developed practices to bring stability to the nervous system, and have tailored these practices through generations of insight, application, and refinement. Yoga philosophy itself speaks to cultivating balance in the body and mind, with the effort focused on letting the deepest layers of the self come to light. In Chapter 6, we'll explore the physical yoga practice as both a trigger and a resource, and discuss the potential for poses to evoke intense emotions and memories. You'll also find postures and sequences that stimulate, soothe, and balance the nervous system.

What Is Yoga?

We've addressed the question "What is trauma?" and the time has come to explore the definition and meaning of yoga. Translated from Sanskrit, the word *yoga* means *to yoke*, or bring together. Despite the image of yoga that the media portrays, the shapes and physical forms yogis practice are only a small part of the practice. Contrary to popular images, yoga is not a practice of contortion or contest. It is a philosophy and practice with deep roots, with wide interpretations and applications, and with many available avenues towards integration and healing. Throughout this chapter and the next, I will highlight the aspects that can both challenge and support those recovering from trauma.

The Eight Limbs

While the word yoga tends to bring images of postures to mind, *asana*, the postural part of the practice, is only part of what constitutes yoga. Like limbs of a tree, yoga philosophy outlines eight avenues of practice, each a step that prepares the practitioner for the one that follows. *Ashtanga* means eight limbs, all part of the path outlined in *The Yoga Sutras of Patanjali*, a foundational yoga text compiled prior to 400 CE and passed down through chanting until recorded in writing (Iyengar, 2008). Each limb offers an opportunity to reflect and cultivate healing, though in the case of trauma recovery, we must be careful in our selection and timing for each limb. Some students and clients will benefit from changing the order of the limbs to meet their needs, while others do better skipping some of the suggested practices. This section serves to help you, as the service provider, to help your students and clients choose which limbs match their needs, and will be of the highest service to their unique path of healing. Figure 5.1 outlines all eight limbs.

1. **Yama**: Restraints, of which there are five:
     - *Ahimsa*: Peacefulness or non-harming
     - *Satya*: Truthfulness
     - *Asteya*: Non-stealing
     - *Brahmacharya*: Restraint of (sexual) energy
     - *Aparigraha*: Non-grasping or non-possessiveness
2. **Niyama**: Observances, of which there are also five:
     - *Saucha*: Cleanliness or self-purification
     - *Santosha*: Contentment
     - *Tapas*: Self-Discipline, often also described as transformative fire
     - *Svadhyaya*: Self-study
     - *Ishvara Pranidhana*: Surrender
3. *Asana*: Postures
4. *Pranayama*: Breathing practices
5. *Pratyahara*: Sense withdrawal
6. *Dharana*: Concentration
7. *Dhyana*: Meditation
8. *Samadhi*: Integration, enlightenment

Figure 5.1 The Eight Limbs of Yoga

Ahimsa and Svadhyaya

While, with sensitivity, each of the eight limbs can be involved in a trauma-informed practice, we will focus in this chapter on the most tangible, accessible aspects of each limb in order to offer students practices in clear alignment with trauma-informed principles. These practices interrelate and build upon one another, so let's take a moment to consider how the first *yama, ahimsa,* and the *niyama, svadhyaya,* set us up to do *asana* in a safe and trauma responsive manner.

Ahimsa

At the heart of many ethical codes is the effort to "do no harm," a phrase that captures the heart of *ahimsa.* If you travel back to the DSM-5 diagnosis of trauma, you'll recall that violence, loss, and threatened death play a role in post-traumatic stress. *Ahimsa,* simply stated, means nonviolence or non-harming. I like to state the word in its positive form, peacefulness, though this is not common in the literature. With this, the healing foundations of yoga clearly counter that of trauma; this first aspect of the first limb of yoga advocates for practicing peace, the opposite of the violence that leads to many experiences of trauma. Highlighting the choices we have between violent thoughts and behaviors and peaceful ones is a necessary component of teaching *ahimsa*. Naturally, saying, writing, and discussing peace come much easier than acting on it, which is why you will often hear teachers call the yoga journey "a *practice*, not a *perfect*." And yet, we strive for peacefulness.

Svadhyaya

Svadhyaya, self-reflection or self-study, helps us with this practice of peace, both in thought and in action. By studying ourselves on a yoga mat, meditation cushion, therapy couch, or in any of the countless relationships and circumstances of life, we are able to shine light on the habits, patterns, and experiences that embody both imprints of violence, trauma, or of peace, *ahimsa*. In becoming aware, we cultivate a wider Window of Tolerance and are able to choose.

When, as in the case of most trauma, violence has become internalized, negative impressions can exist within the mind or as an imprint on the body. As providers, we can encourage our students to notice thoughts and feelings of judgment, shame, criticism, or violence, and to recognize areas that hold wounds, and respond with care. Of course, in order to model the practice of *ahimsa*, we need to become increasingly aware of our own inner world and outer actions, and pay attention to how we perpetuate violence or peacefulness through our teaching.

This practice of choice can, internally in thought and feeling, and externally in behavior, reduce the frequency and propensity for violence in both our inner and outer worlds. With conscious choice we exercise neural pruning, paving pathways in our brains that become habits, beliefs, and when strong enough, world views. Also recall that conscious choice is something that happens within the window on tolerance. Remembering that we do, in fact, have the power of choice, is one thing that can re-connect us to our window, and our sense of agency. This practice can play a role in what many trauma survivors and healing supporters call "taking back power" from the aggressor. By practicing honest self-reflection and making the effort to choose peaceful thought and action, we directly contribute to reducing the re-enactment of traumatic experiences and begin to heal their imprints. How do you encourage self-reflection in your practice, counseling or teaching? To combine these first two concepts, explore ways you can encourage self-reflection that are rooted in peacefulness or non-harming.

Asana

As we move through the eight limbs we come to *asana*, the third limb. This is where we find the postures and shapes that grace advertisements, social media feeds, and the covers of yoga magazines. With the propensity to focus on outer physical form and on accomplishment of tasks, it is easy for American culture, and others, to glom onto the physical practice of yoga and attribute all kinds of unnecessary meaning to it. In the context of the eight limbs, the physical practice is meant to help strengthen and open the body and focus the mind, as a preparation for seated meditation. The word *asana* translates to mean *seat*, and the postures with the longer history are just that – seated positions in which we can reflect and observe the turnings of the mind – in other words, practice *svadhyaya*. Harnessing the energy of the mind is a recurring theme in yoga philosophy and practice. There are many physical practices and purposes for them, which we'll continue to explore as we discuss helpful sequences for trauma recovery in the next chapter.

Pranayama

The next limb, *pranayama*, is the practice of consciously influencing breathing patterns. Breathing practices can directly impact the vagal tone of the heart, and initiate the transition to the ventral vagal complex; this is another bottom-up function of the yoga practice (Brown & Gerbarg, 2005a, b; Porges, 2017; Carter, Bartal, & Porges, 2017). Some research even supports the effectiveness of breathing techniques over targeting neurotransmitters with medication in response to stress, anxiety, and depression (Jerath, Crawford, Barnes, & Harden, 2015). In some forms of yoga, like Kundalini, instructors bring breath practices to beginning students, and focus on repeating different forms of *pranayama* practice. True to the progression presented in the eight limbs, in Iyengar yoga, *pranayama* practices are reserved for more versed, advanced practitioners. Given the connections between trauma, breath, and the nervous system we've discussed, some of the simpler breathing practices may be extremely helpful for new students; however, keep in mind that manipulating the breath is a potent and powerful exercise. As a result, students whose systems are not well prepared often report feeling triggered, overwhelmed, or out of balance after advanced *pranayama* patterns. It is a delicate balance between bringing awareness and gentle changes to the breath, without overwhelming the current state of the body, mind and nervous system.

In my practice, I have seen stimulating practices like *kapalbhati*, or breath of fire, be particularly challenging for those experiencing anxiety and hyperarousal symptoms. I've also seen challenges with other simple practices: holding the inhale or the exhale, for even a short time, can bring about a feeling of overwhelm and/or fear of death, particularly for those who have had a strangle or drowning experience. In addition, with advanced practices like the *viloma* series (interrupted breath), *surya bhedana* (right nostril, or "piercing sun" breath), and *chandra bhedana* (left nostril, or "piercing moon" breath), it is crucial to monitor students for signs of balance in their energy and nervous systems. I would not recommend teaching these practices with those in trauma recovery unless you have extensive experience with them from both a practice and teaching perspective, and feel confident in your skills to help stabilize someone for whom they foster an imbalance.

Having seen the potential for inner discomfort and de-stabilization, I recommend a slow and cautious approach to all pranayama practices. Just like asana, we want to start with foundational practices and repeat them for some time before adding progressive amounts of challenge. It is not that people who have experienced trauma can never engage in advanced practice; we do a disservice to our clients with these types of rigid beliefs. Rather, teachers and students need to be aware of signs indicating that a practice is either improving or overwhelming the current state of the student's system. This takes time, practice, guidance, and attention to detail. Follow the resource link at the end of the chapter to learn a simple and adaptable pranayama practice for new students.

Pratyahara

Pratyahara, or sense withdrawal, is an advanced practice that involves dropping attention in and down, ideally to connect with a deep sense of self, or of spirit, or a peaceful place to rest within. I recommend reserving *pratyahara* for the long-term student of yogic practices, with one exception. The practice of withdrawing senses encourages students to connect with their internal worlds. Consider that those experiencing PTSD are carrying the impact of traumatic experience, on a mental, emotional, somatic, and physiological level. By asking someone to go deep within, yes, they may find a jewel of resilience there – and if they do, that's great and we can support it. However, it is extremely difficult to know what is going on inside the mind and body of someone we have just met, and teaching *pratyahara* to someone in the absence of a strong relationship offers us no bridge to awareness of their internal world. More often than not, people who are seeking the support of trauma-informed yoga have experienced overwhelming emotions and experiences, and being told to "drop in and down" could send them straight into these stressful places. The last thing we want to do is to instruct them to become overwhelmed again, or to disconnect via dissociation, in a place where they are seeking healing. Rather than jumping into *pratyahara*, consider cultivating positive internal resources and building the relationship so that your student/client has guidance and a hand to hold as they slowly step into their own depth, and traverse whatever else may be inside.

The exception comes for those who, as a result of the impacts trauma has on the nervous system, experience sensitivity to sensory input. Urban noise, groups of people, commotion, even technology can quickly lead to overstimulation – even in the non-traumatized nervous system. For those who arrive to yoga saying that their nerves, or bodies feel "fried," simple practices of pratyahara may be appropriate. For most of us, there is immense benefit in letting go of the constant influx of information that comes in through our eyes, ears, nose, mouth, and skin. In a trauma-informed setting, it is important to maintain access to the senses that help people assess for safety – for many, sight and sound are important ways to alert to crisis and orient to safety, and often feeling that anything is restrained can translate *directly to the body* as a lack of safety. Keep in mind that many people are restrained in situations where violence and trauma occurs. This is why we are careful with *pratyahara*. For hypera-roused students, containment of these senses can be helpful – a blanket over the body, hands over the ears or eyes: *this should always be at the choice of the student.* If the student is overwhelmed by stimuli, or asking for ways to reduce input, you may offer a blanket, eye bag, earplugs, or other props to help them feel protected and shielded, rather than intruded upon or denied a sense of safety. As with all of these practices, how the teacher communicates and follows up is crucial, and it is important to watch for signs of either increased distress or relief after we support students in making a choice. Sometimes people are unsure, or unaware, or defer to the teacher's opinion, so notice as much as you can about the state of the eyes, body, and overall energy of a person, even when they report that something is helpful. Everything you can notice and bring into awareness helps in making trauma-informed choices. If you do choose to offer *pratyahara*, and believe it will serve your student or client, be sure to take the slow and steady path and to build clear communication options for them to express comfort, distress, or the need for support.

Dharana

If you choose to skip over *pratyahara*, you can safely focus on this limb. Given the goals of trauma recovery, this limb is more accessible and directly relates to the many of the mental manifestations of PTSD. *Dharana* means concentration. With this practice, we develop a single point of focus. Giving a student something tangible, and either neu-tral or positive, to focus on, gives them clear direction and an anchor to come back to when challenging memories, thoughts, emotions, and feelings intrude. This practice provides respite from intrusions – and something concrete, in present time – to return to when the tides of traumatic experience pull strongly on the mind.

Anything can serve as a point of focus, and the yoga sutras name many such ways to direct the mind to prepare for meditation, or *dhyana*, the next limb. Start with whatever feels most accessible for you and those you serve. Simple tends to be better than complex, and you can choose to stay with simple, or progress into more complex images as a way to exercise the brain's capacity for detail. A colleague of mine starts with an application on her phone that shows a simple bar of light, and lets clients choose a color that feels good to them. With the set-up of my office, I often encourage clients to choose a plant on the windowsill, the golden spoon on my shelf (a gift from the student who taught me Spoon Theory), or the top of a tree outside. Something distinct, colorful, and easy to describe and agree on tends to be most helpful. Consider, of course, not suggesting things that your client may associate with a negative experience. If they report any negative reactions, support them in identifying something that is neutral or positive.

When you exercise *dharana*, for yourself and with your students and clients, you help cultivate a present moment resource, which supports students and clients in orienting to present time and environment. If someone, when not in a triggered state, develops the habit of gazing at the golden spoon on your shelf, for example, it will be much easier for them to access this connection to the present in a moment of overwhelming emotion. Building these skills as a mental and neurological habit supports the capacity to go step by step and stay rooted in psychological resources. Ultimately, this helps the practitioner stay connected to a feeling of present moment safety.

Dhyana

Described as a state of meditation that evolves from the focused concentration practices we just explored, this is, like all else in the book, something that cannot be forced. There are many techniques for meditation: focusing on a feeling of love in one's heart, or on a teacher or deity who embodies healing. Watching the breath, or counting it, is one of the most common bridges into meditative states. Repeating mantras also helps to focus the mind. Each of these serves *dharana*, focused concentration, which prepares and leads the practitioner toward a meditative state. As yoga texts describe it, we practice focused attention to set the conditions for meditation, and practice movement so we can become comfortably still. In the stillness of mind, we can see the depths of ourselves more clearly. The yoga sutras describe this from many angles throughout the text as a truth central to the practice of yoga.

Samadhi

The final limb, *samadhi*, translates to mean enlightenment or integration. Interestingly, in some of the most severe cases of abuse, some people develop dissociative coping mechanisms that lead to a diagnosis of DID.

Many DID therapists work to build communication within the internal systems, or personalities as they were called in past forms of the diagnosis. It is common to hear the term *integration* in this setting, as identities within the person come closer together and, at times, integrate as one. In yoga, the term *samadhi* can refer to both this internal sense of integration and one that transcends the body, and refers to a sense of oneness with all. This limb is often referred to as a spiritual experience, one that the other practices set the stage for, and that lies just beyond our conscious choice for it. While some will inevitably strive for it as a goal, sage teachers share that it is a gift the practice bestows upon the practitioner, a result of dedicated practice, but not something that even an advanced practitioner accesses by simple choice.

Note the difference between this and *spiritual bypass*, which describes the process of jumping straight to spirituality in defense of, or while denying the experience of, more difficult emotions like anger, sadness, and grief. When we use spiritual practices or beliefs to avoid facing our needs or our painful emotions, we become less integrated, and step off the yogic path towards *samadhi*. Every effective yoga practitioner, teacher, therapist, and healing human I know will attest to the importance of experiencing emotions; it is a central aspect of healing. Recall, also, that avoidance is a central aspect of the PTSD diagnosis. Rather than shove ourselves back into discomfort, the way the traumatic event did, we must build a solid foundation of resilience and resource that allows us to feel the deeper, challenging feelings that relate to the traumatic experience. Many seasoned trauma therapists refer to this as being able to "know what we know and feel what we feel" (van der Kolk, 2014). Spirituality, including any experience of *samadhi*, can be an important part of resourcing; and, with *samadhi* meaning integration, seeking enlightenment in denial of difficult emotions does not serve the process of yoga these limbs outline. Integration happens not with denial, but with truth, inclusion, and acceptance.

Yoga as a Trigger and a Resource

Now that you are familiar with the eight limbs, consider the people you serve and how different aspects of the limbs we've discussed may be received as either a resource or a trigger. This is the core of the challenge for a trauma-informed yoga teacher, or therapist using these practices in session. The very same practice that is soothing, calming, and comforting to you, can be uncomfortable, upsetting, and triggering to someone else. This is why you *must* listen to your students and clients and get curious about the cultures they are steeped in. Only then can you guide them in building resources that can help them to process the uncomfortable emotions or sensations related to the trigger. Consider the common instructions in yoga class listed in Figure 5.2, and how students who have experienced specific traumas may hear them as triggers.

Cue	Effect
Close your eyes	Person loses access to sight, which tells them whether or not they are safe
Separate your legs, or fold forward	Vulnerable areas of the body are exposed
Lift your arms up over your head	"Put your hands up," for those exposed to police injustice
Surrender	Military context: giving up at the end of a battle, defeat
Let out a long slow exhale	Some military trainings instruct shooting on a long exhale to steady the hands

Figure 5.2 Examples of Triggering Yoga Cues

The examples are countless and they depend on the populations you serve, the cultures they are a part of, and both the body positions and language that relate to their traumatic experiences. It may be obvious that speaking to the movements of the pelvis could be triggering for sexual assault survivors, but how could you know that your combat veteran student was trained to shoot on a long exhale? Keep in mind, as you learn triggers that apply to groups, that each individual's experience will be unique to them. How can we respond to this wide-cast potential for triggering?

First, we can seek to identify the words, positions, images, and environmental cues that might upset our students or cue them to recall their trauma. This is an ongoing process of education – listening and adapting – and is a wise response to help reduce experiences of overwhelm in the yoga room. The more diverse your population is, the more challenging it will be to identify all of the words, positions, sounds, images, and cultural elements that may remind them of their trauma. Despite our best efforts not to trigger, through the process of practicing yoga difficult emotions will likely arise. Keeping open lines of communication, while offering a number of options to help students find psychological resources through the practice, helps to reduce the number of triggers and guides them in navigating these challenging experiences. Ideally, we can offer both a safe emotional space for students to experience their emotions, and a supportive environment in which we meet their needs and boundaries with respect. As you identify triggers, also seek to define what works best for your particular class or student, what helps them connect to the practice and to themselves in a positive or helpful way. If you're not sure, ask and, as always, observe.

The Yoga Sutras

We have yet to pull from the opening lines of *Patanjali's Yoga Sutras*, which, with *sutra* meaning thread, weaves together pearls of yoga wisdom. The book, while short in length, has immense potential for depth, reflection, and complexity. The three opening lines speak volumes, and clearly relate to goals in trauma recovery (Miller, 1996; Iyengar, 2008; Bryant, 2015):

1.1 *Atha yoga anushasanam*: Now is yoga, or now begins yoga.
1.2 *Yogas citta vritti nirodhah*: Yoga is the cessation of the turnings of thought.
1.3 *Tadah drashtu svarupe avastanam*: Then the seer resides in their own true nature.

These sutras teach us to cultivate present moment awareness and harness mind chatter to still the waves of thought, so we can see clearly to the depths of our being. Just as disturbances on the surface of a lake prevent us from seeing to the bottom, mental fluctuations prevent us from connecting with our deeper layers. Trauma is one of these *vrittis*, as my teacher calls them, meaning whirlpools, or turnings of thought. As we've discussed, in cases of post-traumatic stress, thoughts, memories, and emotions pull us into a past experience. Yoga encourages us to practice presence, to "be here now," as Ram Dass would advocate (Dass, 2010). As we practice *dharana*, concentration of the mind, we develop awareness of its habits: moving to the past, to the imagined future, to memory or fantasy, to planning, or to something else entirely. Concentration practices encourage us to connect with the present moment, which is also one of the most powerful techniques for interrupting intrusive thoughts and memories.

The Yoga Sutras also describe *samskaras* as memories, habits, or imprints in the body, mind, brain, and being of an individual. *Samskaras* are said to stem from experiences, including those of previous lives. They can be positive and helpful, in the case of resourcing, or negative and unhelpful, in the case of intrusions. In yogic theory, as we bring awareness to patterns of posture, thought and behavior, conscious choice and practice offer us the key to create new patterns, to correct negative *samskaras*, and to invite positive grooves and habits to take their place. We can describe the process of recovering from trauma as addressing a negative *samskara*, the painful experience, and building habits to replace this with positive *samskaras*, be they beliefs, experiences, ways of holding the body, or some combination of these.

The sutras describe another helpful practice called *pratipaksha bhavana*, which is similar to cognitive therapy techniques. It translates to mean "cultivating the opposite," which I often describe more colloquially as "flip the thought." For example, if one is practicing yoga *asana* and experiencing self-judgement, a *pratipaksha bhavana* practice would encourage the student to explore the opposite of the negative thought. If the first thought was, "I am so inflexible," the next may be "I appreciate the range of motion that I have." For simple negative thoughts, this practice, particularly when repeated, can create new neural pathways, and slowly reprogram our minds toward more positive and empowering messages. As you may be noticing, the practice involves *svadhyaya*, self-study, as well as *ahimsa*, the practice of peace. It can also impact complex networks of negative thought by beginning to disrupt negative patterns and the snowball effect that often ensues once they begin.

Present-Moment Feeling Awareness

In many cases, coming to the present moment and/or flipping the thought is not substantial to address the deeper emotional needs arising. Emotions are often rich with material, and have a way of processing when we can offer attention and a safe space for them to do so. Recall the examples in Chapter 4 of learning to release, rather than hold, emotions and sensations. If we grew up in a family or culture that denies the usefulness of emotions, or encourages restricting or repressing them, we may need to learn how to feel our way through uncomfortable emotions. Recall also the saying *feel it to heal it*; the popular aphorism that describes our need to cry when we are sad, grieve loss, acknowledge anger, and recognize the complex blends of emotions that often present themselves together. Practices like yoga and meditation that help us pay attention and build awareness also allow us to identify primary and secondary emotions – that's the way we feel, and the way feel about how we feel. Repressing emotions takes energy, and often when we are allowed to feel the full range of stored negative emotion, we often feel a deep release of tension that allows us to enjoy positive emotions all the more.

Like Water on Rock

Many modern cultures carry a fast pace that encourages us to seek rapid results. Technology encourages this, making it possible for us to seek immediate answers and instant gratification rather than ponder questions and sit with not knowing. "The slower you go, the faster you get there" (Kluft 1993) suggests the wisdom of respecting that healing is a process and that, as much as we crave instant fixes, it is exceedingly rare that the healing, growth, and integration clients are seeking can happen in an instant, particularly in the case of developmental trauma. Healing takes time. Healing takes practice. Healing takes patience. Think of these yogic philosophies and practices as water on rock, smoothing out your energy and nervous system in a slow, repetitive, gentle way, over time.

Notice this in your own experience of the practices. Remember too, that as a provider, you are a guide and can help pace the process, but you are not in full control. The person's deep subconscious is often at the helm, and the client may be eager to move forward, wondering if they will ever fully recover a memory, or perplexed about why something from 12 years ago "still" comes up. Patience and persistence on the path of healing can be a challenge, but given the often quite nonlinear trajectory of recovery, they are necessary elements of long-term healing.

One of yoga's biggest gifts is that it is an ongoing practice and a process. This process, this conversation, can be both reparative and preventative. As we take the physical shapes, we have the opportunity to experience our bodies on a daily basis and to become aware of how they are changing. Mentally, we can become more aware of habits and leanings of the mind. Psychiatrist Dan Siegel calls this *mindsight* (Siegel, 2010). Perhaps most importantly, with practice we also have the opportunity to transcend the mind and body, and experience deep layers of peace within ourselves.

***

Three years after the conversation in juvenile hall, Lana showed up to one of my studio yoga classes in San Francisco, ready to practice. The innocence that had revealed itself over the six months in the juvenile program was now hidden under makeup, tucked back in behind eyebrow pencil and the bravado that keeps people from coming too close. "Lana!!" I called from across the room, ignoring the cool exterior and seeing through to the warm heart she had shown me while serving her time. "Lisa!" she called back, eagerness to please filling her face. She proceeded to tell me about her new job, her son, and the yoga class she'd enrolled in at the local community college. "You know, of everything in the program, I think yoga helped me the most. It just helps my mind empty out, and I feel more myself." I remind her, "You know, you could teach one day if you want." "Well, not today," she quips, "stay present, Lisa, it's time for *you* to teach."

Reflection Questions

1   How do you practice peacefulness and self-reflection? Is this different from how you offer these principles to others?
2   What habits of mind pull you out of the present moment?
3   What practices best reconnect you to here and now?
4   Which aspect of yoga philosophy covered in this chapter is the most helpful for you in this moment? Which will best serve those you work with?

Additional resources available at http://howwecanheal.com/y4tr

References

Brown, R. P., & Gerbarg, P. L. (2005a). Sudarshan Kriya yogic breathing in the treatment of stress, anxiety, and depression: Part I—neurophysiologic model. *Journal of Alternative and Complementary Medicine, 11*(1), 189–201.

Brown, R. P., & Gerbarg, P. L. (2005b). Sudarshan Kriya yogic breathing in the treatment of stress, anxiety, and depression: Part II—clinical applications and guidelines. *Journal of Alternative and Complementary Medicine, 11*(4), 711–717.

Bryant, E. F. (2015). *The yoga sutras of Patanjali: A new edition, translation, and commentary.* New York: North Point Press.

Carter, C. S., Bartal, I. B. A., & Porges, E. C. (2017). The roots of compassion: An evolutionary and neurobiological perspective. In E. M. Seppala (Ed.), *The Oxford handbook of compassion science* (p.173). New York, NY: Oxford University Press.

Dass, R. (2010). *Be here now.* New York: Three Rivers Press.

Easwaran, E. (2007). *The Bhagavad Gita: (Classics of Indian Spirituality).* Tomales, CA: Nilgiri Press.

Iyengar, B. K. S. (2008). *Light on the Yoga Sutras of Patanjali.* New York: Thorsons.

Jerath, R., Crawford, M. W., Barnes, V. A., & Harden, K. (2015). Self-regulation of breathing as a primary treatment for anxiety. *Applied Psychophysiology and Biofeedback, 40*(2), 107–115.

Kluft, R. P. (1993). Basic principles in conducting the psychotherapy of multiple personality disorder. In *Clinical Perspectives on Multiple Personality Disorder* (19–50). Washington, DC: APA.

Miller, B. S. (1996). *Yoga: Discipline of freedom: The yoga sutra attributed to Patanjali.* Berkeley, CA: University of California Press.

Porges, S. W. (2017). Vagal pathways: portals to compassion. In E. M. Seppala (Ed.), *The Oxford handbook of compassion science* (pp. 189–202). New York, NY: Oxford University Press.

Siegel, D. J. (2010). *Mindsight: The new science of personal transformation.* New York: Bantam.

Van der Kolk, B. (2014). *The body keeps the score.* New York: Viking.

6 Yoga Practices for Trauma Recovery

Yoga teaches us to cure what need not be endured and endure what cannot be cured.

– B. K. S. Iyengar

Jordan showed up seeking relief from depression through yoga, and wanted to know how yoga was supposed to help. "I went to class and we were lying down the entire time. It drove me crazy! But my sister swears by it and I really want to figure out if it can help me." I gathered from his comments that he may be experiencing a freeze response. In his first session, we began with a standing yoga practice, then moved into some shapes on all fours. Jordan's history was a bit different than most of my clients: no reported history of childhood abuse, but at age 18 he had been in an airplane crash that contributed to a very dysregulated nervous system, and left him coping with a serious Traumatic Brain Injury (TBI). Depression and confusion made it challenging to work and to maintain social relationships, and medications didn't prove to help much. "How does that feel?" I asked, to which he answered, "It's really hard!" We continued with a few basic postures, all the while observing the breath. Coordination proved challenging as a result of the TBI, so we worked slowly. Since Jordan's symptoms indicated a freeze response, we followed the dynamic movement with a long forward fold and some extended exhale breath. "How do you feel?" I asked, after 20 minutes of practice. "Good," Jordan replied. "That was so different than the class I took! We didn't do any of those moves." I nod, knowing the yoga world well, "There are so many ways to practice yoga. Try these at home and if it's working for you we can try some more next week."

***

We've covered the foundational philosophy of yoga, but it would take a pretty complex algorithm to begin to cover all of the potential variations of yoga available. There are lineages, schools, trademarked styles, and sequences within each style. Some practices have strong similarities while others look drastically different from one another. For a trauma survivor who is new to yoga, choosing a class and finding the right type of practice can contribute to feeling mentally and emotionally overwhelmed. As providers, the more familiar we are with the styles, teachers, and studios in our areas, the better, and the wider our scope of understanding of yoga, the more effectively we can serve our clients.

The Sequence for Trauma Recovery

The bulk of this chapter is an effort to respond to the most common question I get from students, workshop participants, clients, and other mental health professionals: "What's the best sequence of yoga poses for trauma?" "It depends" is always the answer, and the variety of both symptoms and needs that clients present is what keeps sequencing, and this work as a whole, complex and fascinating. This truth is challenging and demands that we continually deepen our understandings of yoga, mental health, our clients, and ourselves.

Outside of methods with structured, scripted sequences, there is no one right way to teach a class; the two most important things you can do are to observe the needs of your student(s), and make choices to respond to their needs. While we all want the roadmap to the most successful, healing sequence, prescribed methods become less helpful as the complexity of a person's trauma history increases. The following is not a list of yoga postures, but provides a structure you can refer to when working with traumatized populations:

1   Assess
2   Instruct/Offer
3   Observe/Discuss
4   Adapt
5   Refine

Depending on your setting, each stage will look different. In a class environment, you might **assess** by observing bodies and facial expressions. In mental health and medical environments, and even in some yoga studios, you can review any available assessments or intake paperwork to gather information about the student's needs. In some settings, you'll be able to have a short conversation, exploring the client's experience and hopes for healing. While you need to get a sense of if you can help the person, it is not necessary – and can be harmful – to ask in depth questions about their traumatic experiences prior to working together. In the assessment stage, pay particular attention to the nervous system and decide, based on what you know, where you think it will be most beneficial to start.

You can then proceed to **instruct**, offering direction towards a position or short sequence where they can begin. As they begin to practice, **observe** and, when possible, **converse.** How do they seem to react to what you've offered? Are they engaged, checked out, or tense? What do you notice in their eyes and bodies? Take in as much information as you can, combining it with what you already know about the person and the yoga practice, and then **adapt** in order to meet their needs. You might adapt by offering a physical support, like a block, or blanket, or by offering mental support or encouragement through the *dristi*, gazing point, or through words of affirmation. A genuine "That's it, you've got it," or "nice effort" can go a long way when someone is learning something new and potentially uncomfortable (in group classes, it can help to address these remarks to the entire room to reduce experiences of comparison or competition). If the practice is taking the student out of their window of tolerance, make a change in the types of posture, pace, or environment in efforts to guide their nervous system into the window. As you go, continue to listen, observe, and **refine**, with the window of tolerance in mind. If something doesn't have the effect you're looking for, change it. We'll cover three options for sequences in this chapter, all which speak to our efforts to bring balance to the nervous system through asana. Before we jump into these sequences, we'll explore three ways to prepare: grounding, orienting, and centering.

Grounding

Grounding involves connecting the body with the ground, and the earth below. Just as we ground electrical currents to prevent surges, practicing grounding can help with anxiety and overwhelming thoughts and feelings, bringing you "back to earth," so to speak. This practice is also referred to as *earthing* when it involves direct contact with the earth itself, without any shoe or other surface in the way. With this tactile connection, the feet can actually feel the floor, or earth, and it's easier to access the messages the body is sending about its present state, as compared to the traumatic state. While limited research exists, some health professionals explain that placing our feet in direct contact with the earth creates an opportunity for the earth's electrons to conduct to your body, thereby matching the body's electrical potential to that of the earth. In mental health circles, connecting with the felt sense of ground under the body – even without direct connection to the earth – is one of the most common practices used to support clients experiencing overwhelming emotions and internal experiences. Like orienting, which we discuss next, it provides something tactile and tangible to bring attention to, directing awareness away from intrusive thoughts or feelings.

Most often we use the feet and sit bones as points of grounding, since they tend to already be in contact with something below. However, yoga, and its many shapes, allow us to find grounding in other areas of the body – the hands, forearms, belly, back, and even the head! Still, many people report feeling grounding sensations more strongly in the lower body, so unless this area is triggering or there is a clear reason not to, this is a good place to start. Encouraging a client to notice their back touching the sofa, their sit bones in the chair, or their feet on the floor are common examples. When grounding is helpful for a client or student, encouraging them to notice the positive sensations it brings to the body and mind can be helpful and strengthen their relationship to the practice. The sequence that follows offers an opportunity for each

---

Begin cross legged on the floor or a bolster. Encourage students to notice the sensation of the floor or bolster under them and press into the floor. Invite an added fold forward, of any amount, supporting the hands on blocks, or on the floor just in front of the rest of the body. Encourage students to push into the floor and feel its texture. Transition to hands and knees.

❖ **Opening, Beginner Sequence:**
  • Cat Cow: Press down into hands and shins.
  • Plank on knees or toes: Hands press.
  • Lower to belly: Observe connection of front body with the floor.
  • Low Cobra to Sphinx: Forearms ground.
  • Forearm Plank on knees or toes: Ground through forearms.
  • Child's Pose: Ground into hands.
  • Downward Dog: Grounding through hands and/or feet.
  • Low Lunge, repeat both sides: Grounding through front heel and back shin.
  • Standing Forward Fold: Grounding through feet, option to support hands on chair or floor.
  • Wide Squat (*Malasana*): Option for heels on blanket and sit bones on block. Note the energy of *apana*, moving down.
  • Mountain Pose: Reflect on any shifts, relationship to feet and floor.

❖ **For more physical challenge, consider adding:**
  • Sun Salute A: Same grounding points as above in Plank, Cobra/Upward Dog, Forward Fold, *Tadasana*.
  • Chair Pose: Grounding through feet, connecting with energy of legs.
  • Sun Salute C with Low Lunge option: Grounding through heel and shin.
  • Tuck toes under sit towards heels (sole of the foot stretches).
  • *Vajrasana*, kneeling pose: Untuck toes and sit of heels with tops of feet on the floor (stretches front of ankles, can add a small flat or rolled blanket under the ankle for support, or lean back and lift knees for more mobility).

❖ **Closing:**
  • Staff Pose: Rock paper scissors with your feet (hold hands with your feet).
  • Bound Angle Pose (not recommended initially for sexual abuse survivors).
  • Seated forward fold: Helpful to have option to rest hands on props (belt, blocks, bolster).
  • *Savasana* with option to stay seated, option of support of the wall behind back.
  • Close with soft low chant of "*Lam*," if appropriate. This is the seed syllable of the root chakra.

Check in post-sequence to observe effects on yourself and your student(s). Adapt, omitting anything overly challenging, or including something else that has a grounding effect, to maximize benefits.

Figure 6.1 Sample Grounding Yoga Sequence

practitioner to choose the best grounding point to emphasize stability and connection. You can also access these sequences in the resource link at the end of this chapter.

Orienting

This is a practice that cultivates connection to the present moment through the five senses. Quite the opposite of *pratyahara*, the primary goal of this sequence is to connect with the environment, the space within the studio, practice area, and anything that feels grounding, safe, or soothing. The grounding practice above is, in essence, orienting to the earth. This practice expands to invite other senses and perspectives. Remember that quality of the experience is more important than quantity,

---

Begin with eyes open, in a comfortable seated position, supported by appropriate props. Encourage students to look around the room, notice who and what the space contains – entrances, exits, colors, shapes, etc. Invite students to keep the eyes open throughout class, if they prefer.

❖ **Opening/Beginner Sequence:**
  - From seated: Teach *dristi* – gazing point. Again, color can be helpful here.
  - Cat Cow: *Dristi* forward, then navel. Invite students to orient to neutral or positive sensation by feeling the texture of the floor, mat, or blankets as they meet the palms and shins.
  - Downward Dog: Identify *dristi*; call attention to the hands and feet and, if appropriate, sounds in the environment.
  - Standing Forward Fold: Option to use wall, chair or blocks for support.
  - *Tadasana*: Invite students to note anything new or different they notice in the room or immediate environment, after this short practice.

❖ **For more physical challenge, consider adding:**
  - Sun Salute A: Noting the *dristi* points and sensations outlined above. You can also offer that students orient to your voice, and count or instruct breath throughout the sequence.
  - Low or High Lunge on both sides: Focus on sight, sound, texture, sensation.
  - Quarter-turn Sun Salute – option here to orient students beyond the room: facing north, east, south, west
  - Tree Pose: Single *dristi* is easiest, as an added challenge, students can look around enough to identify a new shape or color. This will make balancing more difficult!

❖ **Closing:**
  - Staff Pose: Orient to floor, sensations, sounds in room.
  - Forward Fold with gaze at big toes: orienting to sensations at back of legs, dristi, or sound.
  - Close with listening meditation (eyes open always okay).

Orienting yourself before, during and after the practice can help. Which way is north in your space? Which direction does the window face, and what is just beyond the room? Orienting to time is another way we can remain connected to the present moment, so counting breaths, saying "we will be here one more minute" or identifying other aspects of the relationship to time during practice can be helpful.

Figure 6.2 Sample Orienting Yoga Sequence

so it is better to offer a few of these than bombard clients with everything at once. To provide an orienting experience note any visual, tactile, and auditory cues that could connect your students or client to the present moment in a neutral or positive way. It may be appropriate to include smells – essential oils are commonly used in yoga spaces. If you choose these, be sure to discuss the purpose prior to introducing it in a group environment, so that students can choose something soothing and so you can ensure that, if there are more than one or two people, people's chosen scents do not invoke a negative response in others. Sensitivities to smell are relatively common, so checking in first is particularly important with this sense.

If you, the teacher, are well-oriented to the space you will be able to guide your students in becoming so. Throughout the sequence, invite students to notice their five senses, and describe in your own words what you experience in the moment, as a model. This may be the cool touch of the wood floors, the coarse wool blanket brushed against your shoulder in a posture demonstration, or the increased humidity and warmth as the practice builds. If you do chose to include scents via oils or incense, you can include smell as a platform for orienting. One studio I frequented for a period of time was just a few doors down from a bakery, and the smell of fresh bread would waft through the windows early in the morning. Making note of these potential "distractions" and including them in the practice of orienting helps make even the most tantalizing pastry scent serve a relevant purpose. Guide your students through these types of experiences with suggestions, offerings, and examples of what they might notice. Noticing and verbalizing your felt experience has the added benefit of helping you connect with your environment. Staying connected to your own experience helps you remain embodied, which reduces the likelihood that you will become overwhelmed by the traumatic experiences of others.

Centering

For many people, the experience of trauma pulls them off center and can even, quite literally, change patterns in the core muscles of the body and impact the sense of power that resides there. From an energy body standpoint, the solar plexus area houses the third chakra, and attention to sensations in this area can help reconnect a practitioner to their inner sense of power. I think of centering as orienting to a deep sense of self and the agency that resides within us – to say yes, or no, to draw a boundary or to pace our healing.

As with any sequence, check in with students before, during and after to observe the effects of the practice. If a student shares that they feel their center more in their heart than in their abdomen, honor that. Over time, calling attention and energy to the center and fostering healthy ego strength contributes to recovery from situations where students internalized a negative belief, or experienced a loss of power.

The grounding and orienting practices prepare students for this internal focus. Should this centering practice bring up any feelings of overwhelm, return to grounding and external points of orientation.

❖ **Opening:**
- Begin seated or reclined, with the invitation to have a hand on the heart or abdomen, observing rise and fall of breath.
- Cat Cow: emphasize rounding and drawing abdominals gently in to connect with core muscles.
- Downward Facing Dog: Emphasize navel drawing gently towards spine to support the lower back, outer hips firm in, front ribs draw towards hip points. This brings attention to core stability.
- Step forward to *Ardha Uttanasana* (halfway lift), attention to the torso with equal length on all four sides.
- Hands to hips: Rise to stand with support of all core muscles (reinforce those addressed in Downward Dog).
- Mountain Pose: Option to ask – where is your center? Invitation to place a hand there.

❖ **For more physical challenge, consider adding:**
- Sun Salute A: Emphasis on moving from center and core stability.
- Sun Salute B with High Lunge: Emphasis on supporting lower back with abdominal support.
- Power Lunge: From High Lunge, tilt the torso forward at a 45-degree angle.
- Lunge Twist: High or low, on both sides.
- Active Intense Side Stretch Pose (*Parsvottanasana*): Hands on blocks emphasizing length on all four sides of waist.
- Twisting Triangle: Maintain length and use obliques to twist.
- Warrior 3 (option for hands on blocks): Find center of gravity; draw navel towards spine.
- *Vinyasa*: With pause in plank; same actions in abdomen as Warrior 3.
- Transition to Seated: Reinforce length on all four sides of torso and core stability; spine long and supported.
- Boat Pose (*Navasana*) to Low Boat Pose (*Ardha Navasana*), option to repeat.

❖ **Cooling:**
- Supported Bridge (releases abdomen).
- Supine Twist (releases lower back).
- Reclined Pigeon (to release hip stabilizers used in standing postures).
- Knees to chest (releases lower back).
- *Savasana*: Option to remain seated, or to lie prone; invitation to return hand to abdomen if helpful.

The effects of a centering practice can be heating and energizing, so when students are hyper-aroused consider moving slowly and bringing more time and attention to the cooling stage of practice.

Figure 6.3 Sample Centering Yoga Sequence

The *Gunas*

The *Bhagavad Gita* describes material nature, referred to as *prakriti*, as all that changes, and *purusha* as the unchanging, spirit, observer, or Seer of that which changes (Vyasa, 2017). *Prakriti* includes three qualities of nature that are present in all things, including bodies, minds, yoga postures, and practices: *rajas, tamas,* and *sattva.* Distinguishing *purusha* from *prakriti* helps us to gain some distance and perspective about our current experiences, similar to a child saying "I have depression" rather than "I am depressed," we can experience the *gunas* without becoming them. *Rajas* is the quality of nature related to movement, and is associated with the element of fire. You'll often hear yoga teachers use this word to refer to energy that is athletic, restless, active, heated, or contains an excess of energy. *Tamas* describes the opposite: stillness, inertia – a *lack* of energy, heat, or movement, and can even convey a sense of restraint or limitation in movement. *Tamas* is associated with the element of earth.

While *rajas* and *tamas* are simply referred to as qualities, neither good nor bad, older texts emphasize attitudes and behaviors related to these qualities, with both more emphasis on the potential negative effects, and with a higher value on the third guna, *sattva.* Suffering is said to arise not because of the guna, but because of our relationship and response to it. As teachers, we can transform the relationship to the *gunas* by highlighting the adaptive, responsive, or functional elements of the guna. For example, as we include grounding, stability and centering in *tamas,* we accept the present condition, rather than wrestling with it, and encourage feelings that relate to a sattvic state. With all trauma symptoms, when we meet them without judgement, identify their function, and make an inclusive and discerning choice about what to do with the experience, we initiate an integrative experience of healing, rather than promoting discord between parts, or experiences, of the self.

Often described as calmness, tranquility, or lucidity, sattva is associated with the element of light. *Sattva* describes something very similar to the window of tolerance – an awake, alert, present, calm, and engaged space. Often after a balanced yoga practice yogis will describe feeling more sattvic – rested, with a peaceful, attentive internal experience. As we cover in the first three yoga sutras, we can liken *sattva* to still waters that are not agitated with rajas or clouded by *tamas;* in *sattva,* the stillness and clarity allow us to see through *prakriti* to *purusha.* Yoga teachers versed in this knowledge seek to cultivate clear-seeing by sequencing towards *sattva,* just as trauma therapists seek to support clients into cultivating their Window of Tolerance. While trauma therapy and yoga practice can appear strikingly different, this is another place in which their efforts converge, where we can translate yoga-speak into clinical language, and vice-versa.

Sequencing for Balance

Note that this ancient model (the *Bhagavad Gita* dates back to 200–400 BCE) offers a perspective similar to Newton's first law of motion, sometimes called the law of inertia: objects in motion stay in motion, while objects at rest stay at rest (Newton, 1999 [1687]). It also bears striking resemblance to the modern-day Window of Tolerance model (Siegel, 1999), and to the tendency for the nervous system to become stuck on, or off. It even reflects the findings of Polyvagal Theory (Porges, 2011), with rajas representing the SNS's activation to fight or flee, tamas being akin to the dorsal vagal complex, and *sattva* describing the ventral vagal complex (Sullivan et al., 2018). It appears that yogis have been onto something, and that modern science is both validating and deepening our understanding of ancient wisdom. Putting all of this together, we can make choices in yoga sequences based on wisdom passed down by yogis in the language of the *gunas* in efforts to activate the myelinated vagal response of the ventral vagal complex. In other words, we can use yoga to foster *sattva*, connection to the present moment and to other beings. Figure 6.4 shows the Window of Tolerance model with the *gunas* and polyvagal terms included.

Combining the knowledge that has been passed down through yoga philosophy and practice with the modern theories of trauma recovery allows us to craft sequences with an effort to bring healing to the whole person. By paying attention to cues in the face and body, listening to the unique challenge of each person, and responding in an effort to bring balance to the nervous system, we provide tools to help cope in the aftermath of trauma, and support self-regulation. The most common mistake I see reflects what Jordan experienced in the case example above: teaching or practicing in a way that does not meet the needs of the nervous system and bring it towards balance. For most people in a fight, flight or freeze response, simple reclining and relaxing does not feel accessible.

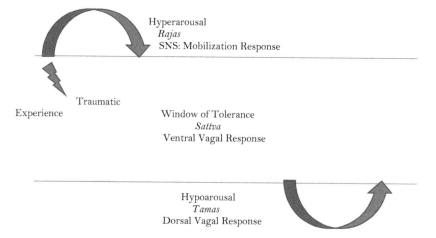

Figure 6.4 Window of Tolerance with *Gunas* and Polyvagal Theory

As a result of the energy that floods the system at the time of the trauma, most of these students, even when they appear depressed, experience an internal sense of agitation. Yogis call this *rajasic depression*. In a yoga practice, it is essential to meet the nervous system where it is and gradually encourage movement into the Window of Tolerance. Figure 6.4 is a visual representation of these efforts.

When we sequence with the *gunas* and the nervous system in mind, teaching students and clients how to pay attention to their own cues, we can offer a practice that meets the person's internal experience where it is, facilitates awareness, and brings balance to the body. Like the arrows in Figure 6.5, we choose practices that meet the student or client where they are, and help them cultivate *sattva*, activate the ventral vagal response, and transition into the Window of Tolerance.

Following are some sample sequences that demonstrate how we can facilitate the transition into this balanced state. You can access the resources that accompany these practices at: http://howwecanheal. com/y4tr.

A Soothing Sequence

Yoga practices teach us that some groups of postures have a soothing, or cooling effect. Forward bends, postures that stretch yin lines of energy (inner arm, inner thigh) and involve lateral movements, longer exhales, the left nostril and side of the body, are all associated with

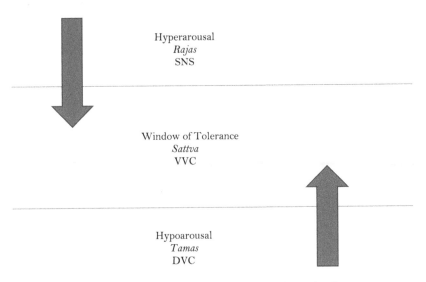

Figure 6.5 Bringing the Nervous System into the Window of Tolerance

cooling, soothing, or *chandra* (moon) energy. In addition, a slower pace, seated postures, and an internal focus on experience all go along with a soothing theme. To the extent that you have training and experience with advanced energetics, you can include these additional aspects into your teaching.

The sequence below is best for those whose systems are in hyperarousal. It reflects the principles of meeting the student where their *nervous system* is, and moving into the Window of Tolerance by weaving in postures known to have a cooling influence. While this is largely effective, triggers and differences can arise, such as feeling claustrophobic in forward folds, in which case we always defer to the student's experience and adapt to find another pathway to the desired result.

Soothing Practice – *Rajas* to *Sattva*
Begin standing in Mountain Pose, bringing attention to the breath. The pace of this class begins energetically, and slows down over the course of the sequence.

❖ **Opening**
- Begin in *Tadasana*, Mountain Pose.
- Quarter Sun Salutation: Dynamic arm movements, inhale reach out and up, exhale hands back to heart.
- Half Sun Salutation: Add halfway lift and forward fold.

❖ **For more challenge, consider adding:**
- Full Sun Salutation: Add plank, *Chaturanga*, Cobra/Upward Dog or use modifications. Repeat three times. With each cycle make the pace a little slower, and increase the length of hold in Downward Dog (moving from 2, to 3, to 5 breaths, for example).
- Warrior 2, Side Angle, Triangle: Repeat on each side.
- Wide Legged Standing Forward Fold (*Prasarita*) with arm variations A (hands to floor) and D (hands to our shins or ankles).
- Tree Pose: Consider arm variations for extra challenge.
- Sun Salutation to Downward Dog to Standing Forward Fold: hold 5 breaths.

❖ **Closing**
- Bridge Pose: Begin focus on the exhale.
- Seated: Staff Pose: Continue focus on the exhale.
- Seated: Forward Fold: Long exhales, releasing any excess energy through the breath.
- Seated: Bound Angle and/or Head to Knee Pose (*Janu Sirsasana*).
- Breath Meditation: 3-count inhale, 4-count exhale.
- Brief *Savasana*, with option to lie prone or stay seated.
- Optional Chant *Om* (this emphasizes the long exhale again).

Trace in this sequence the choices that help students move from *rajas* to *sattva*. Pace, posture, and breath all play a role. When someone is in a hyperaroused, *rajasic* state, it will be difficult to begin with the soothing postures you see here at the end of the sequence, but dynamic movement can help them prepare to sit more peacefully.

Figure 6.6 Sample Soothing Yoga Practice

An Energizing Sequence

The purpose of this sequence is to bring energy to the body and stimulate the nervous system. Postures that are known to be heating and bring energy to the body include backbends, like bridge, cobra, and/or camel, and breathing practices that accentuate the inhale, breath retention, or encourage a fast pace. *Viloma 1, kapalabhati,* and *surya bedhana* are *pranayama* practices with a heating effect that we can use to cultivate energy when sluggish. Even restorative sequences can have an energizing effect when we focus on these types of shapes; *savasana* with the chest lifted on a bolster is a wonderful example.

The sequence in Figure 6.7 is appropriate for someone whose system is in a hypoarousal. It is important to assess, to the best of your ability, whether the client presenting with depression, lethargy, or *tamas* is also

---

Energizing Practice – *Tamas* to *Sattva*
When teaching a practice that bridges from *tamas* to *sattva*, beginning with less movement and postures that are supported and accessible is most helpful for students.

- ❖ **Opening**
  - *Savasana* with chest lifted on a bolster (2–3 minutes): instruct breath awareness and gentle emphasis on inhale. Roll to side to sit up.
  - Seated Twist: On floor or chair, this gently warms by engaging core muscles.
  - Cat Cow: Focus on expansion of chest with inhale.
  - Downward Dog: Option to use hands at wall in "Puppy Dog" if posture is not accessible.
  - Standing Forward Fold: Hands interlaced behind back, if appropriate, or holding a strap, will begin to open the chest.
  - Mountain Pose, *Tadasana*: Lift the area where chest meets the armpits.

- ❖ **For more challenge, consider adding:**
  - Half Sun Salute: Dynamic and heating, yet more accessible for most bodies than Sun Salute A.
  - Sun Salute A: Warms the body and prepares for other standing postures.
  - Low Lunge Twist: Warming, and stimulates internal organs with gentle pressure.
  - Warrior 1: Powerful posture requiring leg strength; can also be grounding.
  - Cobra, Sphinx or Locust Pose (*Salabhasana*) variations: These require mobility in the upper back and stability in the lower/lumbar region.
  - More advanced backbends need different shoulder preparations than we have covered in this sequence, but over time and with proper preparation earlier in the sequence, you can add them here as peak postures.

- ❖ **Closing**
  - Bridge pose: Option to practice on a block or bolster.
  - Supine Twist: Option to support legs with blanket or bolster.
  - Short or Seated *Savasana*. Notice energy cultivated with practice.
  - Option to close with chant *Om.*

Notice that this class moves from the floor to standing, and does not linger on the floor during the cooling phase at the end of class. When cultivating *sattva* from *tamas*, maintaining some of the heat or energy cultivated in the practice can be helpful.

Figure 6.7 Sample Energizing Yoga Practice

experiencing hyperarousal internally, indicating a freeze response. If they are, this sequence may be too stimulating, and could ramp up the energy trapped in the system. Look for signs of agitation – fidgeting, discomfort, short breath, needing to leave the room frequently, and if they appear to be experiencing both hyperarousal and hypoarousal, consider offering the balancing sequence that follows instead.

A Balancing Sequence

The freeze response, in yogic terms, *rajasic depression*, is the most complex and takes attention to the inner experience of the practitioner. If a student is in primarily hyperarousal or hypoarousal (in yogic terms, *rajas* or *tamas*) the best strategy is to meet the energy presenting at the start and gently cultivate change posture by posture, throughout the sequence. Approaching a student experiencing the freeze response with a soothing or energizing sequence risks bringing them further out of balance. Some students may benefit from both sequences above, when using them to respond to the dominant energy in a given moment, while others will become further dysregulated. Our best point of assessment is the state of the body just before beginning the practice. If you observe what looks like a freeze response, a balancing sequence tends to be the best option. From a yogic standpoint, we cultivate balance through balancing postures, long hold inversions, bilateral movements, and equal counts in breathing practices, like *sama vritti*, or alternate nostril breathing, *naddhi shodana*.

I've included a chant at the end of each sequence due to the benefits of prosodic speech recognized by Polyvagal Theory. A simple *Om* or *Aum* is standard practice, or if you want to get more specific you can use chakra seed syllables. Longer words of blessing like *lokah samastah sukhino bhavantu*, which translates to "may all beings know peace" or "may all beings be happy and free," give a positive message of support. Of course, if chanting is scary or triggering for those you serve, skip this part of the practice, or find a way to bring in the same principle. Some traditions sing a song, and occasionally students who feel uncomfortable with chanting enjoy humming instead. Find a way to apply the principle that resonates – pun intended – with your group.

In addition to these active practices, restorative practices are often more accessible for those experiencing a freeze response, or with limited physical mobility. It is possible to use restorative postures to invite balance in the nervous system and energetic body. See Figure 6.9 for two sample restorative sequences.

Other Healing Components

Through training in a variety of practices that support trauma recovery, I have come to recognize the similar theories and practices they share

Balancing Sequence – Cultivating *Sattva*
A balancing sequence can contain both energizing and soothing postures in equal presence, but it can be difficult to track each person's internal experience to these in a group setting. To be safe, at first, choose postures known to have a balancing effect, and slowly add in soothing or energizing elements to the sequence over time, observing the effects.

❖ **Opening**
  • Seated: Even breathing, offer intention (*sankalpa*) to focus mind.
  • All fours: Alternate leg/arm lift; this encourages right and left brain integration.
  • Downward Dog: Even press of hands, even breathing, moderate length hold.
  • Standing Forward Fold: Option to bend knees, support hands, or head, with props (blocks, chair, bolster).

❖ **For more physical challenge, consider adding:**
  • Sun Salute A: Includes both forward and back bending, de-emphasize extremes of spine, emphasize stability and even rhythm of breath and body.
  • Triangle both sides: Moderate breath and hold length for population.
  • Warrior 2 both sides: Emphasize even breathing and equal attention in both arms and legs.
  • *Prasarita* A, B, D: Option to support head, hands or arms on a chair; build tolerance to longer holds over time. Encourage even breathing.
  • Tree Pose: Teach *dristi*, add support of one hand on wall when appropriate.
  • *Urdvha Hastasana*: With arms reaching upward, emphasize even length on all four sides of the torso.
  • More difficult inversions: You may choose to include Handstand, Forearm Balance or Headstand if student and teacher are well-versed. These are heating inversions, they call for the energetic counter pose *Halasana* (Shoulder Stand) cycle to foster balance in the system. Since these inversions carry a higher risk to the joints (wrists, shoulders, cervical spine), they need to be instructed thoroughly and with props initially. Do not attempt to teach these postures without a thorough understanding of them.

❖ **Closing**
  • Forward Fold: Option to support hands or head on props (bolster, block, chair).
  • Cooling inversion: *Viparita Karani*, or shoulder stand on chair. Props like the chair help to make these inversions, and longer holds, more accessible.
  • Focused concentration: Even-breathing meditation.
  • *Savasana*: Option to practice seated, supine, prone, or with supports.
  • Optional chant, *Om* or otherwise, to close.

In addition to choosing postures that are known to have a balancing effect, we can use the language of *sattva*, speaking to any sense of lightness, balance, ease or clarity that comes as a result of the practice. Noticing these elements at the end helps the strengthen students' awareness of the changes that are possible through practice, and gives them an experience of what it means to cultivate balance in the nervous system.

Figure 6.8 Sample Balancing Yoga Practice

with yoga. Eye Movement Desensitization and Reprocessing (EMDR) is an increasingly popular and effective treatment intervention for PTSD (Seidler & Wagner, 2006). EMDR brings focused attention first to psychological resources, then to the distressing aspects of traumatic experience, with bilateral stimulation. Bilateral stimulation, in EMDR, is typically done with eye movements (hence the name), a beeping sound or

Simple Restorative Practice to Balance Excess *Rajas*

Desired Effect: Soothing

- o *Tadasana* with back at wall: Cultivate awareness of back body and breath
- o Standing Forward Fold with forearms on chair
- o *Prasarita Padottanasana* with head on block(s)
- o Downward Dog with forehead on bolster
- o Child's Pose with front torso supported by bolster(s) and blanket(s)
- o *Janusirsasana* with front torso supported by bolster(s) and blanket(s)
- o Seated Forward Fold, *Paschimottanasana* with front torso supported by bolster(s) and blanket(s)
- o Prone *Savasana*, or supine *Savasana* with bolster and/or blankets placed at the top of the thigh

Simple Restorative Practice to Balance Excess *Tamas*

Desired Effect: Energizing

- o *Savasana* on two blocks: one behind thoracic spine (upper back) at low or middle height, the other under the head at middle or high height
- o Supported Bridge Pose on bolster
- o *Viparita Dandasana* on the chair with feet at wall
- o Chair Headstand (or *Viparita Karani*)
- o Prone Twist with torso supported by bolster and/or blanket(s)
- o Chair Shoulder Stand (or *Viparita Karani*)
- o *Savasana* with chest lifted on a bolster (2-3 minutes): instruct breath awareness and gentle emphasis on inhale
- o Roll to side to sit up

Figure 6.9 Simple Restorative Practices to Cultivate Balance

music that moves back and forth between the left and right ears, or by a holding a small pad that buzzes back and forth between the two hands. In treatment, these elements can be paired, or not. Some clients prefer to just use one aspect: tactile, audio, or visual. One theory about how EMDR functions is that the rapid right to left stimulation allows the neural networks to integrate, bringing together resources and challenging memories (Parnell, 2010). As we create space for difficult emotions to process, we also re-connect to positive aspects of memory, and of ourselves.

Most yoga practices contain aspects of bilateral stimulation, moving from right to left, in a rhythmic pace. In this way, yoga may be tapping into this EMDR principle believed to help us process emotions. Many yoga teachers are aware that emotions arise in yoga, and offer some guidance towards positive ways to cope and to relate to the self – forgiveness, compassion, acceptance, gratitude, and letting go are all common themes in a studio practice. There are similarities between yoga and EMDR, though EMDR is a specific and targeted process that requires additional training for mental health professionals to use appropriately.

In addition to sharing similar principles with EMDR, yoga, depending on the teacher and approach, can demonstrate aspects of hypnosis, as well. During my training in clinical hypnosis, the emphasis on facilitating focused attention and absorption rang in my mind as *dharana* and *dhyana* – focused attention and meditation – as described in the eight limbs. Another important component of hypnosis is suggestion; offering options, choices, and encouraging words. As I learned about this approach, I thought back to classes where teachers said things to the effect of, "That's it, ease into it, focus on your breath. Notice what comes to mind and return to your breath. Can you accept your thoughts, your body, your life as they are in this moment?" The hypnotist offers targeted suggestion to support the client in moving beyond a block or accessing their inner guidance. Yoga teachers do this, too, typically in a general way and, if the class goals adhere to the eight limbs, after facilitating focused attention and a state of meditation, or absorption. Soon after I completed my clinical hypnosis training, a yoga student asked me after class if I was a hypnotist. She later said it was something about the rhythm of my speech, which is something that hypnosis training addresses, that reminded her of a hypnotist she had been to. While I *was* trained in hypnosis, the truth was that, more than attempting to integrate hypnosis into my teachings, I was emulating the speech patterns I'd learned from my own yoga teachers.

Biofeedback practices overlap with yoga as well. Becoming aware of tension in muscles and actively allowing them to release is one form of bio-feedback, which is a common yoga teaching. EEG neurofeedback focused on alpha theta brain wave training has also been shown to improve symptoms of post-traumatic stress disorder (Peniston & Kulkosky, 1991). For most neurofeedback teachings, this is an advanced practice, and is meant to support spontaneous resolution of traumatic material. Alpha brain waves are present during times of reduced arousal. When we complete a task, take a rest, take a long shower, a walk in the garden, or meditate we are typically in an alpha state. Theta states occur when the task at hand is "on autopilot" and our brain can disengage to a degree. This is typically the brainwave state that occurs when you're driving on the freeway and forget your exit, or when you're in a daydream. Some people feel a flow of ideas in this state, as censorship and analytic thoughts occur in more highly aroused states. In yoga-induced meditative minds, we tend to see an increase in alpha and theta brainwaves (Elson, Hauri, & Cunis, 1977; Corby, Roth, Zarcone, & Kopell, 1978).

The Energy Body

While the nervous system provides the primary overlap between modern science and the time-tested practice of yoga, a basic understanding of the energy body is enormously helpful in identifying and responding to the needs of clients. Two approaches to the energy body that are common in the yoga practice are the *koshas* and the *vayus*. *Kosha* means sheath, and the word *maya* translates to "made of." The five koshas, outlined in the *Taittiriya Upanishad* are increasingly subtle, and are typically pictured like a set of Russian dolls, one just inside the next (Milford, 1921).

> *Annamaya kosha: Anna* means food or physical matter. This is the material body built from foods we eat that contribute to our muscles, bones, and physical body.

> *Pranamaya kosha: Prana* refers to the energy body and vital life force, much like chi in Traditional Chinese Medicine, it pervades all organ actions and the function of the physical body.

> *Manamaya kosha: Mana* refers to the mind and thought patterns. We address this body when we develop focused attention and seek to manage the fluctuations of the mind.

> *Jnanamaya kosha: Jnana* means wisdom. This is the layer of intuition and knowledge coming from lifetimes of experience. We access this layer in the stillness of mediation.

> *Anandamaya kosha: Ananda* means bliss. This is the deepest layer that exists at the core of all others. It is the spiritual heart and connection to all beings, happiness, joy, and bliss. This is the body we touch in experiences of *samadhi*, or integration.

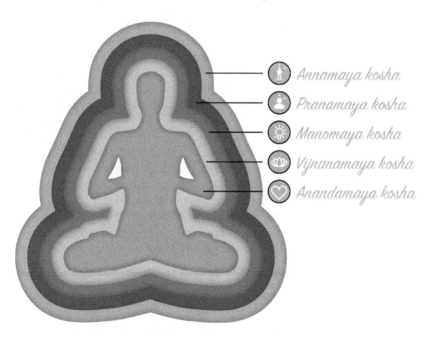

Annamaya kosha
Pranamaya kosha
Manomaya kosha
Vijnanamaya kosha
Anandamaya kosha

Figure 6.10 The Koshas

While *koshas* are layers of energy, the *vayus* describe, as the word translates, winds of energy within the body. These five components describe currents of energy and their function, and yoga postures are often taught in a way that stimulates healthy function of each *vayu* (Sen-Gupta, 2009).

The *prana vayu* centers in the chest and governs inhalation. Its energy is cyclical and, when functioning well, helps us adapt to change. Energy that is blocked here can manifest as fear or anxiety. Observing the breath cycle in a restorative posture like *savasana* on a bolster or *supta baddha konasana* is a helpful way to connect with this energy in the body. As we do in the *tamas* to *sattva* sequence, connect to the lift of the chest, and subtle sensations around the heart center, as the supports allow it to open.

The *udana vayu* centers in the diaphragm, lungs, and throat and is associated with upward movement of energy. It connects to the exhalation, or expression of air, thought, and feelings. It helps us communicate effectively in an emotionally honest and authentic way. It encourages expression and helps emotion move up and out. Postures associated with this *vayu* include anything that lifts the chest, like *dandasana*, staff pose.

The *vyana vayu* is associated with outward movement; it centers in the core of the body and moves blood and lymph to the extremities. This energy is integrative. Dynamic movements circulate blood and lymph, and postures that are expansive bring the internal to the external.

The *samana vayu* directs energy inward to the body center where it can be processed and digested. It connects to the digestive system and assimilation of all that enters the body physically and energetically. Twisting postures that churn the abdomen are said to stoke the fire, or *agni* of the *samana vayu*. The centering sequence above supports the functions of the *samana vayu*. Taking time to turn inward and process thoughts, feelings, emotions, and experiences before moving on to the next "meal" supports the function of this *vayu*.

The *apana vayu* resides in the lower abdominal region and connects with downward, rooting, steady energy. This *vayu* connects with letting go, in a mental, emotional, and physical sense, as it connects to the organs of elimination. Postures emphasizing the *apana vayu* are helpful for grounding, and you will find them in the grounding sequence earlier in this chapter. *Malasana*, the yogic squat, is a classic posture of *apana*, as this is the posture used for elimination for many years before we began using more formal bathroom facilities. You'll find postures that connect to the earth and to a sense of grounding strengthen the *apana vayu*.

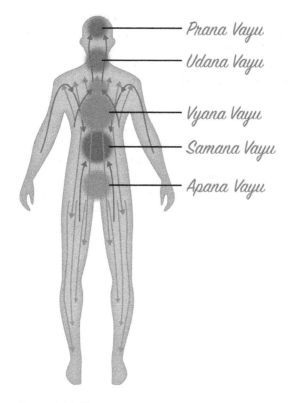

Prana Vayu

Udana Vayu

Vyana Vayu

Samana Vayu

Apana Vayu

Figure 6.11 Vayus

The *koshas* and *vayus* offer an increasingly refined way to choose postures and to recognize the strengths and challenges our clients and students face. By studying the *vayus* and their function, we can bring more options to our students as we seek to support them in balancing their system through yoga.

Through the many avenues yoga offers to practice coping skills, balance energy, and regulate the nervous system, our practice becomes the path of neuroplasticity that allows us to re-create safety within our own bodies. As we learn somatic practices that help us endure, as the B. K. S. quote passed down by so many Iyengar teachers suggests, we create neurological pathways that can, with repetition, become a cure to the dysregulation we seek to heal.

***

After six months of slow pacing and long exhales, Jordan's practice took root. As he became more habituated to these movements and practices, we added in more complicated breath practices and posture variations, with lots of work on coordination to support his TBI. At times he practiced at home, other times the challenge was too great, so we continued in session. We began to explore the practice of *kumbhaka*, the short pause between the inhale and exhale. On days when hyperarousal symptoms were strong, he practiced forward folds and longer exhales, and when he felt more *tamasic* he'd focus on gentle back bending and a short hold of the breath, to lift the *prana vayu*. His symptoms of depression slowly improved, and stubborn negative thought patterns began to shift. While yoga has not cured his symptoms of TBI, his practice has evolved to support his emotional experience and the stability of his nervous system, making the typical challenges posed by work, relationships, and navigating his ongoing medical appointments more palatable. Yoga continues to be a significant source of support for him, as he continues the journey of complex trauma recovery.

Reflection Questions

1   What values do you communicate with your choice of sequence?
2   How do you know if a sequence is "working" for a student or client? Name three things you can observe.
3   Based on what you know about your own nervous system, the gunas, and the sample sequences in this chapter, choose five postures that will help you cultivate balance and put them in the order you think will best meet your needs.

Additional resources available at http://howwecanheal.com/y4tr

References

Corby, J. C., Roth, W. T., Zarcone, V. P., & Kopell, B. S. (1978). Psycho-physiological correlates of the practice of tantric yoga meditation. *Archives of General Psychiatry, 35*(5), 571–577.

Elson, B. D., Hauri, P., & Cunis, D. (1977). Physiological changes in yoga meditation. *Psychophysiology, 14*(1), 52–57.

Milford, H., (1921). *The thirteen principal Upanishads: Translated from the Sanskrit with an outline of the philosophy of the Upanishads and an annotated bibliography.* Oxford: Oxford University Press.

Newton, I. (1687). Philosophiae Naturalis Principia Mathematica as cited in Newton, I. (1999). *The Principia: Mathematical principles of natural philosophy.* Berkeley, CA: University of California Press.

Parnell, L. (2010). *A therapist's guide to EMDR: Tools and techniques for successful treatment.* New York: Norton.

Peniston, E. G., & Kulkosky, P. J. (1991). Alpha-theta brainwave neurofeedback for Vietnam veterans with combat-related post-traumatic stress disorder. *Medical Psychotherapy, 4*(1), 47–60.

Porges, S. (2011). *The Polyvagal Theory: Neuropsychological foundations of emotions, attachment, communication, and self-regulation.* New York: Norton.

Seidler, G. H., & Wagner, F. E. (2006). Comparing the efficacy of EMDR and trauma-focused cognitive-behavioral therapy in the treatment: A meta-analytic study. *Psychological Medicine, 36*(11), 1515–1522.

Sen-Gupta, O. (2009). *Vayu's gate: Yoga and the ten vital winds.* Vijnana Yoga Books. https://vijnanayoga.com/en/our-books/.

Siegel, D. J. (1999). *The developing mind* (Vol. 296). New York: Guilford Press.

Sullivan, M. B., Erb, M., Schmalzl, L., Moonaz, S., Noggle Taylor, J., & Porges, S. W. (2018). Yoga therapy and Polyvagal Theory: The convergence of traditional wisdom and contemporary neuroscience for self-regulation and resilience. *Frontiers in Human Neuroscience, 12,* 67.

Vyasa. (2017). *The Bhagavad-gita (translated into English prose with an introduction by Kashinath Trimbak Telang).* Lightning Source Incorporated.

7   Trust and Relationship

Love without trust is a river without water.
– Harbhajan Singh Yogi

My teacher stood by my side and, as I twisted to the right, assisted me by lifting my lower back and rotating my upper body further to the right. It was beyond where I had gone before. I heard myself let out a yelp. He immediately retracted, asking, "Ti ho fatto male?" (Have I hurt you?) I paused, observing. I was scared, but not hurt. "No," I replied, a little bewildered. What had just happened? I knew that, had I not had a relationship with Gianfranco, the fear I felt would have been unloaded directly onto him. Instead, I noticed and reflected. I had moved beyond my typical movement patterns, but at no time had I felt any pain. As a result of the trusting relationship I had developed with him, I was able to differentiate the two, and to explore the areas in my body where I was unconsciously holding tension. In addition, he learned that this position was a tender one for me and refined his assists and communication accordingly moving forward. As a result, what could have been a disconnect ended up building a stronger sense of trust between teacher and student.

***

In any therapeutic relationship, the most profound healing takes place in the context of trust and requires a combination of vulnerability, intimacy, and respect of individual differences. While methods and tools help us to organize our thinking about the healing path, we must keep in mind that the relationship itself provides many of the healing experiences clients and students seek. As Babette Rothschild, author of *The Body Remembers*, points out:

> These days there's an over-emphasis on method and a de-emphasis on the therapeutic relationship, and claims that trauma can be resolved in one session are an emphasis on method. There are outcome studies

that show the effective resolution of trauma in three sessions, but these are done on clients who have a single standing trauma and a non-complicated background. Such studies are misleading because the vast majority of our clients have multiple traumas and/or come from complicated backgrounds.

(Rothschild & Oakes, 2002)

When relationships are a part of the trauma, they become a central aspect of the healing experience.

In this chapter, we describe what contributes to a healthy relationship between teacher and student, and suggest practices for building healthy attachment, particularly with clients and students who have experienced relational trauma. We also address the importance of power dynamics in the teacher–student relationship, and explore triggers, boundaries, shame, and shame resilience. As you read through this material, consider the concept of rational authority we covered in Chapter 1, and note how you, as a teacher or provider, are in a place of power. Your choices and responses to students and clients matter, and they can forge a connection between you and those you serve that is rooted in respect and service.

Cultivating Healthy Attachment

Traumatic experiences activate patterns of threat and defense in the nervous system. In treatment, we seek not to replicate or exacerbate this experience, but to build a foundation of safety by activating different neural networks. As a sense of safety builds, it becomes easier to tolerate moments of fear or distress, be they related to traumatic memory or based on something occurring in present time. One crucial way we communicate safety is in relationship. When a provider can access a sense of safety in their own nervous system and lead, consistently, by example, the client or student can witness what it is like to feel regulated and to have access to self-regulation tools. By incorporating awareness of our own nervous systems, using our own tools, and including healthy attachment practices, we respond in a way that is both trauma-informed and attachment-focused. This helps lay the foundation for trust, the element Yoga Bhajan declares is as essential to a loving relationship as water is to a river (Harbhajan, 1982).

What is healthy attachment? John Bowlby coined the term attachment after studying development in children across many contexts. He noted that the physical and emotional attachment babies forge with a primary caregiver is critical to their personal development. In infants, Bowlby identified four categories of attachment. **Secure attachment** describes infants who feel soothed and responded to by the caregiver. They will experience some distress when a caregiver leaves, are soothed by the response of other caregivers, and by the primary caregiver's return.

Through their behaviors, infants with a secure attachment display the assumption that the attachment figure will be available to meet their needs, and that their cries for help will be responded to. An individual who experiences secure attachment, "is likely to possess a representational model of attachment figures(s) as being available, responsive, and helpful" (Bowlby, 1980, p.187).

The **insecure ambivalent**, attachment style was identified by Mary Ainsworth (Ainsworth & Bell, 1970). It was also called resistant in early literature. Those with insecure-ambivalent patterns often alternate between seeking and dismissing interaction with the caregiver, and display intense distress when the caregiver leaves. They demonstrate fear of connecting with strangers. When a caregiver returns, the infant may approach them, but may resist contact and not feel reassured by the reunion. Of the styles, the insecure-ambivalent cries more and explores less than the others. This attachment style is often the result of caregivers who are inconsistently available to respond to the needs of the child. Those with **insecure avoidant styles** do not orient to their caregiver while exploring their environment, and display physical and emotional independence from the caregiver. They display no signs of distress when the caregiver leaves. They will play normally with a stranger present, and show very little interest when the caregiver returns. Most often this style results from a caregiver being insensitive to, or rejecting of, the infant's needs.

Disorganized attachment (Main & Solomon, 1990) was identified later in efforts to understand the infants who did not fit into the other three categories. When parents are frightening or frightened, or when they're experiencing mental and emotional challenges that make behavior inconsistent, children become confused. The child then tends to exhibit disorganized behaviors. Unable to make sense of the parental relationship, they respond in mixed expressions of confusion, distress, and freeze, among other contradictory, or incomplete, displays.

Bartholomew and Horowitz outlined four adult attachment styles, which, though slightly different, reflect the four infant styles: secure, anxious-preoccupied, dismissive-avoidant, and fearful-avoidant (Bartholomew & Horowitz, 1991). Most adults experience some of each of these attachment styles; experiences can vary from one relationship to another, and may evolve over time. It is important to note that adults can develop what has come to be called "earned secure" attachment (Main & Goldwyn, 1989; Roisman, Padrón, Sroufe, & Egeland, 2002; Mesman, van IJzendoorn, Sagi-Schwartz, Cassidy, & Shaver, 2016), which develops from becoming aware of attachment patterns and developing healthy, trusting relationships, often with the help of therapy.

As clinicians, teachers, and leaders facilitating mental, emotional, and social health, it is important that we understand what fosters healthy attachment, and make choices to offer the people we serve an opportunity for healthy connection. Dr. Dan Siegel recommends using the four S's as a guide: **seen, safe, soothed, and secure** (Siegel & Bryson, 2011). Feeling seen goes beyond eyesight to describe a sense of empathy and deep understanding, which Dr. Siegel often describes as *mindsight*, the capacity to perceive mind and impact of experiences on ourselves and others (Siegel, 2010). For adults who have not experienced this, or for whom being seen meant being abused, being seen in this way can be both validating and scary, healing and full of risk. Donald Winnicott, who introduced the influential concept of a mother's *holding environment*, famously said, "It is a joy to be hidden, and disaster not to be found" (Winnicott, 1963). We see our clients by listening, practicing full presence with them, and getting to know them over time, not by forcing eye contact or by intruding on their personal space. Patricia Walden, one of my most influential teachers, will often call from across the room to students, myself included, "That's your old pose!" when one of us slips into an old but comfortable, non-helpful movement pattern. Once, after years of not seeing her, I relished in hearing her say "Great job, Lisa. You're maintaining the stability in your lower back." In the context of the trusting relationship, both comments demonstrate that she is paying attention and that she sees the student's physical habits and changes. We can go further to see beyond the physical forms, recognizing our students' efforts rather than results. Comments like "You've been showing up so consistently," offer an opportunity to reflect, and questions such as "How is this feeling for you?" create an opportunity to connect, and see the student or client with greater clarity. As teachers or therapists working in a group setting, it is important that we remain aware of the participants who seem to turn invisible, or shrink away from contact. We don't need to shine a spotlight on them, but it is important to include them in our awareness.

In addition to seeing those we serve, as holders of the environment, we can facilitate a felt sense of **safety** through our choices. Physical, emotional, mental, and social safety are all intertwined, as we've learned from our discussion of the nervous system in Chapter 3. Through neuroception, our brains collect information about the safety of places and other people. For those who have experienced childhood trauma and neglect, the expectation often becomes that other people are inherently unsafe, or that they will not be able to respond to important needs. For this reason, creating safety consistently, and in an ongoing way, is crucial. We can demonstrate safety at a basic level by avoiding choices or actions that may cause a fear reaction. Even when students respond harshly, like the young woman in juvenile hall who unloaded a mouthful of profanities when I asked her if she'd done yoga before (one "no" and about seven other words I'll refrain from echoing), we need to train our own nervous systems not to translate a student's or client's upset into a threat response in our own bodies. Instead, we learn to see these types of responses as a display of fear, and respond with as many cues of safety that we can. This particular young woman nearly fell over in surprise when I responded, "Wow, because you're really good at it." Letting people know that they can feel and be who they are, and that they will not be shamed or reprimanded, all while communicating clear group norms and boundaries that respect the needs of all involved, is a craft that develops uniquely in each environment. We'll discuss the process of creating safety at length in the next chapter.

In addition to feeling seen and safe, healthy attachment in relationship offers us an opportunity to feel **soothed** when something upsetting or disruptive occurs. Since trauma tends to have a disruptive impact, and can bring up many complicated emotions, offering opportunities for soothing is crucial in a trauma-informed setting. Opportunities for soothing can manifest in a multitude of ways, and can differ from person to person, group to group. For this reason, both emphasizing choice and observing the impact of each choice are essential components of a trauma-informed environment. One way I offer opportunities for soothing in my office is by having warm tea and cool water available for clients as they arrive, along with a fountain that offers the sound and sight of running water. This may soothe a deep feeling of thirst, or be a reminder that basic needs are responded to in this space. I also have artwork, plants, books, and art supplies in the waiting room, and lots of pillows and cozy blankets. Could plants, nature, or fuzzy blankets be a trigger? Yes, anything could, which is why it is important that we listen and respond to the unique people we serve. More often, however, soft textures, things that meet basic needs or connect us to nature, and images that offer a pleasing experience foster a sense of soothing. These are external examples, which are important, and through the work, we can also develop internal resources that are soothing. Examples include: the breath, a comfortable gazing point, an image or memory of a soothing experience, a smell, or a tactile experience. For some, having silly putty in hand while talking is soothing. For others, eye contact is upsetting so being allowed to gaze out the window most of the time is helpful. As a provider, identify what is soothing to you, and help your students and clients do the same.

In the world of attachment, secure is a loaded word. Many people over-simplify the attachment categories we've covered, and deduce that they are stuck in one category or another. Recall that earned security is real, and that through effort and attention we can rewire our brains to expect security in relationships. In a similar way, we can offer a secure connection to our students and clients. We can foster inner security by helping those we serve cultivate an inner sense of self-worth and well-being. Consistency is a piece of relational security – by having consistent connection over time, we learn that the person (provider) is there and will continue to be there to help meet our needs. A regular meeting time and day contribute to a sense of rhythm and predictability within the relationship. Clear communication and expectations can also support a secure relationship. Giving notice when you will be away, when a substitute is covering for you, or when something is approaching an end helps students build a sense that you, as a person, care about how the classes or sessions impact their rhythms. Beyond communicating respect, planning for vacations, maternity leave, and other shifts in your presence to the best of your ability, helps communicate care for their emotional and relational needs. Strive to be upfront with your ability to respond to the needs of your clients and students, and to set boundaries that reflect what is sustainable for you. This helps to develop a sense of security.

Triggers in Relationship

One of the reasons physical touch ignites an important conversation within the field of trauma-informed yoga is that it carries huge potential to trigger traumatic memory. Consider, for a moment, complex, interpersonal trauma and betrayal trauma: what if being in relationship is the trigger for memories of traumatic stress? In this case, which is true for far more people than most of us are aware, simply interacting with a yoga teacher, counselor, or clerk at the corner store can be paralyzing. For some, relational and betrayal trauma can manifest in social anxiety, while for others the residue of negative experiences does not become apparent until deeper levels of intimacy become available. Nevertheless, being in connection with others can bring up semi-conscious memories related to upsetting or disappointing experiences of the past.

One of my students described her experience at, ironically, a training for teaching yoga to trauma survivors: "While I was there I felt like I was doing everything wrong, so eventually I got quiet and felt ashamed of my choices." She discovered there were many layers to her experience, including implications of gender, race, and cultural power dynamics, along with the truth that many professional trainings that cover trauma do not prepare participants to cope with their own personal associations with the material. In addition, she shared, "When I left, I felt hypervigilant to do anything in front of my class – it was as if we were being taught that students are ticking time bombs!" Here she speaks to her own experience of feeling seen, safe, soothed, and secure as a teacher. Not having those feelings as a foundation, she noted the stress response in her own system. Her training experience turned on defensive neural networks, rather than the safe and social ones. If she feels hypervigilant in front of the group, it will likely *not* put hypervigilant students at ease, which is what needs to happen to foster healing. When we understand the instructor's experience and healthy attachment dynamics, we can find ways to improve the experience of both teacher and student.

Projection

Imagine the world outside of you like a screen. We have a shared reality that each of us filters through our unique neural networks and senses; our brains function as a lens that helps us select, interpret, and analyze the data we receive. For this reason, two people can have very different experiences of the same set of circumstances. As we filter the information that comes in, we also project our worldview out onto the outside world. As we are sensitized by our upbringing, through culture, or via professional training to dynamics, experiences, or aspects of life, we carry the imprints of these experiences with us and see them more readily in the outside world.

Psychological priming is the simple principle that, if I say the word green to you and show you a picture with five colors, you are more likely to notice the green parts of the picture (Heij, Dirkx, & Kramer, 1990). At a more complex level, our brains learn to associate experiences with emotion and behavior (Schröder & Thagard, 2013). So, if you have positive memories of barbeques with your family on a Sunday afternoon growing up, the smell of barbeque may instantly bring you positive feelings, without the conscious association. Auditory and olfactory senses carry the strongest association; many of us experience this when we hear a song and it instantly "takes us back" to another time and place. These types of associations happen at conscious and unconscious levels, and contribute to our experience of neuroception, which can create an experience of feeling soothed, feeling triggered or feeling something entirely different. The season during which a traumatic experience occurs can trigger associated memories and feelings, just as hearing song from a high school dance can remind us of the experience of dancing with our high school sweetheart (or pining for them, as it may be). Your life experience, in this way, primes your subsequent experiences.

Projection speaks to the truth that we have been conditioned, by experience, over time, and that we bring our worldview and past experiences to new experiences. Simply put, we project what we've learned from the past onto our present. In therapy, we can project these feelings or assumptions onto the relationship, or directly onto the therapist. This is called **transference**, which speaks to the client's experience of the therapist. **Countertransference** speaks to the therapist's, or provider's, experience of the client based on their prior learning and expectations. Each of these terms describes a spectrum of thoughts, feelings, and experiences, and can be positive, negative, or neutral. It is important that we remain aware of these phenomena when in supportive roles, and that we have supports to help us sort out our own projections and countertransference.

To apply this to the yoga class setting, a student may experience the teacher in a way that reflects their early experiences. Perhaps the student feels they must do everything the teacher says, even if their body sends messages of pain, because they grew up in a school and/or family that emphasized deferring to authority figures. Perhaps, as a teacher, you feel scrutinized by students if you grew up in a household where every misstep was met with a negative response. These are examples of how we bring our worldview into the room and project the past onto the present. This can occur outside of traumatic experiences, as well as in direct relationship to them.

Displacement and Enactment

When we are unaware of pain, or it is too threatening to feel it toward a specific person or situation, we may experience a **displacement** of the pain, or an offloading of the emotion, in a place that is different from the source. If someone is having trouble at work but cannot assert themselves with their boss, they may come home and offload the tension or anger directly onto their partner. They may also find it coming out while on the road, or in another place that is less threatening than the workplace, where one's livelihood is at stake. It is an unconscious protective and defensive mechanism, to take out feelings of anger or frustration on less threatening people or objects.

Projective identification describes the process by which someone projects unconscious aspects of the self onto someone they are in close relationship with. This could easily happen between a student and teacher, or therapist and client. These qualities or characteristics can be positive, neutral or negative, but tend towards qualities that carry emotional charge, or are difficult to connect with for some reason. They can relate to traumatic experience, but need not be derived from trauma. This projective expectation about the therapist or teacher can become a self-fulfilling prophecy; once a person is convinced that the assumption about the other person is true, they may create situations that influence the person's behavior to fit into the projection, facilitating circumstances that validate their initial, yet erroneous, beliefs.

When subconscious feelings and experiences become realized in a new dynamic, we refer to this as an **enactment**. This happens in a myriad of ways, including within therapeutic relationships. When clients express having the same experience with different people, one that repeats over time, or when a dynamic they experience outside of the session or class occurs within the class context, there is often healing to be found in exploring the transference, countertransference, and projective identification within the relationship. This is deep psychological work, best done in individual settings with a mental health professional. However, even in the role of teacher, becoming familiar with these dynamics, which increase in strength the more severe and subconscious the traumatic experience or emotion, helps us to say rooted in our own truth and centered in our own bodies.

Trauma survivors have endured painful experiences. When someone has unresolved hurt in their mind and heart, and when you are an unassuming stranger or new person in their life (i.e., new counselor or yoga teacher) it may happen that they displace the pain or project unconscious aspects of self, or of experience, onto you in the form of projection or enactment. Expecting this to take place can help keep you centered, rather than pulled into circumstances in which you behave in a way more consistent with their expectations for abuse than with your own character. Building a positive relationship helps us to minimize and manage these processes, and can help people recognize the root of the uncomfortable emotion, which contains within it a seed of healing.

Shame

Often as a result of trauma, we live with negative beliefs about ourselves and the world that surrounds us. Shame goes a layer deeper than guilt, guilt being the thought or feeling "I did something bad," while shame is the thought or feeling "I am bad." Many survivors of trauma, children in particular, experience self-blame because it is easier to live in a world where they are in control of the outcome of experiences – believing this happened to me because of something I did or some way I am – than live in a world where bad things can happen to good people. If it is just our behavior that is or was bad, we can fix that by apologizing and behaving in a way to try to mend the harm done. When we believe that our very *self* is bad, there is not much we can do to fix that, other than change, run from, or hide from ourselves. For some people who have trouble apologizing and repairing relational harm done, this is the key: differentiating between behavior and the core self. The deeper the negative beliefs of shame go, the more of an impact they have on self-esteem, self-worth, and relationships.

In Figure 7.1, Taylor (2015) relates many of the difficult emotions and behaviors we see in trauma survivors to shame, and helps us to decipher the many ways shame can show up in someone's experience, and in the therapeutic setting. In it, we see how shame can lie at the root of other emotions and behaviors, including but not limited to: fear, anger, distress or disgust, isolation, depression, addiction, and aggression.

One of the most effective ways to identify shame within others is to track it within yourself first. Use this diagram as a tool to understand first your own habits, then those that you serve. Can you see a way that someone in isolation or addiction may feel shame? Can you identify how shame might play a role with clients you serve coping with anger or aggressive behaviors? An awareness of these tendencies and an approach of curiosity can help uncover, and resolve, deep feelings of shame.

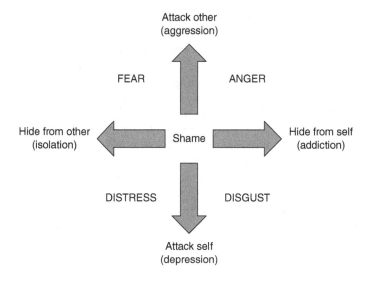

Figure 7.1 Manifestations of Shame

The Opposite of Shame: Ego Strength

If, in response to trauma we cultivate resilience, in the experience of shame, what do we seek to build? If shame is the belief, and related beliefs, "I am bad," then the opposite must be "I am good." The field of psychotherapy would call this *ego strength*. While many in the field of yoga and mindfulness describe the ego as something negative, psychotherapists often view having a strong sense of self as a positive thing, and seek to strengthen the ego and support clients in developing a positive sense of self. If we differentiate the descriptions of ego – the psychological referring to self-worth and the others referring to self-absorption or fear-based thinking – we can understand the conflicting efforts. When people have healthy self-worth, they tend to treat themselves, and others, better. When people become lost in self-absorption and fear, the opposite is true.

We also know from cases of severe abuse and dissociation that conflict between parts of the self can create internal disharmony and make healing in an integrative manner more difficult. With this awareness, promoting conventional understandings of ego as bad make less sense. Rather than battling the ego, an internal aspect of self, we can reframe the goal to create a healthy one that respects both the self and others. In order to build a healthy ego, we seek to build the opposite of shame. The word *pride* can have negative connotations in some contexts; I prefer the term *proudness*. What makes you feel proud? Of yourself, your actions, your choices? When do you feel good about who you are in a balanced way?

These are important questions. If you are in a tradition that battles the ego, consider embracing it instead. How can your sense of being an individual contribute to the collective, and vice versa? How can you support those you serve in feeling a positive identity and strong sense of themselves? Leaders in service to others benefit from joining empathy and ego strength in efforts to support and uplift people around them.

Another experience that counters shame is dignity, the experience of being valued and treated like you matter. In her book *Dignity*, Donna Hicks describes 10 practices that create safety and foster dignity in relationship. They include acceptance of identity, inclusion, safety, acknowledgement, recognition, fairness, benefit of the doubt, understanding, independence, and accountability. We will revisit each of these components in more detail in Chapter 9. These are helpful themes to guide how we relate with those recovering from trauma, in efforts to restore, or maintain, a sense of dignity. By promoting dignity, we express care for everyone's unique experiences and innate human needs. Practicing giving and receiving dignity helps to build relationships based on mutual care and shared value, which also helps to counter experiences of shame.

Shame Resilience

In addition to cultivating ego strength and building a shared experience of dignity, we can practice resilience in the face of shame. Qualitative research on shame has helped us to understand how we can perpetuate it, or free it, with our choices. Brené Brown teaches the following four steps to assist in recovery from shame.

The first step is to **know your triggers**. Perhaps you feel shame when you arrive late to a meeting, or when someone criticizes your work, parenting strategy or dietary choices. Perhaps deeper aspects of your family, identity or background arouse a sense of shame. When these feeling arise, we move to the second step which is to **reality check them**. Would you talk to a friend the way you are talking to yourself? Often, we are more critical with ourselves then we would ever be with a loved one, and we say things in our mind that we would never speak aloud. Practice talking to yourself the very same way you talk to someone you love when you find yourself allowing negative messages to permeate your sense of self. From there, you may choose to take the third step and **reach out to someone you trust**. Despite popular encouragement to be vulnerable at all costs, we do not need to broadcast our vulnerabilities – not everyone has earned the trust to have access to these tender parts of our experience. It is okay to keep sensitive feelings within a small circle of trust; having just one or two people you trust to share your feelings with is enough.

The fourth step is to **speak shame**. Brené Brown states, "shame cannot survive being spoken and met with empathy" (Brown, 2006). Secrecy, silence, and judgment intensify and perpetuate feelings of shame, and empathy is the antidote. When we speak to trusted, supportive friends, we remove the secret belief that we are bad or wrong. During some of my workshops I have given people the opportunity to reflect and to speak something shameful in a dyad, and let them choose to share either their own experience, a common experience of those they serve, or a fabricated one, simply for the exercise of speaking shame. I often receive messages from students days, weeks, and months later reflecting on the power of being heard and met with empathy.

Providers' Personal Development

One of the most important ways to ensure you are doing good work is to actively look for your own wounds, limiting thoughts, residual feelings, and behaviors, and seek a path of personal development and healing. What triggers you, and how do you cope with your own personal experiences of shame? Whether you are holding space for a community, a group, a couple, or an individual, your energy carries weight when you are in a leadership position. As the person holding space, you fill the room and the relationship with your own thoughts, feelings, opinions and, yes, even your own trauma history. For this reason, your investment in personal growth, healing, and awareness is essential.

The false dichotomy of healer/healed is what we call in CBT a *cognitive distortion*: it is the epitome of black and white thinking. We are all human beings, and everyone on this planet has been exposed to some form and degree of trauma. There is absolutely a time to focus on your own healing and not take on the needs of others. At the same time, there is almost always someone we can be of service to, and helping others can be healing in and of itself. For this reason, many people feel called to serve in ways that are personal to their own experience of trauma. Be thoughtful when choosing when and why you choose to serve. If we are aware of our own history and our developing path of service, we can set ourselves up to engage in a mutually healing relationship. When we know to look for it, this type of service work can bring to light our own challenges that lie just outside of awareness. Shine light on the areas of your life that need healing, develop your own path of growth, and practice letting go of patterns that no longer serve you. As you become increasingly aware of the patterns that limit you, you will become more able to see these patterns in your clients, and will develop a wider range of empathy – for yourself, and for the many varieties of human experience.

Too much mental health education centers around developing tools and skills, rather than upon developing self-awareness and trust with support people who can contribute to our evolution as a human being. Therapists talk a lot about the unconscious, and much of the work of both yoga and therapy is about becoming more aware. Occasionally, after completing the long, grueling process of licensure, mental health professionals, perhaps certified yoga teachers as well, risk falling for one of two extreme beliefs: that they are done, healed, or even somehow better than their clients, or that they will never be whole or healed enough to be of service to others. Both perspectives are dangerous; one leads professionals into risky territory of entitlement and enactments of unhealed trauma, the other paralyzes and perpetuates the disempowerment that often pairs with traumatic experiences.

As I write this, leaders in the field of both yoga and trauma recovery are being accused of misconduct – of harming others even as they bring gifts of insight, research, wisdom, theory, and practice to the fields. Not having ongoing support in your own personal development can manifest in a professional "Achilles heel" (Roseman et al., 2017). The best antidote is to remain grounded in rational authority, to recognize that we are all on a healing journey, individually and collectively, and to make our own healing an active practice. Helpful questions to ask ourselves before, during, and after we provide services include: How am I feeling? What am I *not* aware of? What makes me feel anxious, tired, interested, helpful? What motivates me? How does this work impact me? In the moment of teaching or offering counsel, we can maintain awareness of the purpose of our words, while remaining curious about our own words and actions: whom do they serve? This is a foundational question when we feel moved to share a personal experience with someone we serve: is the sharing for them, or does it only serve to meet our needs, or bring attention to us?

As a student in class, in training, or even in therapeutic relationship, it is important that we retain our autonomy and ability to decide for ourselves what feels right. Teachers, therapists, leaders, or gurus who do not allow space for questioning prohibit growth in all directions. Our capacity to question, reflect, and choose lies at the heart of healing. Evolution in families and in fields of service happens when we constantly seek to improve the quality, integrity, and degree of awareness of our choices and behaviors. I have been in yoga classes and witnessed abusive dynamics playing out between teacher and student. When we experience the limitations of our teachers it can be disappointing, and yet, they are human. We can decide how best to respond, when to give feedback, when to leave, when to report, and perhaps most importantly, what to carry forward, and what to leave behind.

As a provider, one of the most effective ways to maintain safety is to stay rooted in rational authority and continue to create experiences of safety and care in your own body. This means actively building a field of self-care and safety, responding to your own challenges, and seeking professional supports to heal in a continuous and ongoing way, as life demands it. When we seek to empower, rather than exploit, we tap into the evolved social aspects of the nervous system, rather than the older protective circuits. In this way, Polyvagal Theory supports our choice to build safety within ourselves, and in social connection.

Boundaries and Scope of Practice

No one person can be everything to another. Caregiver–child relationships are the most dependent, but even as we seek to repair challenges or absences of caregivers, we cannot treat our clients and students as children, feeding them all their meals and cleaning up after their bathroom mess. As healers in a professional role, the more we are clear about what we are able to offer in a sustainable and consistent way, the clearer a student's or client's expectations will be. It is up to us to determine, and refine, the aspects of work that are sustainable, and those that are not. Hours, fees, short- or long-term nature of work, scope of practice, vacation practice, all of these help us to define our role. Along these lines, reflecting on personal and professional content – information about yourself, your loved ones, your experiences – prior to being with your clients can help you discern what you are comfortable with, and what serves the participant's highest good. Note that, once you cast a wide boundary it is much more difficult to retract it. When you are conservative with boundaries initially, you can always choose to extend them later with careful thought.

Many yoga teachers I have worked with express concern about students needing emotional support that they feel is beyond their professional capacity to offer. It can be a challenging conversation when a teacher feels a student needs additional professional supports, particularly in circles where psychotherapy is not common, or there is an echo of stigma attached to seeing a therapist. One helpful way to set this boundary is to engage the student in a conversation about their supports outside of yoga. In this way, you may be able to offer a direct referral, or to remind students of the support they already have. It can also quell the concern the teacher has, knowing that the student is supported in many capacities, clarifying the role of yoga instructor, and differentiating from other service providers. Just as a yoga teacher can offer general physical wellness suggestions but should not offer medical advice, a yoga teacher operating solely in the role of instructor, even with experience in trauma-informed yoga, can practice staying within the ethical and legal scope of practice by referring to licensed mental health professionals.

Mental health providers often express concern about how much yoga they can bring into sessions without specific training in yoga. Some find that clients bring skills beyond their knowledge base, or that they would like to bring in things they, personally, have found helpful. My recommendation is always to participate in yoga-specific training in addition to your personal practice prior to introducing it with clients. Even with post-traumatic stress aside, yoga postures have risks and benefits, and it is important to understand these prior to sharing practices, particularly in a professional capacity. While 200 to 500-hour trainings have become the standard, some trainings have shorter modules, or prepare teachers to offer a specific practice. If you are a licensed mental health professional, be sure to add yoga to your professional insurance as one of your complementary therapeutic offerings prior to including it in your sessions.

For those of you with both yoga teaching credentials and mental health licenses, your challenge may be in differentiating your services based on the context, or on different roles you play. In terms of professional boundaries, be clear about which hat you are wearing, and when you are wearing both. Having written agreements for students to sign that outline your role – whether as a workshop leader in a studio, or as a psychotherapist in private practice – helps make it clear how you are serving, and supports a well-defined relationship. As author Brené Brown asserts (Brown, 2018), "Clarity is kind."

For yoga teachers with public classes, it is possible for ethical questions around dual relationships to arise, if a long-time student would like to become a therapy client, or if one of your clients would like to attend your yoga class. I recommend seeking supervision and consulting with your licensing board, and/or professional association to make these difficult decisions, and to maintain the highest standard of service for the client as priority. Keeping this in mind, and, when appropriate, expressing this to those seeking dual services, helps to communicate that we care even when we cannot offer a service within our professional code of ethics.

Reciprocal Transformation

Often, we are called to healing work because of our experiences and our own healing journey. We may share parallel experiences with those we serve, and want to pass on messages and tools that we have found helpful to assist others in their healing and growth. I certainly wish a book like this had existed 20 years ago to guide me on my professional journey, so this book in and of itself is an example of reciprocal healing, as I share what I have learned in hopes that it serves you personally and professionally. When we keep our own healing in mind and serve those who we feel motivated to serve, we prevent becoming a martyr and prevent experiences of burnout. When we over-identify with those we serve, and put ourselves in their shoes without coming back to our own, we increase our risk for enmeshment and experiences of vicarious trauma. By identifying both the shared experiences, and the different roles and circumstances, you can stay compassionately connected to those you serve, while maintaining the perspective that allows you to support them effectively. By noticing both our shared humanity and our uniqueness, we can connect and support health in both parties simultaneously.

***

By treating me with respect, honoring my discomfort, and responding with care to my experience of fear, Gianfranco strengthened my experience of trust in our relationship. In that instant, I felt seen, soothed, and secure – even though, for a split second, I felt scared. By honoring the experience of going beyond my comfort zone, and restoring a sense of safety quickly and effectively, he was able to communicate care and respect. I have been in classes where students are pressed beyond their limits, and their expressions of fear are met with force, rather than responsiveness or tenderness. With any yoga student, and certainly within a trauma-informed environment, this is not acceptable. We must be aware of how harshness, even simply in vocal tone, can activate defensive neural networks, and communicate a lack of safety to participants on a neurological level, and seek to use our position of authority in service of healing.

Reflection Questions

1 What do you do to develop trust and healthy attachment with the people you serve?
2 Who can you reach out to when you are experiencing feelings of shame?
3 When does your professional role become confusing? What can you do to clarify it?
4 What supports can you access this month that will help you become more aware of yourself?

Additional resources available at http://howwecanheal.com/y4tr

References

Ainsworth, M. D. S., & Bell, S. M. (1970). Attachment, exploration, and separation: Illustrated by the behavior of one-year-olds in a strange situation. *Child Development, 41*(1), 49–67.

Bartholomew, K., & Horowitz, L. M. (1991). Attachment styles among young adults: A test of a four-category model. *Journal of Personality and Social Psychology, 61*(2), 226.

Bowlby, J. (1980). Loss: Sadness and depression. Attachment and loss (vol. 3); (International Psycho-Analytical Library no.109). London: Hogarth Press.

Brown, B. (2006). Shame resilience theory: A grounded theory study on women and shame. *Families in Society: The Journal of Contemporary Social Services, 87*(1), 43–52.

Brown, B. (2018) *Dare to lead: Brave work. Tough conversations. Whole hearts.* New York: Penguin Random House.

Harbhajan S. Y. (July 9, 1982). Lecture by *Yogi Bhajan*. Retrieved from: www.3ho.org.

Heij, W., Dirkx, J., & Kramer, P. (1990). Categorical interference and associative priming in picture naming. *British Journal of Psychology, 81*(4), 511–525.

Hicks, D. (2011). *Dignity: The essential role it plays in resolving conflict.* New Haven, CT: Yale University Press.

Main, M., & Goldwyn, R. (1989). Adult Attachment Interview scoring and classification manual. Unpublished manuscript, University of California at Berkeley.

Main, M., & Solomon, J. (1990). Procedures for identifying infants as disorganized/disoriented during the Ainsworth Strange Situation. *Attachment in the Preschool Years: Theory, Research, and Intervention, 1*, 121–160.

Mesman, J., van IJzendoorn, M. H., Sagi-Schwartz, A., Cassidy, J., & Shaver, P. R. (2016). *Handbook of attachment: Theory, research and clinical application.* New York: Guilford Press

Roisman, G. I., Padrón, E., Sroufe, L. A., & Egeland, B. (2002). Earned–secure attachment status in retrospect and prospect. *Child Development, 73*(4), 1204–1219.

Roseman, M.E., Wise, C., Kinsler, P., Danylchuk, L. S., (2017). *The Tidal Wave Effect: Trauma and Dissociation in the Mainstream.* ISSTD 34th Annual Conference. Washington D.C.

Rothschild, B., & Oakes, L. (2002). The body remembers: An interview with Babette Rothschild. *Psychotherapy in Australia, 8*(2), 26.

Schmidt, T. (2000). Visual perception without awareness: Priming responses by color. *Neural correlates of consciousness*, 157–169.

Schröder, T., & Thagard, P. (2013). The affective meanings of automatic social behaviors: Three mechanisms that explain priming. *Psychological Review, 120*(1), 255.

Siegel, D. J. (2010). *Mindsight: The new science of personal transformation.* New York: Bantam.

Siegel, D. J., & Bryson, T. P. (2011). *The whole-brain child: 12 revolutionary strategies to nurture your child's developing mind.* New York: Random House Digital.

Taylor, T. F. (2015). The influence of shame on posttrauma disorders: Have we failed to see the obvious? *European Journal of Psychotraumatology, 6*(1), 28847.

Winnicott, D. W. (1963). Communicating and not communicating leading to a study of certain opposites. In *The maturational processes and the facilitating environment: Studies in the theory of emotional development (pp. 1–276).* London: Hogarth Press.

8   Trauma-Informed Principles

Real education enhances the dignity of a human being and increases his or her self-respect.

> – A. P. J. Abdul Kalam

I was in DC for a trauma conference and needed a yoga break, so I signed up for a class down the road from the hotel. After walking into the studio and having a brief chat with the volunteer at the front desk, I stepped into class and found a spot – front and center was all that was left. A man entered the room and turned the lights to low. He did not introduce himself, but as he began to speak and guide us in Child's Pose, it became clear he was the teacher. It was a decent practice – some salutations, a few standing poses, a standing balance, an arm balance, and some seated postures towards the end. I've forgotten what was listed on the schedule, but it was essentially a *vinyasa* flow class. Toward the end of class, just as I was feeling the support of the floor and the release in my warm muscles, we came into Happy Baby pose.

A potentially triggering posture, it is an enjoyable one for me, but what happened next was not. The instructor, whom I had never met, and who had not so much as introduced himself to the class, or to me personally, approached me from the front, placed his hands on my hamstrings and inner thighs, and pushed them down towards the ground. Having just presented on trauma-informed yoga practices earlier in the day, I had three minds about this in an instant:

1) I wanted to teach him why he should *never* do this, particularly to a new student without warning or consent.
2) I was glad he wasn't doing this to one of my clients or students who was struggling with post-traumatic stress in the wake of sexual assault.
3) I wanted him off me – NOW.

I hugged my knees to my chest to interrupt his adjustment, and shook my head no. He appeared oblivious and sauntered away.

***

This chapter discusses key concepts in trauma-informed yoga (TIY) including environment, touch, assists, language, sequencing, and modifications. Each category will continue to explore the concepts we've outlined in previous chapters, expanding on potential triggers and resources and how to navigate them in a trauma-informed setting. We focus here on becoming aware of triggers and preventing them in order to build a felt sense of safety for participants, but we cannot prevent all experiences that activate a negative *samskara*, or traumatic memory. Instead, we seek to create an embodied experience of safety, and, when triggers arise, offer supports through the tools we have learned. When a student experiences a trigger, our supportive response to their experience can be healing, and the practice of repairing a challenging exchange with a student by following up with them in a caring and curious manner can facilitate growth, awareness, and connection for both parties involved. It does not do students a service when we, as teachers, become so afraid of emotional reactions that we enact avoidance and stifle our students with our own fear. By cultivating resilience in ourselves and our students, we create an opportunity to honor each person's unique emotional process, even when it does not follow a pre-mapped progression.

Safety

As we sort through the categories that follow, let safety be your guiding principle. While traumatic experiences elicit fear and shock responses, safety helps us to calm those innate responses, cultivating the comfort that allows us to connect. Consider the many layers of safety: physical, mental, emotional, social, cultural, and religious or spiritual. People need to be encouraged and reminded that they are safe to be themselves and will not be harmed at any of these levels.

We can cultivate **physical safety** in a multitude of ways. Protect the physical space where you meet or teach, best you can; though you can never guarantee anyone's ultimate safety, you can take steps to facilitate an experience of it. Many therapists are aware of the concept of containment, which involves having a confidential and protected space to share deeper feelings in private. Both a protected, confidential space, and a space in which students and clients can easily come and go by choice, is important. Consider the boundaries of the space you share with those you serve, and be sure there is access to exits, bathrooms, or support facilities as relevant. Practically speaking, we can contain a space by drawing a curtain, closing a door or window, or drawing other boundaries. Most of these will minimize the impact of outside noises coming in and direct the focus onto the practices within the room. We can also create a sense of safety by allowing students and clients, when appropriate and possible, to leave the room. Even in locked facilities, having a bathroom policy in place, or knowing whom to ask for permission to leave, lets participants know the procedure they need to follow should they need to leave the space, and reduces anxiety related to flight responses and personal autonomy. The simple fact of knowing a path to exit the space can help soothe the nervous system and reassure students that they have agency in navigating their own safety. Physical safety planning could include having emergency evacuation and lockdown procedures in place, should significant physical safety risks present themselves. In addition to containment, exits, and emergency planning, being aware of any objects that pose physical threat – obviously, weapons, but also images, words, or any other objects in the space that feel threatening, should be removed whenever possible. By factoring in our students' physical safety, we allow hard-wired defense mechanisms to stand down while we while we encourage and facilitate the work of healing.

We can create **mental safety** by sending clear messages, setting boundaries, and explaining why we, as leaders, are making the choices that we are. By encouraging independent thought and choice, we respect the autonomy of students and clients, and allow them to choose what feels good and right to them. Encouraging clients and students to think for themselves sets up a respectful dynamic and demonstrates the power of choice that is in their hands. **Emotional safety** stems from both physical and mental safety. When people are accepted as they are, leaders are respectful and inclusive, and the nervous system's tendency towards fear and defense is soothed, layers of emotional experience are more likely to rise to the surface. Emotional safety includes acceptance of emotional style: not everyone has to be verbal, to feel sad in a specific posture, or to feel a certain way given their circumstances and life experiences. In providing emotional safety, we remove judgments of feelings as right and wrong, good and bad. Allowing people to feel and express a full emotional range without negative responses (and, to keep physical safety, without any behaviors that put others at risk), creates an emotional space where it is safe to feel, and to process emotion.

Cultural, religious, and spiritual safety extends these principles to differing cultural beliefs, religious backgrounds, and approaches to spirituality. It is okay for someone to be Christian, Muslim, an atheist, or anything else, and still practice yoga for trauma recovery. It is also common that individuals within any defined group will contain diverse backgrounds and perspectives, so we need to be careful about making assumptions about what it means for someone to identify with a specific culture, religion, or spiritual group. In most situations, there is a dominant culture within a group, and becoming aware of the dominant culture's norms, and inviting other perspectives, is helpful. For those of you here in the US, remember that while American culture may be shared across people of many backgrounds and contexts, it is still a culture with its own values, assumptions, and norms – albeit varying by region. This is true of many places it the world. While we will never exist outside of culture, consider ways you can keep the tone of your TIY classes or sessions culturally inclusive. This topic merits ongoing reflection, further training, and adaptive responses to your unique community.

One important and crucial aspect of safety has to do with the state of our world and its current norms and realities. Right now, the unfortunate reality is that people are marginalized, attacked, and victimized as a result of differences in race, sexual orientation, gender, gender identity, religion, ability or disability, age, body type, appearance, and more. Some leaders choose to post signs in welcome areas directly welcoming marginalized groups, and to set group guidelines in a way that values diversity and protects all involved. Consider how you might best set the tone of safety, inclusivity, and nonviolence in early meetings, particularly in relationship to groups who have been excluded, silenced, or oppressed in your community, or in the world at large. This is an important step in addressing the needs of the nervous system after trauma. Recall also, that a deep sense of safety is foundational in building trust and facilitating healthy attachment, which helps foster the connection that all human beings need.

Choice

Connected to mental safety, **choice** is an essential component of a TIY experience. Most experiences of trauma involve lack of choice, and some involve manipulation or coercion. Keeping in mind that, in a TIY class, it is likely that students have experienced negative circumstances that they did not have control over, helps us to value the centrality of choice. Even if you teach a method with a set sequence, giving students choices within the structure encourages them to ask themselves what they need, and build the muscle that allows them to make choices as an act of self-care and self-support. Aspects of class that can involve choice include breath, gaze, degree of intensity, rest, and the omission of postures in part or whole. When possible, students and clients should be able to participate in the experience by choice, and be allowed to discontinue at any time. When this is not possible, as in some institutional rehabilitative settings, offering choice within the class becomes even more essential. Offering a simple posture, like Child's Pose, or *Savasana*, for those who do not want to follow what the rest of the class is doing provides a way for students to remain an active part of the group while making their own choice about what to do with their bodies. In individual sessions, checking in verbally or through ideomotor signaling – an established mode of nonverbal communication – helps us to track the internal experience of clients, and to support them in making choices that respond to their needs in a helpful way. This concept of choice brings us back to rational authority, reminding us to be authority figures that seek to empower, serve, and work with a student, rather than dominate, overpower, or exploit them. Remember that you are facilitating a healing experience, and what worked for you or other clients may not have the same, and could even have the opposite, effect on the next person. Rather than using techniques on a student or client, or doing something to them, establish rapport and offer the choices that you assess to be beneficial, all the while leaving the decision to proceed in their hands.

Environment

When setting up an environment, consider safety and choice in efforts to create an environment that will feel comfortable for your students and clients. Consider all five senses, along with associations your clients may have to each, and how their brains may interpret the experience at a sub-conscious level. Recall that **neuroception**, the deep brain assessment of safety or threat, is happening all the time and, along with each of these sensory experiences, *your* nervous system contributes to student's experiences in the room. Consider sights, sounds, touch, smells, and, though less relevant, taste, as well as your own physiological and emotional state while you are holding space for others.

When tailoring the auditory environment, notice what **sounds** are common in the room, and how students may receive these sounds. To the best of your ability, minimize noise and distractions, and respond appropriately to inevitable sounds. Environments with significant background noise can be difficult, and some teachers choose to use sound machines with white noise or nature sounds to balance this out, while others choose music. Consider, if you choose to use music, what associations it may stir in your clients. Students in classes with classical Indian chanting have reported it stirring memories of their time serving in the military in the Middle East, so these associations may not always be obvious. If you choose music, be sure to check in with students and, best you can, observe the effect it appears to have on their nervous systems. Their experience is more important than your perception or intention.

Also related to sound, is the use of voice in class. How you use your voice matters, and speaking in a way that is engaging and prosodic will help activate a ventral vagal, or myelinated vagal, response. Inviting students to use their own voices can be a healing opportunity as well; at the same time, some experiences of trauma involve feeling voiceless, so these practices can be challenging. In addition to vocalization, teaching extended exhales can also encourage this positive parasympathetic response. In some cases, extended exhales may be a trigger and reminder of traumatic experiences, as I've been told is the case for those who have experienced combat training which teaches soldiers to fire on a long exhale. In cases like these, we look to other avenues that can facilitate a ventral vagal response. Consider how even a simple *Aum* or *Om* chant could feel difficult, and invite students to hum along, listen, or chant silently to themselves as an option. We'll discuss a few other vocal techniques later in this chapter; you may find these helpful to incorporate, as well.

In terms of visual experience, what is within students' line of **sight**? To the degree that it is within your control, consider including images that will create a neutral or positive response. Consider what is on the walls, what colors are present, and what these may mean to your students. Would images of Hindu gods or goddesses be off-putting for your group? These are common in yoga studios, and if they are present in statues, wall art, logos or otherwise, it can be helpful to explain the meaning the studio assigns to them. How much light is in the room where students are practicing? Will you change the amount of light during class? While darkness can feel soothing, it can also feel unsafe and, like closing the eyes, it can remove the sense of safety that vision provides. For this reason, if you choose to dim the lights, make sure there is enough light for students to assess their surroundings. If the setting allows, you may have eye bags available for those students who prefer to block out all light – a folded blanket or strap also serves this purpose well. If lights go out unexpectedly, as they do in a power outage, find light as soon as possible by opening a door or even using the flashlight function on your cell phone. This is not to say that darkness will necessarily create chaos or panic in a palpable way; students may appear not to respond or to be okay with the experience, yet it remains important that we create conditions that communicate safety at the level of neuroception in order to facilitate a deep sense of safety in the subconscious brain. Whenever we suspect that, for any student, the fear response may be amplified, we do our best to bring the system back to a felt sense of safety.

We take in sensory experiences through all that our bodies come into contact with; therefore, the sense of **touch** is central to the TIY experience. Temperature is a non-contact way that the body experiences the environment. Some practices take place in high heat, while others may be in buildings without central heating or cooling. Consider the impact of temperature, and any health considerations that are relevant to extreme highs and lows in body temperature. It is important to factor in humidity, the moisture created by sweat, and transitions between high and low temperatures. Props create another tactile experience for students, and teachers can use them to ground, soothe, and provide stability. We have many nerve endings in our hands, and can use contact with yoga props to ground through the hands, and to bring the experience back to the present moment. Emphasizing the supportive aspects of the props de-conditions the assumption that using them is a crutch;

instead, when they are accessible, they become a supportive and integral part of a yoga experience.

As such, props should be cleaned regularly, particularly in settings where dust and mold are present. General space cleanliness is important for physical comfort; in spaces where we as teachers are guests, this is more difficult to control. I have shown up early and corralled brooms before teaching in a multi-purpose room where students may find their mat on top of a French fry without a thorough sweeping first. I have also taught in settings where it is possible to call in janitorial service prior to class, to avoid students being exposed to uncomfortable or unhealthy contact with the floor. This practice of maintaining a clean and clear space is one of *sauca* (also spelled *saucha* or *shaucha*). *Sauca* is one of the five *niyamas* that describes the practice of cleanliness; you might incorporate this practice of tending to props and the environment into the discussion of yoga philosophy. Given your unique environment, consider how you might facilitate sensory comfort and incorporate tactile experiences in a positive way.

While **smell** and **taste** can be less relevant in therapeutic yoga settings, there are crucial aspects of both that we can factor in to create a welcoming and safe environment for students. Food is not commonly available while practicing yoga, though workshops pairing yoga with food and drink have become popular in recent years. I discourage the use of substances that could be used as avoidance tools in TIY classes. If you are facilitating a gustatory experience, focus on mindful eating practices, as these support the teachings most clearly. Some teachers prohibit water during class to encourage students' bodies to build heat, and yet, if we recall Maslow's hierarchy of needs (Maslow & Lewis, 1987) and recognize hydration as an essential element of health, it becomes clear how allowing water can help maintain stability by providing for the body's basic needs. Even if water cannot be in the practice space, having it available is helpful, particularly for strenuous classes, or in warm environments.

It is common for students with complicated manifestations of PTSD to experience sensitivity to smells, so considering the **olfactory** experiences of students can assist those students in feeling comfortable in the space. Most studios ask that students refrain from wearing heavily scented products for this reason, and choose not to burn scented candles or incense while students are present. Instead, using a natural mist to clear the air helps humidify the space and minimizes particulate matter for those with sensitive lungs. Similarly, some cleaning chemicals, foods, and animal dander can produce an allergic response, even without strong smells. Do what you can to keep the space free of allergens. I know many yogis who *love* to use candles, incense, and essential oils in classes; if you decide to incorporate these as tools for healing ritual, make this clear before the students enter class so, at minimum, they can opt out if need be.

A less common example of managing odors in class comes from a class I taught in juvenile hall, right next to the cafeteria's kitchen. About halfway through class, a waft of tater tots or pizza would envelop the room, just as the students were beginning to work up a sweat from the movement practices. It was challenging to maintain students' attention, and helpful to address the smells directly, acknowledging that it was distracting and that some students became hungrier, while others (typically those who had been incarcerated longer) responded with disgust and yearned to eat something different. Olfactory responses, those related to smell, can create deep visceral responses, so, while these are less common aspects of the practice, keep them in mind when facilitating your trauma-informed space.

Language

The language we choose has an impact on the environment we create in a room, and our tone, pace, and volume also send messages to students. Often words carry different connotations in different environments; take, for example, the word *surrender*, often used in yoga settings, and place it in the military context, and its meaning changes. Having discussions with students, learning about the cultures your students are a part of, and remaining open to feedback helps us, as teachers, to continually adapt our use of language to build safety and connection.

In yoga teacher training, we are often taught to use clear commands so that students understand what to do. For example, "lift your thighs" instead of "feel your thighs lifting." Direct cueing is helpful in sending clear messages, *and* we need to consider the impact of commands on our clients. As a teacher, how would it feel to include commands with a military population? Indeed, following commands is part of the military culture, so it seems like a good way to fit with the culture. It could also encourage participants to defer to your authority, as they are used to doing, rather than listen to the messages of their own bodies. What if your class is for survivors of sexual abuse; how might commands be received? And if you are teaching to a group of military sexual trauma survivors? In the traumatic experiences related to each of these populations, commands may be given that relate to the experience of being overpowered or harmed. Though those of us in supportive roles make the effort to exercise rational authority, repeated directives can re-create aspects of students' traumatic experience.

We can weave choice into our language by using **invitational language in place of directives**. This may be the slight difference between saying, "Inhale, lift your arms up overhead" and "on your next inhale, sweep your arms up as far as is comfortable for your body today." Sometimes communicating choice requires more words, and other times it is the simple inclusion of a modifier. TIY teachers I know and love often use the words and phrases *perhaps, when you're ready, if it's comfortable, if it feels okay, when it's right for you*, and they remind students throughout classes that the choice for all postures and practices is in their own hands. They also demonstrate postures in progression, and don't emphasize excessive range of motion. Simply calling different expressions of postures all by the same name, instead of labeling them by level or as modifications for people who can't access the "full pose" reorients the student's attention to their capability, rather than placing excessive value on mobility. Even the words "pose" or "posture" can have a negative context in that they describe external aspects of the practice. Since these words in yoga are commonplace, we can choose to integrate other words, like "shape" or "form," and we can speak to the process and experience of the physical shape, while de-emphasizing physical results. Occasionally, it is fun to work towards an outer form – to achieve a difficult arm balance or finally stand on your hands – but overemphasis on result can lead to a struggle with the self, or denial of what is true each day. Many teachers rooted in the Ashtanga method often repeat the aphorism, "Practice, all is coming." The yoga sutras encourage us to cultivate change through *tapas*, or effort, and *abhyasa*, practice, and to relinquish results by surrendering to something greater than ourselves through *ishvara pranidhana*, surrender to a higher power, and *vairagya*, centeredness or detachment from results. This delicate balance is a theme that applies to both the yoga practice and the healing journey (Iyengar, 2008). Posture and breath are, like healing itself, a dynamic experience.

Sometimes, there is common yoga language that we need to adapt in order to effectively teach to a population. When a program I worked with in juvenile hall started teaching at a new girls' unit in San Francisco, the staff on the unit made it clear that the name "downward dog" would rouse a series of jokes with sexual connotations – so we made the decision beforehand to re-name the posture. It was a little confusing for us as teachers, at first, but we got used to it. After establishing rapport with the students, we gradually re-introduced names that they might find amusing, or make fun of, but only after we had established enough rapport and mutual respect to keep the class moving. After months of practice, the students had become more familiar with us and with the practices, and we chose reintegrate the original name Downward Facing Dog, in part to prepare them for yoga classes outside of the juvenile hall setting. If you choose these types of adaptations, consider the impact beyond your time with the students, and when possible, find the right time to disclose alternative names, or simply share the fact that poses at times do carry different labels. In circumstances where teachers decide to adapt names or phrases, demonstrations and context can help students learn. If you are unsure of what words or phrases may be triggering or inappropriate with your specific population, talk to other professionals, or record yourself teaching to a friend and listen to your words through a trauma-informed lens. Who can teach you more about your population or setting, and what might you say differently to students given what you already know?

We've covered the difference between describing posture alternatives as variations or modifications; another important linguistic distinction lies in the differentiation between an adjustment and an assist. We can't discuss this one without a thorough conversation about touch, so let's dive into the controversial topic now: physical contact between teacher and student in trauma-informed yoga practice.

Touch in Trauma-Informed Yoga

To touch or not to touch? It is a hot topic of debate in the field of trauma-informed yoga, with strong opinions, emotions, and experiences supporting the decision to include, or refrain from, physical contact with students. Even appropriate, consensual, helpful physical contact crosses a boundary of intimacy; it brings together the personal space of two people. This exchange, like verbal communication but in a more intimate capacity, is susceptible to miscommunication. We've discussed postures, and being in relationship, as both triggers and resources for healing. Touch, as well, can serve as a trigger and a resource. Touch is particularly triggering when it is unexpected, inappropriate, or non-consensual. Touch that serves as a resource should always be expected, appropriate, and consensual. In determining whether or not touch is a helpful part of someone's healing process, **we must always defer to the experience of the student over the intention of the teacher.**

Touch is an important topic in both mental health and in trauma-informed yoga. In both fields, given the risk of triggers and misinterpretation, many trainings strongly suggest a strict no-touch policy. Since the teacher or therapist is in a leadership role and often has a role of authority, it is challenging for them to invoke touch without imposing on the student. At the same time, many therapists who incorporate somatic work do include touch, in the form of a client pushing into their hands, or by offering the resource of a hand on a client's shoulder, at the client's request. Indeed, it is most challenging to live in a gray area where we need to decide when and how touch might be beneficial with those we serve. For this reason, if you, as a provider, are unsure about the purpose of your physical contact with a client, a no-touch policy is the safest way to ensure that physical contact does not trigger participants or cause other harm. Recall our discussion of boundaries; it is much more challenging to reign in an over-extended boundary than it is to extend a conservative one. While we can repair misunderstandings, and assist students in self-regulating after a triggering experience, **there is no way to un-touch someone.** If, as a provider, you are unclear, unsure, or in doubt, focus on other aspects of the practice that provide healing. If the request for appropriate touch evolves in your classroom, you can revisit the decision at a later date and make decisions with your students that clarify the intention, scope, and practice of physical contact in the classroom.

Due to the risk for touch to trigger traumatic memories or experiences, the safe norm is to avoid it entirely, and yet, we often overlook the range of options between no touch and physical contact between two people. If you feel touch may be of service to your clients, consider beginning with the use of **props as an experience of touch.** The invitation to place blankets, bolsters, blocks, or even a lightweight strap or heavy sandbag, in contact with the body allows the student to have an experience of touch that is completely within their control and does not include the potentially precarious aspect of human contact. These props can bring heightened awareness to an action or part of the body, can serve as supports, and can serve to increase a student's experience of comfort. Choosing to use props in this way sets the stage for expected, appropriate, consensual contact between the student and objects in the yoga room. This approach emphasizes a trauma-informed relationship to contact with props, and builds a foundation for other forms of touch, should they become a part of the practitioner's experience at any point in their practice.

More vulnerable is the practice of **self-touch,** which also carries the possibility to soothe and foster healing. Self-touch allows for hands-on assistance without physical contact between two people. In this practice, teachers offer students an opportunity to use their own hands to connect with their body, either in a way that feels soothing or in a way that informs a healthy position within a given *asana.* Examples include inviting a student to place a hand on the heart or abdomen, if it feels good to do so, or inviting them to place a hand on the lower back to feel its shape, or onto the top of the thighs to ground. Resourceful self-touch, the kind that feels comforting rather than instructive, is a good place to start as it can help bring a sense of soothing to the nervous system. Instructive self-touch is best offered with a message of how the change in shape will help the student, to emphasize safety and reduce avoid over-identification with the outer form. If you choose to incorporate instructive self-touch, search for cues that emphasize the safety and well-being of students. Offering the option for students to place a hand on their lower back to help keep it from rounding, while informing them that this will support the spine being in a safe position, gives them a clear reason for choosing the self-assist. As with other practices, we offer these options as invitations, keeping choice and the decision to participate with the student.

Some trauma survivors, as is the case in somatoform dissociation, feel disconnected from areas of their body that were treated violently or relate to some aspect of their traumatic experience. In these cases, even placing a hand on these areas may bring up emotion related to trauma, or highlight the feeling of disconnect. Offering the opportunity for student to place *their own* hands on their own bodies keeps control of the physical experience – pun intended here – in the students' hands. Many students in TIY classes report feeling soothed or connected to themselves when placing their own hand on their heart or abdomen with care, while others report a variety of reactions and experiences ranging from positive to neutral to negative. We cannot know how each person will experience these practices, but can offer structure that creates options for deepening positive experiences and managing difficult ones. This practice adds a human element, without involving another human. Consider self-touch to be an ongoing resource for students who benefit from it and prefer not to participate in any shared physical contact.

Some teachers and programs in trauma-informed yoga and trauma treatment have navigated a path that provides necessary healing experiences that *do* include physical contact between two people. Indeed, touch is the primary mode of communication humans engage in; we grow for our first 9 months of life inside another human being, and need to be held in early days and months in order to thrive. Just as touch can trigger the threat response, it can also influence the stress response in a positive, resourceful way. When incorporating touch into trauma-informed yoga, Meghan Delaney-Zipin, a yoga teacher and physical therapist based in Boston, Massachusetts, describes the importance of differentiating between what we usually call an adjustment or assist, and supportive touch (Delaney-Zipin, 2018). A **hands-on adjustment or assist** includes physical touch that intends to inform movement patterns, teach actions, or change the position of the body. The purpose of supportive touch is to provide a soothing experience for the autonomic nervous system. Meghan uses both forms of touch in her trauma-informed yoga classes at Peony and the Bee Yoga at The Wellness Room in Newtonville, Massachusetts. In a physical assist that intends to serve the student in developing a better long-term movement pattern, a trained and skilled teacher like Meghan can direct the student's body and invoke therapeutic changes in awareness and movement patterns. As I described in my experience with Gianfranco at the beginning of Chapter 6, this can be a scary experience! Trust in relationship and thorough training in anatomy and physiology prepare the teacher for this type of assist.

Supportive touch is different, in that it typically involves grounding, breathing with the student, observing the shifts that take place in the student's physiology and responding in an attuned way. Meghan asserts, "A hard and fast commitment to never touch sensitive populations for fear of doing harm also eliminates the possibility that hands-on healing can be an entry point to comfort, breath, kindness, and ease" (Delaney-Zipin, 2018). Meghan incorporates supportive touch with students recovering from grief, for whom part of their experience of trauma is having lost the daily experience of positive touch that their partner offered. In her training *In Good Hands*, she outlines recommendations for providers who have decided with their students that it will be helpful to incorporate touch into their TIY experience:

- Don't touch unless *you're* comfortable.
- Don't touch unless *you're* grounded.
- Don't touch unless *you're* clear in your intention and poised to move ahead.
- If you're not comfortable or confident touching bodies, practice on friends, family, or students with whom you have an existing relationship. Ask for feedback.

This reiterates the importance of developing your own body awareness, maintaining awareness of your intention and personal comfort, and opening multiple communication lines between teacher and student.

Throughout these stages and aspects of touch in TIY, consent remains a crucial foundation. Consent can only occur when someone is fully informed of the purpose, potential risks, other options, and potential benefits related to an activity, and they agree, give written permission, or say "yes." In some circumstances, like in a psychotherapy practice, a written informed consent agreement is warranted. If your students or clients sign an agreement, be sure to review it in conversation, as it is common for people to skim legal forms without fully understanding the scope of the material covered in the document. Just like when you sit in an exit row on the airplane, a verbal "yes" removes ambiguity that may come with nods or casual responses like "yeah," "okay," or "uh-huh." Consent is always revocable by the person who granted it, and it helps to clarify avenues that the practitioner has to revoke consent, and ask how they would like to communicate any changes that arise. It is important to not assume consent because of nonverbal communication, past experience with a student or client, or non-responsiveness.

When considering the risks and benefits of incorporating touch, get to know your population: the needs of someone who has suffered physical abuse are different from those who've experienced neglect, or sexual assault. Trauma related to hand-to-hand combat is different from armed combat, and both are very different from traumatic loss and grief. Consider what you know about your clients and students, both as members of a group, and as individuals. Becoming versed in potential triggers and exploring the unique experience of each individual will help you make decisions about how touch may trigger, and how it may play a role in healing. All traumatic experiences are unique in their impact and the ensuing needs they foster, so listening to the needs of students and clients gives us information about the nature of the trauma and the best policies and practices to facilitate healing.

Yoga and Body Image

Even without touch, our bodies can carry negative imprints, intense emotions, and harmful thoughts gathered through experience, culture, and power imbalances that exist in the world. Yoga is one way to connect with the body and to explore exactly what it holds in terms of emotion, memory, and felt experience. In addressing the body, we must keep in mind that healthy body image is rarely taught, and is often discouraged by media portrayals of idealized and airbrushed models – some of them in yoga clothing. I've heard students call themselves too fat, too thin, too athletic, too weak, too light, too dark, too old, too young, too bland, too extreme, too smart, too stupid, too bad, too good, and so on and so forth. We all have negative thoughts at times, and it is easy to classify ourselves as not "___" enough. The words we assign here, whatever they are, put us at odds with ourselves, and at times, with our bodies. Yoga, at its heart, is about befriending the body. The more we can teach, model, and lead with self-acceptance, the better. This is easier said than done. "Love your body" messaging can, at times, feel inaccessible. When people can't quite access self-love, or body-love, consider this progression:

1   Witness consciousness: developing awareness of types of negative thoughts;
2   Non-shaming (interrupting negative thoughts, this prepares for *pratipaksha bhavana*);
3   Neutral observation – becoming aware of texture, temperature or position;
4   Appreciation: focusing on function or form, thanking the feet, legs, etc.;
5   Exploration: when a positive mantra feels empty, explore looking for evidence that supports positive qualities. For example, ask, "*Why* am I strong?" This orients the mind to search for evidence in support of strength.
6   Celebration: celebrating aspects of the body, along with any small experience of positive connection to it;
7   Love: *metta* practices, focusing outward first tends to be more accessible, then focusing inward as it becomes accessible.

As with the yogic limbs, love comes as a result of these practices and cannot be forced. Wherever your student, client, or group is, meet them where they are in their body–mind relationship and guide them toward *ahimsa*, or peacefulness, with the appropriate practice. Often this takes acceptance on the part of the teacher, to witness where students are, offer a healthy challenge of healing, and accept the progress the practice offers day by day.

Sequencing

A thorough yoga teacher training and mentorship is the best way to learn the craft of sequencing and, yet, too often, trauma is not a part of the conversation in these settings. If you are teaching *asana* practice, the anatomy and teaching skills covered in training are essential, so that you know how to maintain physical safety across the many shapes yoga takes. This section, and this book, in no way substitutes for this type of training. Once you've learned the basic principles of sequencing *asana* and *pranayama* practices, the conversation becomes how to most skillfully apply this to trauma recovery. Each point in this book sets you up to do this well, yet, there are infinite combinations of postures, variations, and bodies that may enter a TIY yoga class. In order to choose what is best for each, we can revisit our discussion of the Window of Tolerance, Polyvagal Theory, and cultivating *sattva*. Refer back to Chapters 5 and 6 for sequences that offer resources, balance the *gunas*, and support students in widening their Window of Tolerance. Helpful guiding questions include:

- What will bring this person's nervous system into balance?
- What practices will cultivate *sattva*?
- What will build a strong sense of rapport, respect, and trust?
- What can provide comfort or a resource?
- What will activate the more recently developed aspects of our nervous systems (ventral vagal complex)?

Asking these questions will help you choose what's next, even if something surprising and out of your control occurs during class. I was once in a deep *savasana* when a neighbor to the yoga studio stormed into the room yelling about someone parking in his spot (it turned out, it was someone at the restaurant next door). I'd expect we all experienced quite a startle response, but the teacher was able to contain the intruder, set a clear boundary, send the person out, and then comfort us with his words, presence, and response. Helping people recover from a disturbance in this way serves both to model recovery, and to foster a soothing experience.

In addition to questions about the perfect TIY sequence, I also often get questions about how to help a student or client when they are triggered. You may incorporate grounding to the earth below, or orienting to a sound, sight, or smell in the room. Practices that call energy back to center can be beneficial, but most important is that you guide your decision and response based on the answers the questions above. These questions can guide your response in any yoga class, private session, or even in your own life.

Opportunities for Communication

As we covered in the chapter about relationships and attachment, it is important to seek to understand the people you serve. In order to understand, observation and communication must occur, and there must be an anonymous or non-confrontational way for students to share their experience with leaders. As we discussed in Chapter 6, relationships thrive when healthy communication is encouraged and accessible. **Feedback loops** are ways for students and clients to share their experiences with you, and they can exist in many forms. Surveys, suggestion boxes, and feedback forms are all great examples of feedback loops. These can become an integrated part of the program that students participate in, in efforts to listen to the clients and respond to their needs. While it is wonderful to encourage students to give direct verbal feedback to teachers, know that not all students will feel comfortable with this, and that having anonymous suggestions boxes or online surveys is a better way to glean honest feedback from participants. Direct verbal expression can be challenging for a number of reasons related to trauma, so assuming that a student will be verbal and assert their needs as they arise discounts the impact that so many traumas have on voice and agency.

Bringing Voice to Yoga

Many people recovering from trauma report feeling challenges in finding their voice, which can manifest verbally, or as a sense of blockage in other areas. Finding and freeing the voice is a helpful exercise for most anyone, and another way to explore the subtleties of breath, as well as physical, mental, and emotional restrictions. Through practicing vocalizations in a playful and non-judgmental way, practitioners often find a growing sense of freedom and stress relief. Finding freedom expressing air, humming a note, or singing *On Top of Spaghetti* can help connect with different qualities of voice, while the dyadic support of psychotherapy and similar close relationships can provide a space to speak the unspeakable. Often those who are able to bring voice to their suffering find inspiration to share this gift. For some, the healing journey means that they take on the role of healer, and find themselves speaking up for those who are exposed to violence, trauma, or cut off from power. Consider how you can offer opportunities for the people you serve to experience gentle vocalization, and explore how their voice, or lack of it, impacts the relationship you have with them.

Molly Mahoney, therapeutic voice teacher based in San Francisco, California, guides trauma survivors to connect through simple practices first (Mahoney, 2018). The following is an example of a gentle vocalization exercise you might try; you'll find the link to access resources, including this practice, at the end of this chapter.

How to Find Your Voice (Literally):

- o Find a comfortable position, seated or reclined.
- o Gently place your hand on your Adam's Apple. This is your larynx.
- o Swallow. Notice how buoyant and flexible it can be. Behind this shield of cartilage are your vocal folds, which buzz to create your singing and speaking voice.
- o Hum softly and feel this buzzing sensation.
- o You've found your voice!

Figure 8.1 Finding Your Voice

Consider when it may be helpful to incorporate practices like these into the work you are doing.

Organizing Recovery

Since trauma often involves experiences of chaos, and each person's healing path is unique, it is helpful for us to have a road map to healing to organize our approach: Judith Herman's three-stage model of treatment gives us just this (Herman, 1992, pp. 34–35). These stages weave together in a less linear way than any model could provide; yet, this framework can help us stay grounded in the face of confusion, and can help us to make choices about how to best support new students and clients. **Stage One** emphasizes the importance of resourcing and creating stability. Resourcing involves cultivating a sense of safety, identifying effective strategies for self-care, and determining strategies for self-soothing and self-regulation. The secret to this model is that we are always cultivating Stage One qualities. When a foundational sense of stability and safety is created through Stage One efforts, we move on to process work. **Stage Two** is the time for processing difficult emotions and, when necessary, revisiting coping skills built up during Stage One. In this stage, we support a client in digging into deeper negative emotions and moving through them – remembering, mourning, grieving, and honoring difficult emotions like anger, sadness, and confusion. When most of the processing work is done, **Stage Three** brings us to the integration phase, in which we support clients in integrating the trauma into their narrative, and consciously choosing to invoke ongoing supports for growth and healing. When in doubt, we can return to stage one, and build foundational coping skills and resilience factors.

Titration and Pendulation

Many exposure-based techniques overlook the phenomenon of dissociation, which can lead complex trauma clients to flood with memory or sensation, triggering dysregulation in the nervous system. In a dissociative freeze response, the client reports feeling nothing, and the therapist perceives the symptoms to have disappeared. This is a loophole we need to watch for. With clients who have experienced complex, developmental trauma, instead of flooding them with exposure, we can invite small pieces of the trauma to move through, little by little, day by day. By biting off small, chewable pieces of emotional material, we allow each piece to digest. This is called **titration**, and it helps prevent dissociate defenses, and others, from activating.

Dissociation occurs as a protective mechanism, so that the whole person does not have to hold the trauma. The following quote by Rainer Maria Rilke reminds me of the practice of **pendulation**. He writes, "Move back and forth into the change. What is it like, such intensity of pain? If the drink is bitter, turn yourself to wine" (Rilke, 2005). When emotions become too impactful or bitter, a dissociative mechanism can create changes in consciousness in order to protect against intense affect. Pendulation occurs when we move into discomfort, pay attention to it, and *before* it brings overwhelm (or we feel the need to change ourselves to cope), transition out to a resource, bringing the present moment experience back to safety. This is relevant to EMDR therapy, as well, since EMDR and other processing tools can assist the client in accessing traumatic memories and related emotions. We practice pendulation when, instead of diving into negative or overwhelming emotions without support, we weave in and out of resource and process (Stage One and Stage Two), continuously building foundations of safety and support as the difficult memories and remnants of experience move through the body.

Each of the elements of TIY we've covered in this chapter are important to reflect upon, ideally in an ongoing way. If you work in a group program where there are multiple teachers, it is okay for them to have different approaches and styles but these core elements should ideally be discussed and agreed upon prior to teaching a trauma-informed class. This will help prevent uncomfortable situations in classes and deliver a consistent message of support to students. In moments of confusion, return to the words of former president of India A. P. J. Abdul Kalam (2004), quoted at the opening of this chapter, and ask yourself, "Which choice will better promote the dignity and self-respect of this student?" This will guide you toward the trauma-informed choice.

***

When I share the Happy Baby story in a training environment, I hear countless experiences outlining the ways in which people's bodies, personal space, and personal choices have been disregarded and disrespected. I encourage people to follow up, as I often have, by suggesting that studios implement a policy for physical assists by invitation only.

While voicing discomfort helps, the onus is on the teacher and studio to make decisions that are trauma-informed, and to be crystal clear about the level of contact a class entails. As the field of trauma-informed yoga grows in reach, I hope to hear fewer and fewer of these stories of trigger and re-traumatization, particularly since in these environments so many people arrive seeking healing. As teachers become more aware of the range of experiences students can have on the mat and how trauma impacts those experiences, studios and teachers can make conscious choices that support healing for students with a wide range of backgrounds and experiences.

Reflection Questions

1 List three things you can do to promote physical and emotional safety in your students'/client's environment.
2 Name two feedback loops that would best connect you to the population you serve.
3 Name a posture, cue or word that may uniquely trigger the group you serve. What can you replace this with?

Additional resources available at http://howwecanheal.com/y4tr

References

Delaney-Zipin, M. (2018). *In good hands: Incorporating touch into trauma-informed yoga*. Boston (12–13).

Herman, J. L. (1992). *Trauma and recovery*. New York: Basic Books.

Iyengar, B. K. S. (2008). *Light on the Yoga Sutras of Patanjali*. Delhi, India: Motilal Banarsidass Publishers.

Kalam, A. P. J. Abdul. (2004) *The pursuit of truth*. Retrieved from: https://architexturez.net/doc/az-cf-21864.

Mahoney, M. (2018). *How to find your voice (literally)*. Retrieved from http://mollymarymahoney.com/.

Rilke, R. M. (2005). *In praise of mortality: Selections from Rainer Maria Rilke's Duino Elegies and Sonnets to Orpheus*. New York: Riverhead Books.

Part III

Growth

Keeping Joy Alive in the Face
of Trauma

9 Accessing Resilience

*The most beautiful people we have known are those who have known
defeat, known suffering, known struggle, known loss, and have found
their way out of the depths. These persons have an appreciation, a sensitivity, and an understanding of life that fills them with compassion,
gentleness, and a deep loving concern.*

Beautiful people do not just happen.

– Elisabeth Kübler-Ross

Gina came to work with me after being attacked late one workday evening,
walking the short distance between the bus stop and her home. I'll spare
you the violent details; suffice to say that she was seriously wounded
physically and, for good reason, was feeling hypervigilant. At the time
we started working together, she could be scared out of her boots by a
cute puppy coming out from around a street corner. During one of our
sessions, she had just been startled on her way into the office, and was
feeling quite shaky. "What can I do to feel normal again?" She asked,
with an earnest search for relief in her eyes.

I gathered the "tappers" – they're an EMDR tool that buzzes back and
forth between the right and left hands, and offered them to her to hold.
Knowing the drill, she said, "I definitely need something positive right
now." We had resourced before with feelings related to being in nature
and being with friends, but I sensed she needed something stronger today.
"What comes to mind now that helps you feel comfortable, relaxed, or
peaceful?" She sat for a moment, closing her eyes to reflect. In an instant
her eyelids flung open again, "Baby goats!!" she exclaimed. Her enthu-
siasm was contagious, and, as I asked her to describe the details of the
fur, their sounds, and their spirits, her entire affect changed. She became
ebullient and warm, rather than retracted, protective, and fearful. We'd
found a switch.

I began to guide her with questions to connect with the positive feeling state. When you think of baby goats, what images do you see? What
do the goats look like? Which emotions arise in their presence? Where

do you feel those feelings in your body, and how does it feel to touch the baby goats? How do you think and feel within yourself when you are holding a baby goat?

"It's like my whole body turns soft, like it melts into a puddle," she mused. "I feel so warm and safe in my heart. Like they need my care and it's so easy to love them. Their little eyes look up at me and I just. . . melt." As we went through this resourcing process, she took a few deep breaths, and her posture shifted from sitting clenched and hunched forward to sitting back with an open chest and heart. "Much better," she shared after the set of resourcing was complete. "I can still feel the fear but it's further away. I wish I could really go snuggle a baby goat right now. Is there a petting zoo nearby?" Lucky for her, there was a little farm just up the hill from my office, and I was pretty sure they had some baby goats on hand.

***

The concept of resilience has become increasingly mainstream in mental health culture over the past two decades. Academic programs and departments focused on resilience, post-traumatic growth, and positive psychology have grown in number, size and reach, and mental health groups are more likely to take a "strength-based" approach than ever. As we make the transition, as a field and as a society, from the question "what's wrong?" to "what happened?" to "what's right?" the next logical question to ask is "what helps?" Supporting clients in moving from expired coping mechanisms, ones that served an adaptive function in the past but are causing pain or discomfort in the present, necessitates a perspective of resilience and a deep belief in their capacity to heal.

The biggest misconception I hear about resilience is that we either have it or we don't. It is common for clients early in our work together to say, simply, "I am not resilient," while others will ask, "How can I become more resilient?" There are both risk factors and resilience factors, more of each than we can list, and researchers and theorists in this field attempt to understand, organize, and categorize both. We can simply define a **resource** as anything that brings relief, support, or positive experience to the individual, in mind, body, or spirit. Accessing healthy coping skills and resources are key components of resilience building. "What lifts you up?" is a common question to ask to help people identify the people, places, practices, and experiences that provide psychological resourcing and promote mental, emotional, and physiological health. While it's helpful to identify as many resources as possible, often just one or two powerful ones suffice to support a healing experience. As Gina described her experience of baby goats, her body and internal experience shifted in a way that I hadn't seen with any other resource practice; there was something powerful and personal about this one. By identifying this potent resource, she found significant relief from the fearful state initiated by her experience of being attacked. Identifying resources, in all of their forms, helps us to access our own unique path of resilience and carve out a positive path forward.

Over the past two decades I have worked with clients of all levels of ACE and resilience scores, and have found that resilience consists of a series of conscious and unconscious choices that help us to access internal and external resources, along with situational factors that facilitate our capacity to respond to overwhelming stress. The dictionary definition of resilience remains "the capacity to recover quickly from difficulties; toughness;" but the field has evolved to value slow, steady efforts to build resilience, and to honor vulnerability in the process. By studying those who experience quick recovery, we've identified some of the skills and resources that can help those who continue to struggle. It's important to note that those who appear resilient are not always feeling so internally, and may experience their symptoms in a different timing or manner than others expect. A 9/11 survivor I worked with talked about the deep need to return to work, primarily because it made life feel somewhat normal again, and connecting with colleagues helped soothe the experience of losing other colleagues when the towers fell. She shared that she *appeared* to bounce back by returning to work so quickly, but felt like it was the only way she could keep herself from "falling apart." About six months after the attack, deeper emotions and somatic implications of her experience surfaced, and she took some time off work to focus on her personal healing at that time. She shared that people would often say, "You're so resilient!" and internally she would think, "If you only knew."

Integrating deep emotional experience is a process that is difficult to map since we are all uniquely wired and process emotions through different senses and experiences. Verbalizing, creating art or music, writing, drawing, meditating, moving the body, and spending time alone are all examples of ways that people can process traumatic material. Something helps you process when it moves some of the energy or emotion related to the trauma, and allows for a deeper sense of integration, acceptance, release or relief following the traumatic event. A variety of supports can help us to cope with emotions that come with difficult life experiences.

Active and Passive Coping

In early stages of developing resilience, we often refer to coping skills: what will help you get through this difficult experience in a healthy way? Coping skills come in both active and passive forms. **Active coping** involves seeking out resources to support ourselves through difficult feelings, emotions, and experiences. Seeing a therapist, taking up a sport, talking to a friend or loved one, or expressing emotions through art are all examples of active coping. Active coping mechanisms require an awareness of the stressor and our conscious attempt to try and reduce stress.

Passive coping generally involves avoidance, withdrawal, and wishful thinking. Abusing substances like drugs, alcohol, or food is one way that we attempt to cope in a way that does not address the root of the emotional experience. Ignoring the problem or thinking that it will magically disappear if you look away from it are other ways we attempt to cope passively. While drinking, binge eating, and drug use are actions, these behaviors often relate to unconscious avoidance of the deep emotions related to trauma, rather than awareness of feelings and experiences followed by active solution planning. While people seek out these behaviors to bring comfort, they often create further problems, and add to the experience of stress in the long term. For this reason, seeking active coping methods that reduce overall stress is more conducive to long term healing.

Developmental Assets

Early on in my career I worked in a housing development notorious for its gang activity and crime. The kids there had inhumanely high ACE scores. Most of the youth I worked with there had experienced trauma from a very young age, with few supports to cope with the stress and continue to meet necessary developmental tasks. Two 16-year-old young women, who also happened to be identical twins, stood out to me. Despite their many ACEs, they embodied humor, heart, creativity, connection, and bravery. They were a gregarious duo, so it was easy to recognize some of the major resources they had: each other; dancing; connecting with adults; asking for help; a mother who loved them dearly. Their choreographed Janet Jackson routines were off the charts. These young women gave wonderful, real life examples of Developmental Assets (Scales & Leffert, 1999). In this book, the authors outline both internal and external resources that help youth meet healthy developmental tasks and go on to create a thriving adult life.

There are numerous ways to conceptualize and categorize the variety of resilience factors and assets, and if we divide them into two groups, internal and external, we can further explore details and applications of each asset. **Internal assets** tend to be psychological and emotional, but they can also be physical by way of genetic predisposition. In the book, *Developmental Assets*, Scales and Leffert describe the following four categories of internal assets:

- Commitment to Learning
- Positive Values
- Social Competencies
- Positive Identity

Each of these categories include subcategories to help us identify the asset and support it as part of a child's development. **Commitment to**

learning can involve being motivated to achieve, engaged with school, feeling a connection to the school, and reading for pleasure. **Positive values** encompass caring, honesty, responsibility, integrity, equality, and restraint. **Social competencies** range from planning and decision making, to the ability to resist peer pressure, to the capacity to resolve conflict. Empathy, sensitivity, and friendship skills fit in here as well. **Positive identity** can involve a sense of personal power or self-esteem, as well as a sense of purpose and hope for a positive future (Scales & Leffert, 1999).

External assets tend to be relational, communal, and related to activities or relationships with the outside world. They include the following categories:

- Support
- Empowerment
- Boundaries and Expectations
- Constructive Use of Time

Support can come from many places – the family, a neighbor, the neighborhood or school, even peers. Having good communication within the family, and parents who are involved with the schooling process, also offers a sense of support. **Empowerment** entails feeling safe in the community and feeling valued by adults. This can involve being offered meaningful roles in the community, or being involved in community service activities. **Boundaries and expectations** refer to the family, community, and school having clear rules and high expectations, as well as the child having access to role models and positive peer influences. **Constructive use of time** includes involvement with sports, music, theater, clubs, organizations, and time at home (Scales & Leffert, 1999).

As you read, you may have ideas for related or additional assets – add them to your list of things to look for and cultivate in those you serve. Paying attention to developmental assets helps us bring a solution-focused approach to both youth and adults; as we look for and bolster the available internal and external assets, we cultivate resilience and growth.

Re-Iteration and Post-Traumatic Growth

On a recent zip lining expedition with a few students I've been mentoring, we found ourselves deep in a redwood forest in the Santa Cruz mountains, here in California. A local gestured to a nearby tree that had been struck by lightning and explained, "That is what we call a re-iteration," he pointed to the place where the lightning had struck and the trunk sprouted to the left to continue its reach skyward. The tree did not move on as before, but became an entirely new version of itself, as we often do in the wake of traumatic experiences. The impact of the lightning strike did not end the tree's growth, but it impacted it, and the tree continued to proceed in a slightly new vector. We humans often do a similar thing in the wake of trauma.

The field of post-traumatic growth (PTG) arose from qualitative observations that many who have experienced trauma, as upsetting and dysregulating as the experiences are, also report making meaning and identifying how the very same experiences led to personal growth. PTG describes the perspective shifts and choices for positive change that often come in the aftermath of significant trauma, and includes not only what helps people get through life's difficulties, but what helps them thrive as a result of challenge. Five common themes in the field of PTG include **personal strength, new possibilities, relating to others, appreciating life** and **spiritual change.** The field of PTG reflects, and seeks to operationalize, what Dr. Kübler Ross (1975) observed about painful experiences creating "beautiful people."

It is common for trauma survivors to hear phrases to the effect of "I can't even imagine how awful that was." In truth, people who have not endured similar experiences often have no concept of how challenging it is to navigate the path of healing. When one is faced with the unimaginable and finds resources and supports to meet the extreme demands of this challenge, a sense of **personal strength** can follow. A client of mine who lost a child once said, "If I can make it through this pain, I can endure anything." Towards the end of our time working together she'd taken up body-building based on this premise. "It helps me to feel the intensity come and go, and I do it almost every day. It's like I've come to accept that intense feelings are a part of my daily life now, and that's okay. I can breathe through them now." Many find strength in exercise, sports, or in creative endeavors like theater, music, or art. Others feel strong when connecting with, or helping others. It can be helpful to ask clients and students: What helps you to feel strong? How do you cope with intensity, both emotional and physical? Often, when sensations and emotions feel uncomfortable, we choose passive coping behaviors that also have drawbacks – using drugs, alcohol, or distracting with unhealthy relationships to people or activities. Facing these emotions and finding more active ways to cope can help to develop an embodied feeling of strength, or a widened Window of Tolerance.

Many people report experiencing a shift and reordering of values in the wake of trauma, and with these shifts come **new possibilities.** With experiences that impact or threaten life, we can experience an organic shift in perspective related to our time on the planet, our relationships, and how we invest our energy. Perhaps things that were meaningful before the traumatic experience no longer feel engaging, while other topics become more compelling. When Gina identified the resource of baby goats, she not only found something to help her feel good in the moment, but initiated a shift in her lifestyle away from the city and closer to farm animals. Like the re-iteration of the tree, life-as-usual may not continue, but other opportunities that allow for more meaning, depth or perspective may cultivate growth in new directions.

Social supports are a huge way that we move through difficulty in life, thus the way in which we **relate to others** may change. Difficult experiences may lead us to reach out for professional help, or to confide in a friend. We might also cultivate a deeper sense of compassion for others who are experiencing difficulty, which opens the doors for new connections and can even contribute to relating to the world at large in a new way. Consider how a difficult experience may reorganize relationships to family, friends, community, and society at large. Individuals and groups that are helpful and healing often take center stage in the wake of trauma, while less meaningful relationships can fall away. In addition, we can learn how to reach out and ask for, or provide, help. Both supporting and service-based roles can become more central, and can deepen our connection to other beings.

When there is an experience that highlights the reality of our mortality, we can develop a much deeper **appreciation of life**, even in the smallest detail of it. Hamilton Jordan describes this in his book *No Such Thing as a Bad Day*.

> After my first cancer, even the smallest joys in life took on new meaning—watching a beautiful sunset, a hug from my child, a laugh with Dorothy. That feeling has not diminished with time. After my second and third cancers, the simple joys of life are everywhere and are boundless, as I cherish my family and friends and contemplate the rest of my life, a life I certainly do not take for granted.
>
> (Jordan, 2001, p.248)

As traumatic events highlight the vulnerability of life, they can lead us to treasure moments of beauty, connection, or peace that we had previously taken for granted. **Spiritual changes** often follow traumatic experiences and evoke questions of mortality, afterlife, and spiritual meaning. We may find ourselves asking, "Why did this happen?" or "Where do people go when they die?" These questions are deeply personal and can have significant implications for how we understand ourselves, the world, and beyond.

Mapping Resilience

Four core components of resilience have become clear to me, and, while I'll present them in a linear fashion, reality is not so neat and organized. A key foundational component is being **open to change**. Life is a series of transitions, some more difficult than others, and those who accept this and cultivate adaptability tend to have an easier time letting go of what "should have been" and embracing what is or was. While this process is rarely easy, practicing openness and acceptance can help facilitate ease in the midst of a deep transition. From this place of acceptance, Identifying **active coping** strategies is a clear support to healing. Finding **external resources** in supportive relationships, spiritual practices, creative outlets, and movement practices while cultivating **internal resources** like self-worth, self-compassion, hope, and perseverance builds support from the inside out, and the outside in. The final piece that for some takes time, is to combine present-oriented practices, like yoga, meditation, and other mindfulness disciplines, with future-oriented goals. In these practices, people practice being in the moment and connecting with what is, while at the same time building healthy neurological functioning for the future. When we **combine present-oriented practice, with future-oriented goals** we can bring relief to our days while slowly, patiently building self-awareness and neurological resilience.

Reciprocal Transformation

Many of you reading this are in roles of service and support to others. As we heal, a desire to share healing modalities that have served us can grow, and we might offer yoga, therapy, or other healing modalities to those who are traveling on similar paths. It is important for us to reflect on our own healing journey and to understand our own triggers in order to do this work well, and yet both the *wounded healer* and *healed healer* archetypes are incomplete. We are all continually learning and developing, and while there may be significant markers along the healing journey, we can also continue to heal and grow while in a service role. In her book, *Wisdom, Attachment and Love in Trauma Therapy: Beyond Evidence-Based Practice* Sue Pease Banitt describes "wise therapists" as those who recognize their shared experiences and are aware that clients can play a role in the therapist's growth, both personal and professional (Pease Banitt, 2018). In this way, it is helpful for us to be aware of the themes we connect with and what the work brings up for us on a personal level. This awareness cultivates opportunity for those in healing roles to access support outside of work and to pass through iterations of healing. I call this process **reciprocal transformation**, meaning that the process of healing can positively impact both parties, at times in similar, or parallel, ways, and other times in complementary, or less direct, ways. There is no prescription for this work, but maintaining awareness of shared healing offers depth and a positive focus for all parties involved. As Carl Jung stated, "The meeting of two personalities is like the contact of two chemical substances: if there is any reaction, both are transformed" (Jung, 1933, pp.49–50).

Healing is Not Linear

Often when people are seeking healing they are in pain, and want solutions fast, which, of course, is understandable. While I have seen some modalities work wonders for specific people, I have yet to find a magical panacea that resolves human emotions and obliterates suffering following a traumatic experience. Often, planners come to therapy with a hope for a simple step by step process and a checklist that will bring them back to "normal." While some methods employ homework and checklists, and we can use these, I have found it essential to expect a nonlinear trajectory. When we set up a rigid expectation of our healing process, it is often based on limited, conscious information, and does not leave space for our awareness to expand. As Molly Boeder Harris, founder of The Breathe Network, shares, "The nonlinear process that begets healing causes many people to question their capacity for resilience. . . In my experience, healing is an ongoing, lifelong *practice* that requires intentionality, consistency, and endurance." (Boeder Harris, 2018). We can create additional suffering by expecting progress when we are not ready for it, or by attaching to a way of seeing ourselves that is based on life prior to the trauma. We can also fall for the expectation that life will one day become perfect and free of stressors or challenges; which is simply not the case for any growing human being. Rather than setting ourselves up to struggle and experience additional inner conflict or disappointment, we can choose to honor our earned resilience, and witness the process of healing as it unfolds. As a vine winds toward the light, often the path of healing moves into unexpected places as it progresses.

Resilience is Not Denial

Another important aspect of any conversation about resilience to differentiate it from bypass, or denial. Sometimes, awful things happen. Focusing on resourcing, developmental assets or PTG is in no way meant to take away from the truth of pain or suffering. Compassion and empathy for difficult feelings are necessary for those in deep shock, trauma, or grief, and if we, as providers, skip to resilience as a defense against feeling the difficult realities that life can bring, we do a disservice to ourselves, and to those we serve. Resilience is not simple positive thinking or an attempt to manifest healing through denial, avoidance, or **spiritual bypass**. Spiritual bypass, a term coined by John Welwood (Welwood, 1984), later expounded upon in the text *Spiritual Bypassing: When Spirituality Disconnects Us from What Really Matters* (Masters, 2010, p.2). In it, the author writes:

> Spiritual bypassing is a very persistent shadow of spirituality, manifesting in many forms, often without being acknowledged as such. Aspects of spiritual bypassing include exaggerated detachment, emotional numbing and repression, overemphasis on the positive, anger-phobia, blind or overly tolerant compassion, weak or too porous boundaries, lopsided development (cognitive intelligence often being

far ahead of emotional and moral intelligence), debilitating judgment about one's negativity or shadow side, devaluation of the personal relative to the spiritual, and delusions of having arrived at a higher level of being.

Just as we watch for dynamics of rational or irrational authority, or seek to remain out of the roles defined in Karpman's Triangle, we must remain aware of the pathways of spiritual bypass, both within ourselves, as space-holders, and in those we serve. When we identify that spiritual bypass is taking place, we can gently, in time, refocus on the emotions and realities that we'd rather avoid, and envelop them back into our awareness, along with their accompanying emotions, body sensations, and narratives. This practice of bringing parts of the self together, rather than apart, sets the foundation for an experience of holistic healing.

While psychology can be deduced to a scientific study of the mind and emotions, for many clients, colleagues, and even for myself, healing manifests more as a form of art. Perhaps this is why poetry and images can resonate more deeply for those of us healing after experiences of inexplicable violence, pain or loss. The following poem, "Blessing for the Brokenhearted," from Jan Richardson's book *The Cure for Sorrow*, speaks to both the enormity of loss, and the essential role of love in accessing resilience, and the will to continue living (Richardson, 2016).

Blessing for the Brokenhearted
There is no remedy for love but to love more.
—Henry David Thoreau

Let us agree
for now
that we will not say
the breaking
makes us stronger
or that it is better
to have this pain
than to have done
without this love.

Let us promise
we will not
tell ourselves
time will heal
the wound,
when every day
our waking
opens it anew.

Perhaps for now
it can be enough
to simply marvel
at the mystery
of how a heart
so broken
can go on beating,
as if it were made
for precisely this—

as if it knows
the only cure for love
is more of it,

as if it sees
the heart's sole remedy
for breaking
is to love still,

as if it trusts
that its own
persistent pulse
is the rhythm
of a blessing
we cannot
begin to fathom
but will save us
nonetheless.

We need not deny pain to connect to love, or deny suffering to access joy; these are overly simplistic deductions of human experience and of the realities of life. When logic or science fail to encapsulate the depth of your experiences in life, consider how the arts may play a role. For many, they can facilitate self-expression and enhance the experience of resilience. If either of these proves true for you, I encourage you to include the arts in your healing practice.

***

After working with Gina for about one year, she decided to move. By this time, we had built a number of positive resources, including baby goats, among other farm animals, natural landscapes, mostly of the desert variety, as well as friends, family, and fictional characters. As we prepared to close our time together, we noted how many of her resources were about to become a part of her daily reality. She was moving to a house in a small town in the desert, and planned to raise farm animals and invite friends to come stay on long weekends. We marveled at this conscious choice for change: why not live in a way that feels supportive? She had shifted from creating resources in her mind to manifesting them in her world, surrounding herself by a felt sense of safety and support. Many years have passed since the move, during which she has sent the occasional baby goat photo back to my office. While her experience of being attacked had many negative implications, it also led to her choice to live in an environment that feels supportive and healthy for her – body, mind, and spirit.

Reflection Questions

1   Write out a definition of resilience as it applies to your personal or professional experiences with it.
2   Name a healthy active coping practice that works well for you.
3   Name two or more internal assets you see in the population you serve.
4   Name two or more external assets your clients or students have access to.
5   What forms of art or poetry do you find helpful, for yourself or for those you serve?

Additional resources available at http://howwecanheal.com/y4tr

References

Boeder Harris, M. (2018). *My story*. Retrieved from: www.mollyboederharris.com/.

Jordan, H. (2001). *No such thing as a bad day*. New York: Simon and Schuster.

Jung, C. G. (1933). Modern man in search of a soul, trans. W. S. Dell and Cary F. Baynes. New York and London: Harcourt Brace Jovanovich.

Kübler-Ross, E. (1975). *On death and dying*. New York: Macmillan.

Masters, R. A. (2010). *Spiritual bypassing: When spirituality disconnects us from what really matters*. Berkeley, CA: North Atlantic Books.

Pease Banitt, S. (2018). *Wisdom, attachment and love in trauma therapy: Beyond Evidence-based practice*. New York: Routledge.

Richardson, J. (2016) "Blessing for the brokenhearted" from *The cure for sorrow: A book of blessings for times of grief*. Orlando, FL: Wanton Gospeller Press, janrichardson.com.

Scales, P. C., & Leffert, N. (1999). *Developmental assets: A synthesis of the scientific research on adolescent development*. Minneapolis, MN: Search Institute.

Welwood, J. (1984). Principles of inner work: Psychological and spiritual. *The Journal of Transpersonal Psychology*, 16(1), 63.

10 Beyond Self-Care
Sustainable Systems

It is no measure of health to be well adjusted to a profoundly sick society.
— J. Krishnamurti

Zoe, a trans woman teaching yoga and life skills to youth in continuation schools, came to see me for support with vicarious trauma and burnout. In an early session, she shared that she felt the most positive while hanging out with her friends, and yet, she noted,

> "when I go to work, all of a sudden I have to deal with people who don't understand who or how I am. Some people avoid me, others overdo their interest. It makes the work so much more difficult because I have to put so much effort into managing who I am and how they make sense of me."

Doing social justice work is hard enough on its own, and Zoe wanted to support the youth she served and be a positive role model. She knew that what she taught, and what students learned in this program, was not always supported by their friends and their communities. While there were small moments of progress and connection, Zoe often expressed feeling overwhelmed, and up against forces that were much larger than her capacity to change. "It's hard when I am working within a context that does not support them, and does not support me. I really love the challenge of this work but without support, there is only so long I can do this." Despite a rigorous self-care practice including yoga, positive social community, and expressive creative arts, Zoe's experiences feeling unsupported at the systemic level contributed significantly to her experience of burnout.

***

Culture matters. Culture of families, organizations, societies, and everything in between. When we exist within a culture we learn rules of behavior and social engagement and adapt to its norms and mores, often without conscious awareness. Academic departments have culture. Workplaces have culture. Families pass down larger cultural traditions, and create their own rules for engagement and behavior. We are steeped in these cultures throughout our lives, and they impact our beliefs, behaviors, and feelings about the world.

When stress arises or trauma perpetuates as a result of systemic issues, it is easy to feel powerless to create change. Personal self-care is important, but will only go so far if we live in a toxic environment. This chapter serves to identify systems and their relationships to one another, and to encourage choices that facilitate healthy systems, whenever possible. We will also explore boundaries and self-care practices that bolster practitioners in the face of challenging work.

Ecological Systems Theory

Bronfenbrenner's Ecological Systems Theory provides a model that emphasizes the importance of context on a developing child. This theory describes how different systems interact to form their environment, and helps us to notice how each layer of a system can impact development in positive, negative, and neutral ways. Though the model focuses on youth over the course of development, the systems do not disappear at age 26, and we can continue to apply the model to adults; though some of the systems change with age, the structure of the theory remains applicable. The Ecological Systems Theory describes five levels of systems: the microsystem, mesosystem, exosystem, macrosystem, and chronosystem (Bronfenbrenner, 1979). As the opening quote to this chapter suggests (Krishnamurti, 1975), adapting to an unhealthy system, while life-saving in the short term, does not serve us in the long term. Consider, as you read, how you can encourage healthy systems at each level.

The **microsystem** describes those systems closest to the developing child, the ones that they have the most direct contact with, and create their immediate environment. This typically includes family, school, peers, and caregivers, and for adults can include the workplace as well. Relationships within the microsystem are bi-directional, meaning that an individual's behavior directly impacts others within the system, and vice versa. In this theory, the microsystem is the most influential.

The **mesosystem** layer speaks to the reality that groups within the microsystem interact with one another. The reality is that one's family, school, and religious center, for example, can also exist in relationship to one another, with this relationship impacting the developing child or adult. The mesosystem models these connections and interactions between the various elements of a person's microsystem. For example, the relationship between a parent and teacher has an impact on the child, as can the relationship between caregivers and peers. As these elements interconnect

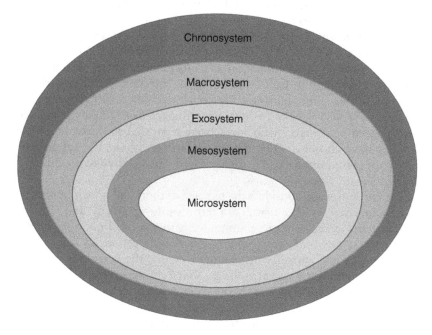

Figure 10.1 Ecological Systems Model

and assert influence upon one another, they change the experience of the developing child. A parent and teacher with good communication and shared understanding of the child can help, while a conflict between parents of the child and a child's friend may limit the potential depth of a friendship. When we look to the mesosystem, we can look for ways to support the systems in relationship to one another, and thus support the person at the center of the system.

The **exosystem** includes systems that the child is not directly a part of, yet impact them nonetheless. A great example is the parent's workplace: while the child may never so much as pay a visit to their parents' place of employment, things that happen there – success, conflict, stress – can impact their quality of life and life outcomes. A teen client I worked with for three years moved to Colorado when his mother's job transferred her there, despite his desire to remain in California. In this way, the system around the parent can have a significant impact on the child's life, including school, friendships, and even home, state, or country of residence.

The **macrosystem** includes social and cultural norms and values. In the United States, there is a strong emphasis on work as an aspect of identity. The question, "what do you do?" or "what do you want to be when you grow up?" shapes the way we think about ourselves as we develop.

Similarly, political inclinations and attitudes shape the way we think as we grow and relate to those around us. In the US, as in many countries, adults in different areas model different ways of thinking, speaking, and engaging with others. A client I've worked with for years who was raised in Georgia often finds that her misunderstandings with friends and colleagues here in California come back to cultural differences in expression and communication between the south and the west. The macrosystem also speaks to how laws impact us. Families who face immigration challenges, who have been separated by law, or whose families have chosen to flee dangerous areas without the support of legal paperwork, often experience increased stress related to the difficulties of their immigration status.

The **chronosystem** considers the passage of time, and how it applies to each of the systems. Age matters in terms of development, and impacts how systems at the other levels interact with the child and eventually, the adult. At this level, we also consider how larger social movements like the civil rights movement, or more recently, the #metoo movement bringing awareness to sexual violence, shape the experience and choices of the developing person. Each of these are beyond the scope of the other systems, yet can have a direct impact. Many of my private practice clients experienced difficulty when #metoo gained popularity, as they struggled with triggers related to stories being shared, and felt pressed to decide if and how to share their own stories. These social movements and changes over time can have a direct impact on the mind, body, and emotions of an individual.

Healthy Systems

One of the most outward displays of trauma I've seen in the yoga studio setting came from a young man who displayed erratic movements during the class I was teaching, yet remained on his mat. I did my best to respond to his needs in the classroom setting, checking in a couple of times, standing nearby him as a resource, and letting him know it was okay to take the variations he was taking, even though other students were not accustomed to this degree of specialized sequencing in this particular class. He approached me directly after class, which I was happy about, since I hadn't had the opportunity to get to know him or become aware of his needs before class. He shared that he had been "traumatized by his PhD program in psychology," and that he was working through the shame and isolation he had experienced there. I've had other clients in private practice speak to negative impacts of academic department cultures, yet I remained surprised when he referenced this as the primary root of his trauma. Of course, a 10-minute conversation after a yoga class is not the place for his full history to arise, and yet, according to his comments, there was something significantly upsetting about his experience in this academic system. Healthy systems, and their counter-part, can exist across professions and across the sociological spectrum. The fact that a program seeks to treat trauma, or teach yoga, or teach psychology in this instance, does not inoculate it from perpetuating unhealthy dynamics.

What are the qualities of a sustainable, healthy system? In order to understand what works for service programs, we can look to what we know about treatment of trauma and dissociation. What works to heal on the smaller scale? Things we've covered in earlier chapters indeed apply – rational authority, dignity, healthy attachment, and communica-tion practices that support healthy and balanced nervous systems. Recall that "**Rational authority** is based on competence, and it helps the person who leans on it to grow" (Fromm, 2013 [emphasis added]). Add to this the ten elements of **dignity** (Hicks, 2011) and we have a clear outline for supporting healthy, balanced relationships within systems.

The ten elements of dignity begin with **acceptance of identity**, which means that everyone has freedom to express their authentic selves with-out negative implications. By accepting individual identities, all parties involved have equal value, and we accept similarities and differences related to race, gender, class, sexual orientation, age, physical ability, and religion, along with any other identifying factors. **Recognition** high-lights the importance of generous praise for talents, thoughtfulness, hard work, and support, and of giving credit to contributors for their ideas and experience. **Acknowledgment** involves actively listening, validating, and responding to other's concerns in a timely manner. **Inclusion** entails making others feel that they belong, while **safety** speaks to an environ-ment free of physical and emotional harm. **Fairness** means that people are treated with equality according to agreed upon boundaries and poli-cies, while **independence** allows people to feel in control of their actions, choices, and lives. Focusing on **understanding** means that what every-one thinks and feels matters, and that there are avenues to listen to and understand differing points of view.

By also offering others the **benefit of the doubt**, we begin with the premise that others have positive intentions and are doing their best; this simple act of presuming that others are trustworthy sets us up to be in the more modern circuit of the nervous system – the ventral vagal response, rather than in the ancient, unmyelinated dorsal vagal circuits. By seeing people as trustworthy we reduce the experience of being evalu-ated, which allows defensive neural networks to stand down. Finally, **accountability** ensures that proper awareness and practices are in place so that people can take responsibility for their actions and apologize, repairing the relationship if any violations of dignity do occur. Add what we know about healthy attachment, the ability to feel seen, safe, soothed, and secure (Siegel, 2010), to these principles and we have a number of solid foundations from which to build healthy systems.

Healthy systems are ones that are rooted in human dignity, rational authority, and healthy attachment, and that support the biopsychosocial health of members. A system must also have access to the appropriate resources in order to support its members. Many systems of service struggle to maintain financial stability, and this stress can impact employees, as well as those served. Defining the population served and scope of offering can help, as can positive management practices and effective company structures. Models of nonprofits that create job opportunities for those they serve facilitate experiences of empowerment for participants and help to maintain sustainable financial models. Africa Yoga Project, an organization based in Kenya that offers yoga classes and trains local yoga teachers, provides an excellent model of this type of effort.

Just as a negative school or home environment can negatively impact a young person's development, a professional culture that is unjust, emotionally toxic, chronically underfunded, or inefficient will leave employees subject to burnout and vicarious trauma. For this reason, it is important to consider the elements of health we discuss here in contrast to the environment of your place of service, be it a yoga studio, psychotherapy clinic, or independent practice. If you are in a position of power and are able to make decisions about the environment, you can continually strive to improve the health of the group and the organization, implementing policies rooted in rational authority, dignity, healthy attachment, and sustainability. If you are not in a position of power, you may choose to advocate or enlist those who carry influence to make changes that will impact the workplace. At times, you may choose to leave a toxic system to support your personal health. Should you be in a place to shape culture, and we all are in different, even if at times small, ways, consider how you can encourage healthy dynamics and practices within the systems you participate in.

Systems of Oppression

Systems of oppression are those that sideline the voices of people based on race, religion, ethnicity, gender, age, country of origin, language spoken, physical abilities, and other identifying details. They lack rational authority, and often involve insults to dignity. Many have roots in human rights injustices and outright exploitation. At the time of this writing, many systems of oppression are coming to light and receiving attention via the #metoo movement, Black Lives Matter, March for Our Lives, and Keep Families Together efforts. In each of these examples those who have experienced oppression or harm based on gender, race, age, or legal status, protest along with allies in efforts to create change in systems. Culture, at any level of the ecological systems model, can promote inclusion or separation. Diversity and inclusion are based on love and amplify our capacity to connect to healing states in the nervous system. By contrast, separation and oppression enable positions based on hate like homophobia, transphobia, or ableism, all of which invoke fear, and thus elicit the threat, or dorsal vagal, response. In order for our nervous systems to have the opportunity to heal, we must be aware of and address these levels of oppression and their relationship to trauma.

Recall that the simple act of being evaluated can incite an experience of threat in the nervous system. Step into the shoes of a young African American male, for the moment, and consider the messages he has received over the past 18 years in relationship to law enforcement. Do you think he feels safe or fearful when a police officer approaches? Most anyone approached by these types of authority figures will feel the threat of evaluation followed by a quick analysis of behavior along with thoughts like "Am I doing everything right? I don't want to get in trouble." Add to this stress that comes with the reality many youth have learned through observation, "Even if I am doing everything right, this officer may still hurt or kill me." This level of fear brings enormous threat and stress to the nervous system. The realities of racism and oppression contribute to this individual experience, again taking the nervous system away from states of healing and re-igniting systems of stress and trauma. In order to fully recover from the impact of trauma as a society, we need to look at the many levels of oppression and continuously work to provide equal safety for all people.

Systemic Challenges in Healthcare

Often, healthcare systems do not identify clients who are experiencing complex PTSD, and thus do not offer appropriate solutions that meet their needs. While each country has its own models of healthcare, colleagues describe this challenge occurring across a number of countries and regions. When we understand deeper relational needs in the wake of trauma, we can move towards an integrated, collaborative, and consistent model, providing what was not there for many people with complex PTSD: community, and a supportive, healthy family feel. For those with the most severe symptoms, it can be difficult to find affordable care. Unfortunately, many hospitals can create experiences in which survivors feel misunderstood and experience circumstances that are re-traumatizing, rather than soothing and supportive.

For this reason, it is important to continue to advocate for access to and continuity of care, and to provide wrap around services whenever possible. This helps to build an empowered system, one that models health so that the participant – be they a teen in juvenile hall or an adult in an inpatient program – can recognize what health feels like, and, hopefully, find it again in their life beyond treatment. The presence of dysfunction can contribute to feeling overwhelmed, and it can feel, in trying times, like the only option is to collapse into apathy. This is how dysfunctional systems gain power, and persist.

Vicarious Trauma, Ecological Systems, and Self-Care

As trauma-informed care has become more popular among mental health professionals, so has awareness of **vicarious trauma**. Also referred to as burnout, compassion fatigue, or secondary trauma, this occurs when a professional is exposed to the details of trauma through the workplace, and begins to experience symptoms of post-traumatic stress themselves. This experience is so prevalent that the DSM-V now includes professionals exposed to details of trauma within the diagnosis for PTSD. It's easy to understand how experiencing trauma on the job carries weight – for example, if a counselor was at a client's school at the time of a drive-by shooting. This is, in fact, a direct experience of trauma. Vicarious trauma occurs when the clinician is not necessarily there for the traumatic event, but absorbs the impact through contact with institutions, groups, and individuals following the trauma. It can be difficult to measure these impacts as they are indirect, but they are real nonetheless, and come with symptoms that mirror those outlined in connection with PTSD, complex trauma, and developmental trauma.

In order to support personal self-care, we can look to Bronfenbrenner's model and optimize to the best of our ability at each level. While we cannot control the families we are born into, we do have choice over what we take part in, perpetuate, and create in our own circles of family, be they biological or otherwise. At this level, we bring positive intention to the **mesosystem**. How can you bring a positive culture into your family, school, yoga studio or workplace? At the level of the **exosystem,** we may be able to facilitate healthy communication between elements of the mesosystem. Whether it's collaboration between training at a yoga school and a clinic, or family and religious center, when we work to promote collaboration and complementary relationships, we reduce stress on the person at the center of these systems.

At the level of the **macrosystem**, consider the many cultures you are, or have been, immersed in. Culture can carry resilience factors, and can perpetuate cycles of violence through belief or tradition. This is where cultivating self-reflection, and nurturing the "baby," or resilience factors, while washing away the "bathwater," or imprints of violence, serves future generations. Through this practice of awareness, discernment, and choice, we can carry forward supports and reduce the cultural norms that make it difficult to recover from post-traumatic stress. We can then turn to the **chronosystem**, and consider how our involvement with circumstances and social movements of the moment might feed or drain our energy. Given the times you are living in, what do you need to do to care for yourself? Does it support your well-being to be more or less involved, and what is the most effective way for you to invest your energy? Consider your media exposure and sources, as well as groups you connect with that are involved with social movements. Even technological evolution has its role to play; at this level, we can reflect on how our relationship with technology impacts our mental and emotional health.

Personal Self-Care

Typical conversations surrounding self-care speak to the individual level: what can you do to take care of yourself? Massages, creative hobbies, time with friends or in nature are common themes. For you, yoga and self-reflection are likely part of your self-care routine at this level. In addition to these peaceful and nourishing forms of self-care, we have the more difficult aspects of self-care, which include things like setting limits, saying no, making a difficult decision, having a challenging conversation, or relieving someone of a personal or professional role. There are count-less examples of self-care, I encourage you to, at the individual level, identify at least one in each of the following categories:

- **Physical:** Exercise, sports, dance, movement practices, rest, stillness, and any physical supports that facilitate comfort, which can manifest as a good mattress, a clean comfortable home, nourishing foods, or a water bottle you carry around to keep hydrated.
- **Mental:** Meditation, positive thoughts, intellectual stimulation, reading, mantra, or time to sort through thoughts and mentally organize. A calendar, a good book, an engaging learning experience, or blank space for the mind to drift are all examples of what might feed your mind.
- **Emotional:** Anything that supports you in connecting with positive emotions like humor, joy, hope, or awe, or helps you to feel difficult emotions like anger, sadness, grief, or regret, can facilitate emotional well-being. Perhaps it's therapy, a good cry in the shower, or explor-ing the world through a new activity.
- **Social:** Family, friends, clubs, groups, therapy, staff or colleagues, or any other people or pets that offer a sense of support can fit here. Since loved ones often offer a sense of emotional comfort, these may overlap with things you identified as emotional supports.
- **Creative:** Art, movement, dance, painting, collaging, ceramics, building things with your hands, songwriting, singing, poetry, writ-ing, drawing, coloring books, gardening, or anything that allows you to create in the way that serves you best. It need not be "artsy" to be creative.
- **Challenging:** What is difficult for you to do but makes you feel much better when you can do it? Setting a limit, establishing

boundaries, leaving a toxic relationship, or saying no when you need to. Consider a challenging practice that will bring relief in its aftermath.

- **Energetic:** Acupuncture, shiatsu, tai chi, yoga, and other practices incorporate awareness of the energy body and seek to bring balance and healthy flow to the body's energies. Which of these serves you, and how can you incorporate awareness of energy into your self-care?

- **Spiritual:** prayer, religious ceremony, ritual, time in nature, time in community or *sangha*, images or *mantra* related to Goddesses or Gods, scripture, spiritual songs, poems or music. Connecting with a higher power, deeper meaning, or transcendental experience are all avenues to connect with spiritual self-care.

Note that each of these relates to our neurological function and can have an impact on the nervous system. When considering the impact of post-traumatic stress on your body, mind and spirit, look to these forms of self-care to determine what will be most helpful for you, moment to moment, year to year. This will help mitigate the impacts of vicarious trauma, and set you up to live in a field of health, rather than trauma.

A Field of Health

Should you feel lost along the way to creating a healthy, resilient system, workplace, or life, come back to a vision of health, in all its forms. When we see health as it already exists, and seek to cultivate it, we engage in strength-based practice, and apply the theories of resilience we've discussed here to our path forward. Remember, our brains are wired to pick up on problems and threats to our well-being, so it's easy for both an agency to become captivated by problem-solving and for an employee to become fearful that there is something they've done that will be a threat to their livelihood. It's also easy for us to become lost in preventing vicarious trauma, rather than modeling, best we can, a life that is healthy, resilient, or even joyful. If we orient to the long-term hope for ourselves, and for those we serve, and build actively towards it, we keep our attention fixed on solutions.

When you have the end goal of success in mind, it is easier to handle mistakes and mishaps because you are more willing to correct and redirect them. By weaving health into the fabric of your life, your work, and the systems you are a part of, you both model, and offer, healthy experiences to those you serve. In order to pave the way for systemic change, functions of resilience and health must outweigh systems of trauma. In addition to bolstering against the negative impacts of trauma, we can hold a vision of positive growth, and stay aligned with healthy courses of action.

***

Zoe and I worked together for a little over two years, and she was able to make choices that supported both her personal self-care, and the development of her workplace as a system. We began by identifying her internal resources, which included a deep sense of care and social justice, along with a feeling of purpose in her work. She then identified a few key boundaries that were important to set with colleagues, and made a point of giving people positive feedback when they behaved in ways that were supportive of her experience at work. She also identified family members and friends who lift her up and leave her feeling full of energy, and invested more time with them during her time outside of work. Finally, she applied for a role within the company that gave her more agency over decisions and policies, and, after multiple interviews, was awarded the position. From this position, she was able to bring in trainers that helped to shift the culture, and connected with colleagues in related fields who were doing similar work. By prioritizing her personal health and looking for ways she could shift the ecological systems that impacted her life, her experience of burnout decreased, and was replaced with more feelings of empowerment. As she gained power to impact the system of her workplace, she felt more gratified and less overwhelmed, and expressed feeling that she was part of the solution, instead of engulfed in the problem. This reduced her symptoms of fatigue and hopelessness. Three years after we terminated our work together, she sent me an update and shared that three youth who had graduated from her program had moved into social justice advocacy roles, and that this gave her a boost of validation; it made her feel that her efforts over the years made a lasting positive impact. She shared that this helped her to maintain a hopeful outlook, not only on her personal and professional future, but on the progress she was seeing slowly, but surely, take place in the systems at hand.

Reflection Questions

1 Using Bronfenbrenner's model, label the current systems surrounding those you serve. What supports or external resources become apparent?
2 Which of the elements of dignity are present in your workplace? Which are not?
3 Name your three top self-care practices in each category. Identify what is non-negotiable in order for your work to be sustainable.

Additional resources available at http://howwecanheal.com/y4tr

References

Bronfenbrenner, U. (1979). *The ecology of human development.* Cambridge, MA: Harvard University Press.

Fromm, E. (2013). *To have or to be?* London: A&C Black.

Hicks, D. (2011). *Dignity: The essential role it plays in resolving conflict.* New York: Yale University Press.

Krishnamurti, J. (1975). *Freedom from the known.* As quoted in Mark Vonnegut, *The Eden express: A personal account of schizophrenia* (p. 208). New York: Book Digest.

Siegel, D. J. (2010). *The mindful therapist: A clinician's guide to mindsight and neural integration.* New York: Norton.

11 Cultivating Joy

Surely joy is the condition of life.
– Henry David Thoreau

"Why is everything about safety??" Joy exclaimed, "I want to be happy, healthy, thriving, and JOYful!!" We laughed at her intentional pun. While Joy still felt impacted by the assault that led her to work with me 10 months prior to this conversation, she wanted to go beyond focusing on safe and comfortable resources. "I want to *thrive.*" She began to say, at least once a session. So, we began to explore the meaning and possibilities of joy, using EMDR resourcing and attuning her attention to moments of fulfillment, joy, and play in her life between sessions. For an additional 6 months, we continued to work through upsetting triggers, and build resources of safety and comfort, but we did not stop there. As her embodied experience of safety grew, she became increasingly curious about how she could have more fun in her life. After all, what do mammals do when they do feel safe, and there is no cause for threat systems to activate. They play! Joy enjoyed homework assignments like building sand castles, expressing gratitude to loved ones, and pursuing meaning through her work. She beamed each time she shared a moment of joy with me, and even began to recall memories of playfulness and joy she experienced as a child. As we built on the positive resources of curiosity, exploration, play, purpose, and joy, her posture and expressions slowly changed. One day, after a session full of both intensity and these positive resources, she turned back before leaving to say, "I feel *lighter.*" I nodded, observing the changes in her face, body, and voice. "Something is shifting," I replied, and she nodded, beaming, and left.

***

Themes of positive psychology are present throughout this book, and in this approach to bringing yoga and trauma recovery together. This chapter serves to reframe safety, a common goal in trauma recovery and TIY, as a necessary step along the way to freedom of expression and joyful living, rather than the end goal of recovery. Contrary to popular opinion, a joyful person is not one without any troubles, but one who has cultivated a wide Window of Tolerance and the capacity to feel the full range of emotion. Often, working through our own trauma history liberates us to connect with ourselves and others in a new way, and to appreciate the wonders of life. Simple joys can come from pleasurable experiences or moments of happiness, but they can also come from cultivating play, curiosity, exploration, and awe. We'll explore each of these themes in this chapter, and end with suggestions of how to cultivate habits that contribute to happiness and joy.

Why Play?

Play contributes to proper brain development, and is an essential aspect of learning and development (Shonkoff & Phillips, 2000). It happens across cultures and throughout child development, but its presence often becomes scant in adult life. Often culture teaches adults to dismiss play as childish or silly, when in fact play is an essential part of our brain function and development. Dr. Dan Siegel and his colleague David Rock identify play as one of seven essential daily brain functions necessary to promote healthy neurological function across the lifespan (Rock & Siegel, 2011). In addition to maintaining daily brain health, play supports healthy development early in life, and researchers contend that recent increases in child psychopathology directly relate to decreased opportunities for play during development (Gray, 2011). As Vygotsky (1978) noted, play "contains all developmental tendencies in a condensed form and is itself a major source of development."

While we tend to think of play as the opposite of study, play itself is an experience of learning. Albert Einstein is quoted as saying, "Play is the highest form of research" (source unknown). Playful learning is enjoyable, intrinsically motivated, and exists *without goal or function* aside from the satisfaction of the behavior itself: this is how it differs from classroom-based learning. Play is process-oriented and freely chosen. Like an ideal trauma-informed yoga class, play is voluntary; if there is pressure or coercion, the experience is not playful. Play is active and engaging, physically or mentally. Rather than taking away from learning or being a break from it, as we frame recess times during the school day, play builds the foundation for lifelong learning. While experts continue to expound a powerful argument for play, the actual time children spend playing continues to decrease (White, 2012).

What can we do to promote play in overworked youth and deprived adults? Luckily, play comes in many forms, and can be **structured** through games and activities or **unstructured** and completely freeform (think back to our discussion of top-down and bottom-up processing). **Social play** involves interacting with other adults, children, or even pets. As we interact with others, play develops within the connection and gives us the experience of attuning to and responding to others. Social play can be structured, as in a game of hide and seek, or spontaneous and self-directed. **Physical play** involves movement of the body, take for example a game of twister, or siblings prancing around the living room for no particular reason. **Mental play** involves memory, thinking or planning. Card games are excellent examples of mental play – be it Solitaire alone or a round of Go Fish in a group. Mental play can also be freeform, as when children create a song or a new language without preconceived structure. A non-betting group poker game is an example of structured, social, mental play. When external rewards become involved in the form of bets, goals or rewards, the purpose of play shifts from experience to result, making it less playful. **Imaginative play** involves creating new identities, roles, dynamics, and worlds in which the player can explore different ways of being. While some adults discourage children from engaging in fantasy, it can be an excellent way to practice creativity, and to engage with deeper layers of consciousness.

Looking back to Dr. Stephen Porges' description of the ventral vagal system and its role in social contact and experiencing pleasure, we see how a sense of safety, both physical and emotional, precedes the capacity for play. By engaging the ventral vagal system, we allow physiological defenses to disengage so that we can explore physically, mentally, and socially. When the ventral vagal system is dominant we can access the imagination for the purpose of exploration and play, rather than for protection against danger. These recent developments in our understanding of human physiology support the necessity for safety, and give us a sense of what is possible once we do feel safe.

It may be that your focus in a therapy session or TIY class remains on safety; the purpose of this chapter is not to encourage you to bypass this step. Instead, as you create safety, look for moments when students and clients feel enough comfort that they begin to explore any element of play. Iyengar yoga teacher Carrie Owerko often brings the theme of play into her teaching in creative ways. She shares:

> I began to bring play into my teaching because play is how I problem solve, create things, find joy, and it is one of the best ways I know to facilitate the learning process. Try this if you dare: get a group of adults to skip around the room for a just few minutes and see what happens. It is like magic. They cannot help but laugh and smile. Skipping is just one way. Play is infinite. That is what I love about play. The possibilities are endless.
>
> (Owerko, 2018)

Play is elective and always occurs by choice, and most of us exist within cultures that value work over play. By keeping an awareness of the essential nature of play in human development, you can provide opportunities for those you serve to experience play without fear, shame, or judgment, all of which would reactivate defensive neural networks. Your awareness of play as a possibility gives your students and clients permission to move into their own experience of growth beyond safety, when the timing is right for them.

Curiosity and Exploration

Think back now to our conversation about attachment and the importance of being seen, safe, soothed, and secure (Siegel & Bryson, 2011). When a child develops secure attachment with a caregiver, or an adult earns secure attachment through corrective experiences, the safety created by security contributes to exploration across the lifespan (Feeney & Van Vleet, 2010). Indeed, when we know we have a base of safety and comfort, it is easier to tolerate the stress of the unknown and to step into it, confident that whatever we find, we will be met with support, or a soothing presence, upon our return.

As with play, exploration can be physical, mental, or social. It may be structured, as a planned group tourism trip is, or unstructured, like a hike in the wilderness without a map. We might explore different ways of thinking about ourselves, others and the world, or even different paradigms and fields of study. Mentally, we can explore by trying on different lenses through which we view life and our experiences. Socially, we can explore connecting with others, or types of relationships. We can also explore our role in families, friendships, and the larger world.

This exploration of roles in society at large, particularly as they relate to identity and professional development, can bring up a conversation about passion and purpose, or as Joy described it, fulfillment. Some people have a strong sense of passion for a particular activity or role. Someone might say, "I've always known I was a writer," or, "I just can't get enough of playing the guitar." For these individuals, a sense of passion or purpose tends to feel accessible. For others who don't experience a strong sense of either quality, these concepts can feel grand and overwhelming. Recall that in trauma recovery, we do our best to prevent contributing to an overwhelming experience, since trauma tends to offer enough of that already. In cases when passion, purpose, or fulfillment feel too grandiose, encouraging exploration and curiosity proves to be more helpful. Author Elizabeth Gilbert writes about developing curiosity in the face of the unknown, and actively choosing curiosity over fear (Gilbert, 2016). This can apply to our response to difficult emotions, and to positive ones alike. Encouraging curiosity towards emotional experiences, interests, and life as a whole offers a way for both student and teacher, client and professional, to remain open to what comes next. From the secure base of safety, we allow those we serve to extend into curiosity, with the knowledge that safety is there to return to.

Awe

The psychological study of awe is young, and we are learning about the many benefits of the emotion. Awe is connected to feelings of wonder, reverence, and vastness. We are "in awe" in the face of things we don't understand, that are physically large, or that span across time. We may feel awe atop a mountain, standing in front of the great pyramid of Giza, or witnessing the birth of a child. Art and music can inspire these feelings, too. Experiences of awe transcend our understanding of the world, and often leave us feeling small in comparison to the vastness we perceive, but at the same time foster feelings of connection to something larger than ourselves.

As we learn about the physiology of awe and its impact on the brain, its role in trauma recovery becomes increasingly clear. Maltreatment in childhood is associated with chronic physiological markers of inflammation (Coelho et al., 2014), while recent research demonstrates that positive emotions like awe predict lower levels of inflammatory cytokines (Stellar et al., 2015). One aspect of awe that is only beginning its scientific journey is the study of goosebumps – a universal human experience that often occurs alongside the emotion of awe, and that many people experiencing during synchronistic moments. Researchers are also finding that awe increases a sense of connection to others, or a greater whole (Piff et al., 2015). Awe, indeed, contains an element of emotion similar to the yogic description of *ishvara pranidhana*, or surrender to something greater. This greater connection encourages transcendence of a smaller sense of self, and may even encourage prosocial behavior (Piff et al., 2015). With awe comes questions related to post-traumatic growth: why are we here and what will we do with this precious life? It encourages us to be curious and to explore the wonders of the world, and of ourselves.

During the healing journey, we may seek experiences of awe for the benefits to well-being that they bring, or we may bring a sense of awe to our own journey. Many clients, Joy included, report feeling awe for the natural world, including the healing capacities of the body. Joy marveled at ancient redwoods, mountain peaks, wide meadows and vistas, and the patterning and color of a single wildflower. She also appreciated her own biology and its ability to heal, and its attempts to keep her alive in the face of trauma. Another client named Ryan, who had endured ritual abuse as a child, shared feeling a sense of awe at his own capacity to endure and continue living. Joseph, a young yoga student in a therapeutic school, expressed awe at the capacity of his own body to learn to balance in tree pose. "It's only been a few weeks, but I'm getting better!" He pronounced with pride. "It's so cool to see things change; it makes me wonder what else is possible."

Consider how experiences of awe arise for you, personally and professionally, and take note of your clients' and students' expressions of awe. If you're in a role to offer experiences that foster these feelings, consider how they may benefit those you serve. Something as simple as watching a plant or a class pet growing, or looking out at the sunset can have a deep positive impact if it invokes the wonder of awe.

Happiness

The pursuit of happiness is a foundational element of the US Constitution, and a central theme for many in trauma recovery. Why is happiness a worthy pursuit? In *The How of Happiness* Dr. Sonja Lyubomirsky defines happiness as "the experience of joy, contentment, or positive well-being, combined with a sense that one's life is good, meaningful, and worthwhile" (Lyubomirsky, 2008). She notes that beyond feeling good, happier people tend to exhibit more sociable behaviors, be more cooperative, and are more likely to have long-term relationships. They also demonstrate more flexible and creative thinking, have stronger immune systems, and are physically healthier. Research even indicates that happy people live longer, and that by becoming happier, we increase our experiences of joy, love, contentment, and awe (Lyubomirsky, 2008). When we cultivate happiness, we benefit not only ourselves, we also impact our families, friends, partners, and communities at large.

If happiness is associated with so many of these positive life experiences, what can we do to cultivate it? You may notice that many of the following suggestions relate to our discussion of resilience; they also happen to be practices that researchers themselves have found helpful in their own lives (Newman, 2018). They fall into physical, mental, and social categories. One of the physical practices that consistently demonstrates improvements in mood is exercise. Moving the body and circulating blood, oxygen, and energy stimulates the release of endorphins, which can have a positive impact on mood and feelings of well-being (Thorén et al., 1990). For those with limited physical mobility, humor is another avenue towards positive physiological states. Even in the absence of jokes and punchlines, laughter yoga provides a bottom-up practice that studies show is at least as impactful as exercise on happiness levels (Shahidi et al., 2011). Consider how you might incorporate healthy movement or more opportunities for laughter into your life.

A popular mental practice for cultivating happiness is gratitude. It is said that "what you appreciate appreciates," and while researchers have not measured external life changes, they have confirmed that practicing gratitude improves feelings of well-being (Wood, Froh, & Geraghty, 2010). Training your mind to notice what goes well during the day, or counting the larger blessings you see in your own life, increases subjective well-being (Emmons & McCullough, 2003). You can use lists, smartphone reminders, creative writing, letters to loved ones, and countless other approaches to identify and, if you choose, share your experience of gratitude with others.

Mindfulness practices are a popular way to increase feelings of well-being and happiness, and they come in many forms. Physical practices like yoga and tai chi are often described as moving meditations, and we can learn to eat, communicate, and even wash the dishes with mindfulness. A key aspect of mindfulness is the ability to be with what is happening in the present moment. Some research indicates that self-compassion is an essential component in the relationship between mindfulness and happiness; as we learn to accept the fluctuations of the mind and return to focus without self-chastising, we become more compassionate with ourselves (Hollis-Walker & Colosimo, 2011). Accepting mind wandering and attention to problems as biological truths and choosing to cultivate positive, optimistic thinking is an excellent practice of *pratipaksha bhavana*, exploring the opposite. Loving kindness, or *metta* meditations take this to another level, allowing us to focus on feelings of love and warmth towards others, and towards ourselves. Consider how you can integrate mindfulness practices that support happiness and well-being into your teaching and life, noting what is challenging for your students and beginning with a practice that allows them to successfully integrate these habits of mind into their current way of being.

Social connections come in many flavors, and practices that support higher levels of happiness include developing awareness of high-quality connections (Stephens et al., 2011). High-quality connections are subjective – if an interaction has value and meaning to you, or stands out in your experience, it may be a high-quality connection. These connections can occur with loved ones or strangers, and can last seconds or be ongoing. To increase the positive emotions related to these exchanges, notice the person, what brings the feeling of quality, and any positive associations or body sensations that arise as you connect. Savoring the experience afterwards, and taking mental note of each exchange, helps attune your mind to these positive experiences. Social relationships are significant correlates and predictors of happiness in children, so consider how cultivating and recognizing quality social connections may positively impact the developmental needs of those you serve (Holder & Coleman, 2009).

We have covered a range of positive emotional experiences in this chapter; each are opportunities to bring feelings of lightness and joy into your life and work. Joy itself is a lesser-studied emotional experience, but I find it connotes something deep and lasting that happiness does not. Joy may be a mixture of happiness, play, curiosity, and awe, or it may have entirely its own quality in your experience. Perhaps the joy Thoreau referred to in his essay "Natural history of Massachusetts" (Thoreau, 1842) connects to the ancient wisdom of the *anadamayakosha*, or bliss body, lying at the center of our energetic bodies. Perhaps it is something we can all access, if we seek to connect with it. In the years before my grandfather passed away, he shared his experience of joy early in life, when he decided to become a minister. As a young man attending a church service, he experienced a moment of overwhelming love and joy – the Holy Spirit itself – and this experience moved him to dedicating his life to sharing these emotions with others, through ministry. What brings you joy in your work? How can you cultivate this and share it with those you serve, in a way that feels relevant to their life and development? By simply holding the opportunity for joy, you create space for those you serve to feel something other than the complexities of emotion and experience that arise as a result of traumatic experiences. While negative emotions narrow our focus to help us respond effectively to threat or challenge, positive emotions broaden our outlook and allow us to build connections that will enhance our future success (Fredrickson, 2009). In your search to create safety for students and clients, do not overlook their capacities for joy.

***

After months of mapping out what a joyful, meaningful life looks like, Joy was ready to end therapy. "You know," she shared "I feel like this experience has helped me become more alive. I appreciate things about my life, and myself, that I never even noticed before." She shared how our focus on cultivating joy impacted her parenting style, and brought opportunities for her to play with her 8-year-old daughter in a new way. "I don't want anyone to have the power to take the fun out of my life, or my family's life," she shared, "How will my daughter grow up if I walk around afraid all the time?" While the resources of safety we identified early in treatment remained fundamental, the experiences of joy she cultivated in her life made a lasting positive impact. "I'm happy that I've learned to live my life well – even if I can't prevent bad things from happening, or bad people from existing. I *can* prevent them from stealing my joy."

Reflection Questions

1   How might you bring play into your work?
2   What inspires a feeling of awe within you?
3   Describe three things you are genuinely grateful for in this moment.
4   What are you curious about in your professional or personal life?

Additional resources available at http://howwecanheal.com/y4tr

References

Coelho, R., Viola, T. W., Walss-Bass, C., Brietzke, E., & Grassi-Oliveira, R. (2014). Childhood maltreatment and inflammatory markers: A systematic review. *Acta Psychiatrica Scandinavica, 129*(3), 180–192.

Emmons, R. A., & McCullough, M. E. (2003). Counting blessings versus burdens: An experimental investigation of gratitude and subjective well-being in daily life. *Journal of Personality and Social Psychology, 84*(2), 377.

Feeney, B. C., & Van Vleet, M. (2010). Growing through attachment: The interplay of attachment and exploration in adulthood. *Journal of Social and Personal Relationships, 27*(2), 226–234.

Fredrickson, B. (2009). *Positivity.* New York: Harmony.

Gilbert, E. (2016). *Big magic: Creative living beyond fear.* Penguin.

Gray, P. (2011). The decline of play and the rise of psychopathology in children and adolescents. *American Journal of Play, 3*(4), 443–463.

Holder, M. D., & Coleman, B. (2009). The contribution of social relationships to children's happiness. *Journal of Happiness Studies, 10*(3), 329–349.

Hollis-Walker, L., & Colosimo, K. (2011). Mindfulness, self-compassion, and happiness in non-meditators: A theoretical and empirical examination. *Personality and Individual Differences, 50*(2), 222–227.

Lyubomirsky, S. (2008). *The how of happiness: A scientific approach to getting the life you want.* New York: Penguin.

Newman, K. (2018). *Nine scientists share their favorite happiness practices.* Retrieved from: https://greatergood.berkeley.edu/article/item/nine_scientists_share_their_favorite_happiness_practices.

Owerko, C. personal communication, April 20, 2018.

Piff, P. K., Dietze, P., Feinberg, M., Stancato, D. M., & Keltner, D. (2015). Awe, the small self, and prosocial behavior. *Journal of Personality and Social Psychology, 108*(6), 883.

Porges, S. W. (2011). The Norton series on interpersonal neurobiology. The polyvagal theory: Neurophysiological foundations of emotions, attachment, communication, and self-regulation. New York: Norton.

Rock D. & Siegel, D. (2011) *The healthy mind platter.* Retrieved from: www.drdansiegel.com/resources/healthy_mind_platter/.

Shahidi, M., Mojtahed, A., Modabbernia, A., Mojtahed, M., Shafiabady, A., Delavar, A., & Honari, H. (2011). Laughter yoga versus group exercise program in elderly depressed women: A randomized controlled trial. *International Journal of Geriatric Psychiatry, 26*(3), 322–327.

Shonkoff, J. P., Phillips, D. A., & National Research Council. (2000). The developing brain, in *From neurons to neighborhoods: The science of early childhood development* (Ch. 8). National Research Council and Institute on Medicine. Washington, DC: National Academy Press.

Siegel, D. J., & Bryson, T. P. (2011). *The whole-brain child: 12 revolutionary strategies to nurture your child's developing mind.* New York: Random House Digital.

Stellar, J. E., John-Henderson, N., Anderson, C. L., Gordon, A. M., McNeil, G. D., & Keltner, D. (2015). Positive affect and markers of inflammation: Discrete positive emotions predict lower levels of inflammatory cytokines. *Emotion, 15*(2), 129.

Stephens, J. P., Heaphy, E., & Dutton, J. E. (2011). High quality connections. *The Oxford handbook of positive organizational scholarship*, 385–399. Oxford: Oxford University Press.

Thoreau, H. D. (1842). Natural history of Massachusetts. *Dial*, *3*(1), 19–40.

Thorén, P., Floras, J. S., Hoffmann, P., & Seals, D. R. (1990). Endorphins and exercise: Physiological mechanisms and clinical implications. *Medicine and Science in Sports and Exercise*, *22*(4), 417–428.

Vygotsky, L. S. (1978). *Mind in society*. Cambridge, MA: Harvard University Press.

White, R. E. (2012). *The power of play: A research summary on play and learning*. Rochester, MN: Minnesota Children's Museum.

Wood, A. M., Froh, J. J., & Geraghty, A. W. (2010). Gratitude and well-being: A review and theoretical integration. *Clinical Psychology Review*, *30*(7), 890–905.

12 Closing Thoughts and Recommendations

Now this is not the end. It is not even the beginning of the end.
But it is, perhaps, the end of the beginning.
                                                    – Winston Churchill, 1942

I stood tall, my parents at my side, in my cap and gown with graduation paraphernalia surrounding me. Two hundred and seventy-two units later – in classic overachiever fashion – my graduation day had finally arrived. We gathered in front of the steps of Ackerman Union, home of the student store and a common connection, eating, shopping, and passing point for any UCLA student. Ash, a fellow Communication Studies graduate, brought her family over to mingle with mine while she and I basked in the glow of our hour of celebration. What a long road it had been! Her parents joined our conversation and proceeded to ask The Question: "So, what are you going to do with your degree?"

Multiple emotions arose instantly: I felt sheepish, unsure, hopeful, and falsely confident. After a pause and quick mental note of these emotions, I answered honestly, "I could tell you now, but that won't be what happens. Why don't you check back with me in 10 years and I'll let you know how things go?" The mother smiled, and the father nodded, and they proceeded to share bits of their own stories. "That sounds good – after all, I studied accounting," the father chuckled, glancing over at Ash. "Then I met your mother and moved clear across the country. Who would have guessed I'd go into landscaping? My degree at least helps me keep up with the books!" Her mother nodded and shared:

"You know, for the longest time I wanted to be an architect, but I studied business because I thought it would be more secure. It was boring, and after a few years I ended up in graduate school studying education. I never thought I'd love teaching so much."

I decided, at that moment, to try and get comfortable with not knowing the outcome of my life, and instead, to breathe into the unknown, and keep stepping forward, until it became the known.

***

This book is part of a process and an evolution of a field. In it, I have brought together theories and philosophies of yoga and trauma recovery to provide an integrated foundation from which you can make choices about how you want to teach, and how you can develop in your personal and professional life. While I would love to say this book is comprehensive, there are many adjuncts, complexities, and tangents that I have chosen to omit. The blessing of a field that encompasses physical, mental, emotional, energetic, spiritual, and mystical is that it is wide in scope; the limitation being that to do anything well, we must dive deeply into it. I encourage you, as you move forward, to choose the aspects of this work that carry the most significance and interest for you, and to immerse yourself in the theory and research as you invest in experiences, which teach beyond the capacity of books or lectures.

In order to apply the principles of yoga practice to trauma recovery, it is essential that you practice, personally. You can read all the books and do all the research but without a felt sense of how the practice of yoga impacts you, your teaching will be hollow and the power of your presence as you speak to the material will dwindle. I have learned this firsthand, the times I have chosen "productivity" over practice, or been swept away by the excitement of travel and teaching to the point where my own practice needs to fit in the cracks. We can easily reach a point where things feel repetitive and boring. It is part of the process to plateau. Continue your practice, even if in a different way, and be curious about what comes next. In these moments, practice, as I did my college graduation day, not knowing what will come next.

As hopefully this book has successfully emphasized, *how* your practice looks, and what it contains, is up to you and your trusted teachers. It may be a five-minute meditative seat, focused concentration on a meaningful mantra, or a round of sun salutations in the morning. *Your yoga practice does not have to be* asana. If you do practice *asana*, the shapes you take with your body will likely need to change in order to adapt to your body as it weaves in and out of life experiences, relationships, and phases of life. I encourage you, as this burgeoning field continues to evolve, to invite a sense of play to your own unfolding. Not only does this keep you grounded in the far opposite of trauma, but it allows for creativity and insight to blossom in unexamined places. This new field is ripe for growth, and by keeping your own energy light, curious, and open, you may discover insights and nuances that contribute something valuable to the development of the field. As my friend and colleague Mel Salvatore-August often says in her classes "hold it lightly."

While holding your work with a light and open mind, I also encourage you to hold what you know with steadiness and confidence. This work has strong theoretical foundations, and continues to gain support from research and the contributions of senior teachers. This is a field in which we never know all the answers, but continue to discover them, piece by piece, person by person. The truths we find can seem antithetical, submerged in their own context and impossible to replicate, and yet, they are real. Stand grounded and supported by the depth of these two fields, even when you don't know how they will evolve, or what will arise with the next student or class.

A Brief Review

Think back over what you have learned throughout the course of this book. We began with a focus on **foundations**. We rooted this approach in mental *health* and cultivated an understanding of ACEs and their relationship to both trauma and resilience. We then moved on to define what exactly we mean by trauma, enough to know what the problems are and to acknowledge the many ways that trauma can manifest. From there, we took a close look at theories of the nervous system, tracking how they apply to trauma and recovery and how principles of somatic psychotherapy offer opportunities for healing. We then moved into exploring **applications** of trauma theory, looking at the connections between it and yoga philosophy, and exploring how yoga postures and sequences can respond to the needs of the nervous system and the mind in the wake of trauma. The following chapters outlined the centrality of trust and relationship, and the many ways we can be responsive to trauma in group classes and individual sessions. After diving into trauma-informed practices, we moved into a discussion of sustainability and **growth**. We defined resilience and identified ways to develop it in ourselves, as well as in students and clients. Our discussion of self-care acknowledged the impact of systems on our individual well-being, and discussed ways we can not only nurture ourselves privately, but interact with systems in a protective and generative manner. We wrapped the discussion of growth by noting the value of moving beyond safety, incorporating opportunities for play, curiosity, exploration, awe, and joy when the timing is right.

The field of trauma-informed yoga, of yoga and trauma recovery work paired together, is established. It exists and is growing – rapidly, from what I see. The question remains: how do you choose to relate to this work? Is it central or peripheral to your life? How much is it personal, and to what degree is it a professional endeavor for you? Most of us are survivors of trauma, in some capacity. If you continue to grow into this work professionally, I encourage you not to lose sight of your personal experiences and your own journey of healing. As each of us cultivates consciousness and self-awareness, we become better able to lift up those around us.

Recommendations for Future Research

If you are a student, or are connected with a research lab or university, consider how your studies may contribute to the growth of this field. We have the collective knowledge of generations regarding the energetic impacts of yoga postures, yet we could use more research on the impact of specific postures. Perhaps you would like to measure the physiological changes that happen with inversions, forward folds, backbends, or specific sequences. Or perhaps you can find a way to test and differentiate the state of the nervous system and its fluctuations. By offering and recording responses to yoga postures targeted to improve symptoms, we can deepen our academic knowledge and compare this to what yogis have passed down in the form of knowledge gained through teaching and practice.

Here is a dream study of mine, in case you feel inclined to pursue it: recruit participants in therapy for developmental trauma (or PTSD related to early childhood experiences, at the very least). Measure their PTSD symptoms, via Clinician-Administered PTSD Scale for DSM-5 (CAPS-5) or another validated instrument. Collect a client report and treating therapist observation, and based on this report divide the group into subgroups based on symptoms: one group for primarily hyper-arousal symptoms, another for primarily hypo-arousal symptoms, another for participants experiencing both (a freeze response or *rajasic* depression). Then subdivide each nervous system category group into three more groups: control (no yoga), a group exposed to a simple, standardized yoga practice, and a group practicing sequences tailored to balance the nervous system. Collect as much information as possible: physiological data, participant report, therapist observation, further or repeated CAPS or other inventories, and anything else your research team deems relevant. With adequate funding, you could even use fMRI data to observe the impacts of different types of postures and sequences on neurological states and patterns. Observe and analyze the data and (much time, energy, and effort later) voila! You've completed my dream research experiment.

By continuing to gather information and conduct quality research in these areas, we begin the path towards validating protocols that could then integrate seamlessly into hospitals, psychiatric treatment centers, and in programs supporting those confronted with different manifestations of trauma. If you are interested in designing a research study, I invite you to connect with me via the website in the resource link below; and if you complete the study outlined above, please do reach out to share your findings!

Thank You

If you've come this far in the book, I am willing to bet that yoga, trauma recovery, resilience, and healing play a significant role in your life.

You have invested time and energy into learning, whether through study, research, personal practice, teaching, or a combination of these. I'd like to acknowledge your efforts here, as they all too often go unnoticed. Thank you. Thank you for showing up for yourself, and for taking this journey with me. I wholeheartedly encourage you to share what you know with those it may benefit; for we cannot wait until we know everything before we extend support to those in need. How you can use your experience and the information in this book to serve yourself and others?

Though we've focused on theory and philosophies here, as teachers and therapists we quickly recognize how the practice of healing is an art. In this work, we weave together information, practice-based insights, intuition and responsiveness in relationship, and more, to create something unique and irreplicable. Accepting the artistic nature of this work does not diminish it, in fact it lends to its power. As Brené Brown shares in her book, *Braving the Wilderness* "Art has the power to render sorrow beautiful, make loneliness a shared experience, and transform despair into hope" (Brown, 2017). Your healing artwork is powerful.

There is immeasurable heartbreak in this world. Recognizing our humanity, vulnerability, resilience, and strength is necessary for our collective healing. I have found this to be true: the more we hide the pain, the more we hide the light of love. I've heard the rhetoric that love will "win," but perhaps there was never a war, and such language only serves to fuel the divide. I believe that love exists, and that it manifests as the still small voice within each of us, and would like to close by sharing this belief with you. Love cannot be broken, but it can be drowned out by loud noise. It is always there, whether in the background or foreground, so it is not a matter of chasing it, or making it happen. Yoga and meditative practices allow us to be quiet enough connect with the love that is already there: ever-present, ever-comforting. Call it by any name you prefer. It is with you now, and, while sometimes it takes some digging and practice, it will respond when you seek to connect with it.

***

We can plan and dream, but we never fully know where the future will take us, and how we, and the world, will evolve in our lifetime. Not even the most intuitive of my friends could have predicted that my life would unfold to bring these two passions so closely together, or that a field surrounding yoga and trauma recovery would be born. Yet within a decade, I am able to respond to Ash's dad's question: I teach mental health practitioners and yoga teachers to integrate trauma theory and yoga practices, in a way that promotes resilience, and facilitates healing. As Joseph Campbell is often quoted to have said, "If you can see your path laid out in front of you step by step, you know it's not your path. Your own path you make with every step you take. That's why it's your path" (source unknown).

I often wish I could go back, and whisper the details of the deeply complex and personal career to my younger self. "Yoga and Trauma Recovery? Cool!" That's what my 22-year-old self would have said. Many students echo the sentiment today, and wish to pursue similar work. I am eager to see how the field continues to evolve, and what these students' journeys bring to the world in coming decades.

In a memorable moment, 10 years after Ash's dad posed the question dreaded by so many graduates, I found myself before the steps of Ackerman Union, ready to climb to the third floor to attend an Interpersonal Neurobiology Conference. The conference, hosted annually by Dr. Dan Siegel, whom we've referenced throughout this book, hosts hundreds of clinicians, yogis, mindfulness fanatics, and spiritual enthusiasts. In it, presenters combine cutting-edge research in neuroscience with theories of human development, psychology, and resilience, and exchange ideas about how the body, mind, and spirit all play a role in healing. As I climbed the stairs, I wished Ash and her parents could join me in that moment, so that we could look into the rearview mirror together and marvel at how the dots had connected.

Often, life leads us down a path, and before we know it, we've arrived somewhere we didn't even know was a destination. From there, we can begin again, and continue to explore and learn. I hope that this book, and others like it, support you on your unique journey, and help you to skillfully integrate yoga and trauma recovery into your personal journey and professional practice. I wish you well in your continued efforts to learn, reflect, and cultivate healing. *Namaste.*

Reflection Questions

1   What is next for you? How do you see your work connecting to, or evolving the field of yoga and trauma recovery?
2   How you can use our experience and the information in this book to serve yourself and others?

Additional resources available at http://howwecanheal.com/y4tr

References

Brown, B. (2017). *Braving the wilderness: The quest for true belonging and the courage to stand alone.* New York: Random House.
Churchill, W. ([1942] 1943). *The end of the beginning: War speeches by Winston S. Churchill*, Volume 3. Compiled by Charles Eade. Boston, MA: Little Brown.

Glossary

Active listening   the practice of listening without interruption while paying attention to the speaker and considering their experience.

Adverse childhood experiences (ACEs)   stressful or traumatic events that occur during childhood, including abuse and neglect.

Afferent neurons   neurons that relay messages from the body back to the CNS.

Alexithymia   difficulty identifying and describing emotional experiences.

Allostatic load   the accumulation of stress as a result of being exposed repeatedly to difficult experiences without adequate time for regeneration and repair.

American Psychological Association (APA)   professional organization of psychologists in the United States; members include scientists, educators, clinicians, consultants, and students.

Asana   the word translates to "seat" and is now used to refer to the many physical postures of yoga.

Ashtanga   the "eight limbs" of yoga that include: *Yama, Niyama, Asana, Pranayama, Pratyahara, Dharana, Dhyana, Samadhi.* Also refers to the physical practices taught by Pattabhi Jois.

Attachment   a deep and enduring emotional bond that connects one person to another across time and space.

Attachment-focused   therapies that seek to strengthen the relationship between the youth and caregiver, or that reflect on the connection styles of the client, often using the therapeutic relationship as a way to observe patterns and cultivate earned security.

Attachment trauma   a significant disconnect with a primary caregiver, most often caused by loss, incarceration, deportation, abuse, neglect, or emotional unavailability on the part of the caretaker.

Autonomic nervous system (ANS)   a control system regulated largely by the hypothalamus, the ANS acts primarily unconsciously and regulates bodily functions such as the heart rate, digestion, respiratory rate, pupillary response, urination, and arousal.

Betrayal trauma   occurs when the people or institutions on which a person depends for survival significantly violate that person's trust or well-being. Childhood physical, emotional, or sexual abuse perpetrated by a caregiver are examples of betrayal trauma.

Bottom-up processing   facilitated by attention to the body, bottom-up processing creates space for the body's tension, impulses, and memories to be experienced and released.

Center for Disease Control and Prevention (CDC)   a federal agency that conducts and supports health promotion, prevention, and preparedness activities in the United States, with the goal of improving overall public health.

Central nervous system (CNS)   the complex of nerve tissues that controls the activities of the body, comprised of the brain and spinal cord.

Chakras   the word translates to "wheel" describing the primary energy centers in the body. The seven primary chakras are the root, sacral, solar plexus, heart, throat, third eye, and crown.

Chandra   a Sanskrit word meaning "moon."

Chandra Bhedana   a calming breathing exercise, also known as Single Nostril Breathing, this pranayama exercise involves inhaling through the left nostril and exhaling through the right.

Citta   a Sanskrit word referring to the mind and mental properties.

Complex trauma (C-PTSD)   a psychological condition thought to occur as a result of repetitive, prolonged trauma involving sustained abuse or abandonment by a caregiver, or other interpersonal relationships with an uneven power dynamic.

Containment   refers to the capacity to internally manage the troubling thoughts and feelings and behavior that arise as a consequence of stress. Also applies to external, environmental factors that provide a sense of safety or confidentiality.

Countertransference   in a therapeutic relationship, the mental, emotional, and somatic reaction of the provider to the client's process and presentation.

Developmental Trauma Disorder (DTD)   a psychological condition resulting from abandonment, abuse, or neglect during the early years of life. It can disrupt cognitive, neurological, and psychological development, and impact attachment to caregivers and others.

Dharana   the sixth of the eight limbs, *Dharana* translates to mean "holding steady," "concentration" or "single focus."

Dhyana   the seventh of the eight limbs, *Dhyana* translates to mean "meditation."

Dissociative Identity Disorder (DID)   Formerly termed "Multiple Personality Disorder," DID is a psychological condition in which a person's identity is fragmented into two or more distinct personality states. People with this condition are often victims of severe abuse.

Dristi a specific gaze or focal point employed during meditation or within the yoga practice, with the purpose of focusing attention.

Dyad (dyadic) something that consists of two parts, or a pair, often referring to two-person communication.

Earthing the practice of placing the body in direct contact with the natural earth.

Efferent neurons neurons that transmit messages from the CNS to all parts of the body, instigating action.

Enactment the process of acting out unconscious emotions in relationship or experience.

Enteric nervous system (ENS) located around the digestive tract and often referred to as the "gut brain," this system controls the gastrointestinal system and involves neural circuits that modulate immune and endocrine functions.

Epigenetics the study of changes in gene expression that do not involve changes to the underlying DNA sequence, which in turn affects how cells read the genes.

Eye movement desensitization and reprocessing (EMDR) a psychotherapy treatment designed to alleviate the distress associated with traumatic memories.

Hatha A style of yoga known for the effort to balance opposites and manage the mind through the practice of posture, breath, and meditation.

Hypothalamic–pituitary–adrenal (HPA) axis a central stress response system in the brain which includes the hypothalamus, the pituitary gland, and the adrenal glands.

Ideomotor signaling an established mode of nonverbal communication.

Interoception the ability to sense, experience, or feel what is happening internally in the body.

Intergenerational trauma also referred to as historical or transgenerational trauma, this occurs when the reaction to trauma is passed down through genetics, thoughts, beliefs, worldviews, and culture.

International Society for the Study of Trauma and Dissociation (ISSTD) an international, non-profit, professional association organized to develop and promote comprehensive, clinically effective, and empirically-based responses to trauma and dissociation.

Jnana a Sanskrit word that translates to mean "knowledge" or "wisdom."

Karma a Sanskrit word meaning action, work or deed, also referring to the principle of cause and effect.

Kapalabhati commonly referred to as "breath of fire," *kapalabhati* is a breathing technique involving short rapid breaths assisted by the movement of the abdominal muscles.

Kriya a *kriya* is a series of postures, breath, and sound that work toward a specific outcome.

Kumbhaka   the pause between an inhale and exhale. The pause following the exhale is called the *bahya kumbhaka*, while the pause following the inhale is called the *antara kumbhaka*.

Metta   a practice of loving-kindness, goodwill, benevolence, or friendliness, often directed towards a person or group of people.

Myelin   a fatty sheath coating the axon that protects and helps send signals faster and more efficiently.

Nadi Shodana   *Nadi* is a Sanskrit word meaning "channel" or "flow" and *shodhana* means "purification." Also known as Alternate Nostril Breathing, this is a powerful breathing practice with wide-reaching benefits.

Nadis   the Sanskrit root "*nad*" translates to mean "channel," "stream," or "flow." Breathing techniques and postures in yoga are intended to influence the flow of energy within these channels. *Ida* and *Pingala* are the primary *nadis* of the body.

Niyama   observances, of which there are five; *Sauca* (purity), *Santosa* (contentment), *Tapas* (perseverance), *Svadhyaya* (self-study), *Isvarapranidhana* (surrender to the divine).

Parasympathetic nervous system (PSNS)   one of three divisions of the ANS. Sometimes called the rest and digest system, the PSNS conserves energy as it slows the heart rate, increases intestinal and gland activity, and relaxes sphincter muscles in the gastrointestinal tract. In Polyvagal Theory, the PSNS governs immobilization.

Peripheral nervous system (PNS)   connects the CNS to the limbs and organs, essentially serving as a relay between the brain and spinal cord and the rest of the body. The PNS is divided into the SoNS and the ANS.

Post-traumatic stress disorder (PTSD)   a psychological condition that can occur following the experience of a traumatic event such as a natural disaster, a serious accident, a terrorist act, war/combat, rape or other violent personal assault.

Prakriti   A Sanskrit word that describes the prime material energy of which all matter is composed.

Pranayama   Practices that involve manipulating the breath or energy.

Pratipaksha Bhavana   A practice described in the yoga sutras (2.33), translated from Sanskrit as "cultivating the opposite."

Pratyahara   the fifth of the eight limbs, translates to mean "sense withdrawal," often practiced by covered the eyes or ears.

Presence   the state of being connected to present moment experience.

Proprioception   the ability to collect and synthesize information about the position of the body in space.

Proudness   A positive sense of accomplishment, or of feeling proud of one's self, efforts, or work.

Purusha   a Sanskrit word meaning that which is constant or unchanging, often translates as soul or consciousness.

Rajas one of the three *gunas*; the element of prakriti associated with passion, energy, and movement.

Rajasic depression describes the type of depression where restlessness, agitation, or anxiety are also present or predominant.

Rational authority a leadership style based on competence, in which the person with more power or authority helps the person they have power over to grow.

Reptilian brain includes the main structures found in a reptile's brain: the brainstem and the cerebellum; controls vital functions such as heart rate, breathing, body temperature, and balance.

Resource an experience, relationship, or aspect of self, real or imagined, that supports the client in accessing positive biopsychosocial states, or assists in coping with challenging emotions or experiences.

Resourcing practices that help clients develop their psychological resources, or connect them to supports and positive states during times of stress.

Sama vritti a Sanskrit term meaning "same rotation," most often used to describe breath practices that are equal in count for both the inhale and exhale.

Samadhi the eighth and final limb, translates to mean enlightenment or integration.

Samskara physical, mental, emotional or energetic patterns related to movement, thought, feeling, or systems within the body. These patterns are thought to be a result of previous thought, action or experience, in this lifetime or before.

Sangha a community or group of people with shared spiritual purpose.

Sattva one of the three qualities of nature, *sattva* describes a state of harmony, balance, awareness, intelligence, or neutrality.

Somatic nervous system (SoNS) part of the PNS; manages voluntary body movements and involuntary reflexes like a blink, knee jerk, or gag response.

Socioeconomic status (SES) an individual's or family's economic and social position in relation to others, based on income, education, and occupation.

Solution-focused an approach or therapy that brings attention to practical pathways to solve immediate problems, rather than discuss cause of suffering or history at length.

Somatoform dissociation dissociative symptoms that involve the body and range from reduction to complete loss of sensory perception or motor control. Can also involve sensations in absence of present moment stimuli: pain in some part of the body, a sense of being touched, smelling or tasting something, etc. These sensations can be related to traumatic memories.

Spiritual bypass   describes the process of using spiritual principles in defense of, or while denying the truth of emotions like anger, sadness, grief or resentment.

Spoon Theory   a metaphor used to explain the reduced amount of energy available for activities of daily living and productive tasks that may result from disability or chronic illness.

Strength-based   a clinical focus on the positive qualities, resources, and supports and inherent strengths of individuals, families, groups, and organizations.

Substance Abuse and Mental Health Services Administration (SAMHSA) a branch of the US Department of Health and Human Services that leads public health efforts to advance the behavioral health of the nation. SAMHSA's mission is to reduce the impact of substance abuse and mental illness on America's communities.

Surya Bhedana   an energizing breathing exercise, also known as Single Nostril Breathing, this *pranayama* exercise involves inhaling through the right nostril and exhaling through the left.

Sympathetic nervous system (SNS)   part of the ANS that activates the fight or flight response when exposed to significant mental and emotional stress, or when a situation arises that threatens physical safety.

Tamas   a quality of nature related to darkness, inertia, inactivity or heaviness.

Top-down processing   a cognitive process that initiates with our thoughts, which then flow to the body and senses.

Transference   in the therapeutic process, when the feelings, desires, and expectations of one person are redirected and applied to another person.

Trauma-informed care   an organizational structure and treatment framework that involves understanding, recognizing, and responding to the effects of all types of trauma.

Trauma-informed yoga (TIY)   an approach to yoga that integrates awareness of post-traumatic stress, including the causes, symptoms, and pathways to recovery. TIY prioritizes the biopsychosocial, spiritual, and energetic needs of the student or client over the goals of the class or instructor.

Traditional Chinese Medicine (TCM)   a style of traditional medicine built on a foundation of more than 2,500 years of Chinese medical practice that includes various forms of herbal medicine, acupuncture, massage, exercise, and dietary practices.

Vayus   a Sanskrit word describing energetic "winds" within the body, the five primary vayus are the *Prana Vayu, Vyana Vayu, Udana Vayu, Samana Vayu*, and *Apana Vayu*.

Viloma   in Sanskrit, "*vi*" means against, while "*loma*" means hair, making *viloma* mean against the natural flow. *Viloma* is a breathing technique that interrupts the inhale and/or exhale with a series of pauses.

Vinyasa   a method of yoga in which movements form a flowing sequence in coordination with the breath; often translated as "movement with breath," "gradual progression" or "placed in a skillful way." As a noun, *vinyasa* refers to the sequence of *Chaturanga Dandasana*, upward dog and downward dog taught in this style of class.

Vrittis   a Sanskrit word meaning "churning," "whirl" or "cyclical movements," in Sutra 1.2 *"yogas citta vritti nirodha"* referring to the mind as turnings of thought, or "mind stuff."

Yama   the first of the eight limbs of yoga, encompassing five practices of restraint: *Ahimsa* (non-harming or peacefulness), *Satya* (truthfulness), *Asteya* (non-stealing), *Brahmacharya* (restraint of energy, often in regards to sexual behavior), *Aparigraha* (non-grasping).

Resource: Yoga for Trauma Online Training Program, www.howwecanheal.com/y4t

Index